Garfield takes up space

BY: JIM DAVIS

BALLANTINE BOOKS · NEW YORK

Published in the United States by Ballantine Books, a division of Random House, Inc., New York, and simultaneously in Canada by Random House of Canada Limited, Toronto.

Library of Congress Catalog Card Number: 90-93221

ISBN: 0-345-37029-5

Manufactured in the United States of America

First Edition: March 1991

10 9 8 7 6 5

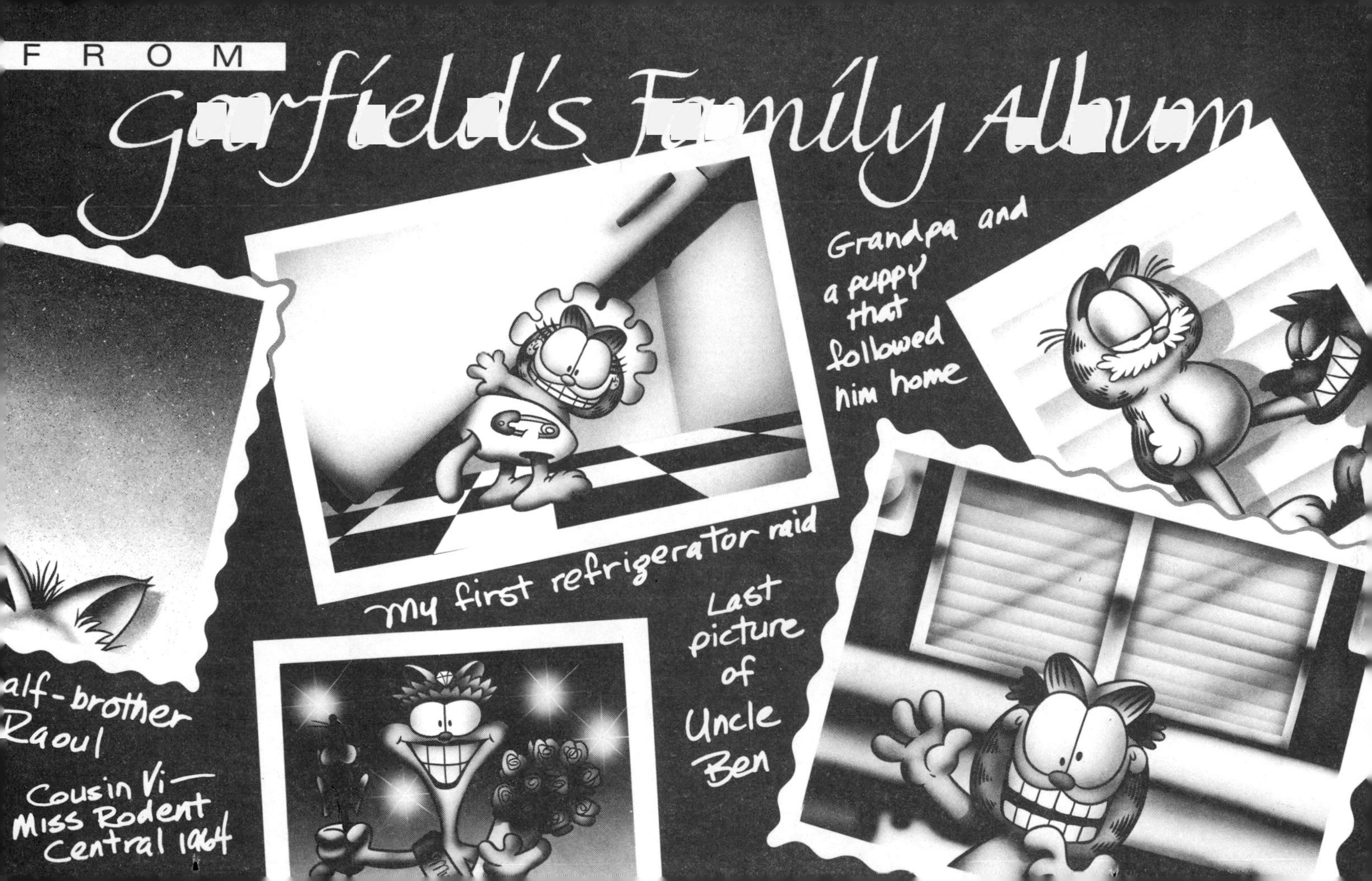
FROM
Garfield's Family Album
My first refrigerator raid
Grandpa and a puppy that followed him home
alf-brother Raoul
Cousin Vi— Miss Rodent Central 1964
Last picture of Uncle Ben

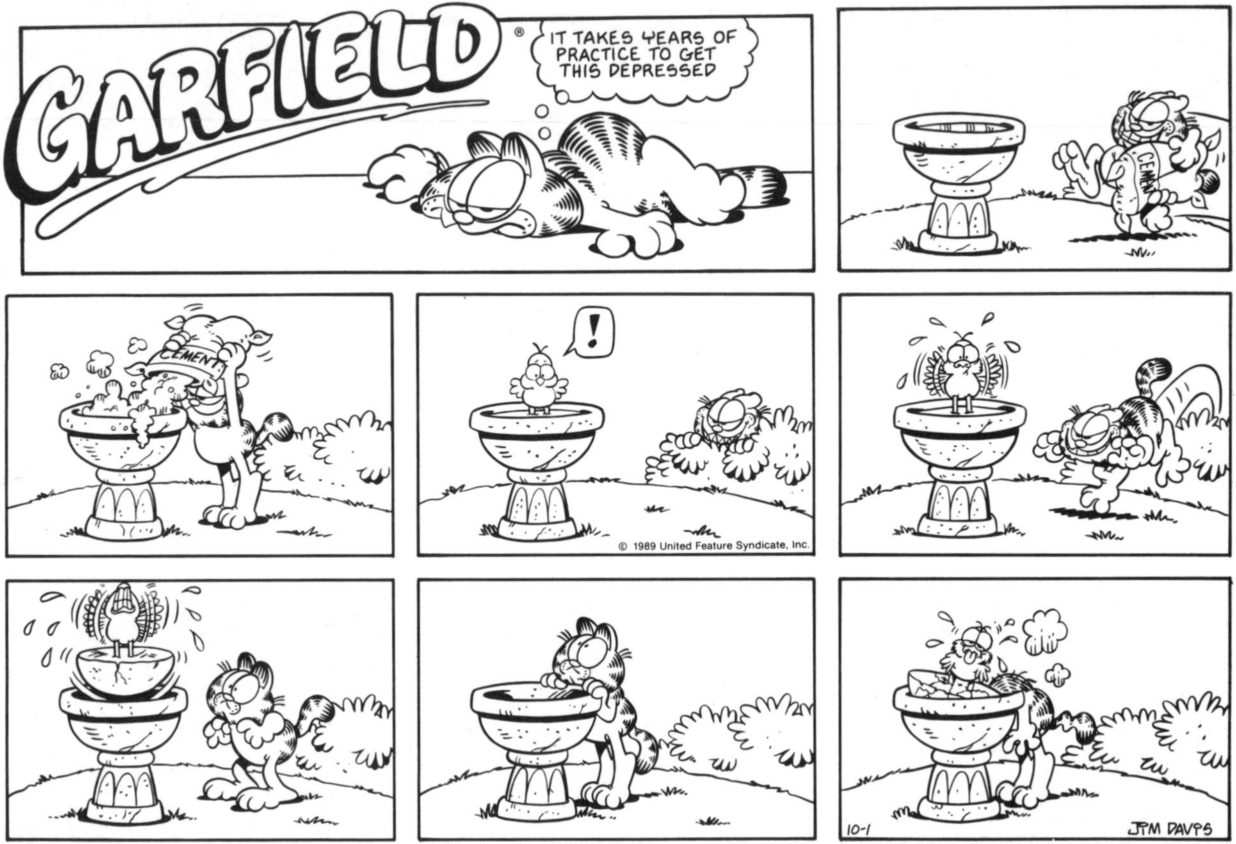
GARFIELD®
IT TAKES YEARS OF PRACTICE TO GET THIS DEPRESSED
CEMENT
CEMENT
!
© 1989 United Feature Syndicate, Inc.
10-1
JIM DAVIS

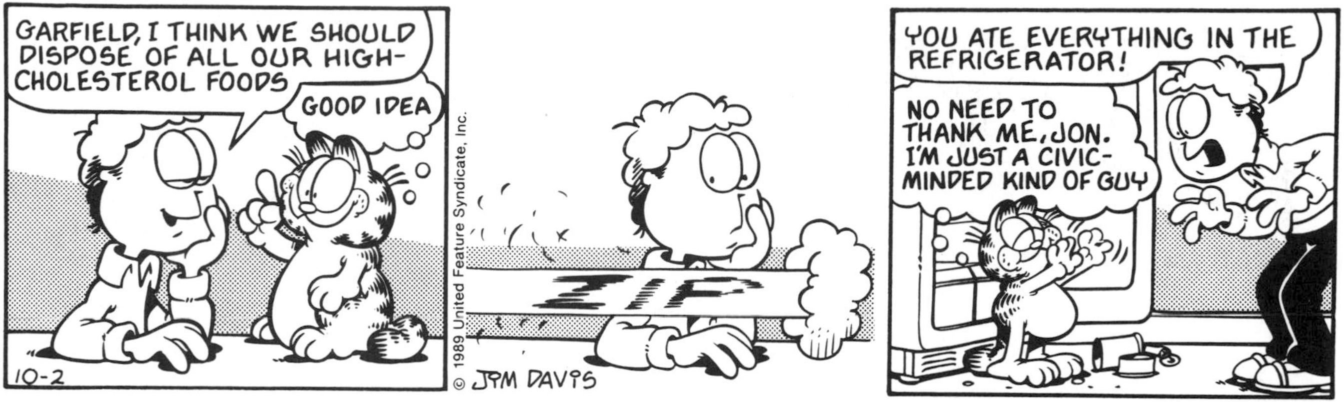
GARFIELD, I THINK WE SHOULD DISPOSE OF ALL OUR HIGH-CHOLESTEROL FOODS
GOOD IDEA
ZIP
YOU ATE EVERYTHING IN THE REFRIGERATOR!
NO NEED TO THANK ME, JON. I'M JUST A CIVIC-MINDED KIND OF GUY
10-2
© 1989 United Feature Syndicate, Inc.
JIM DAVIS

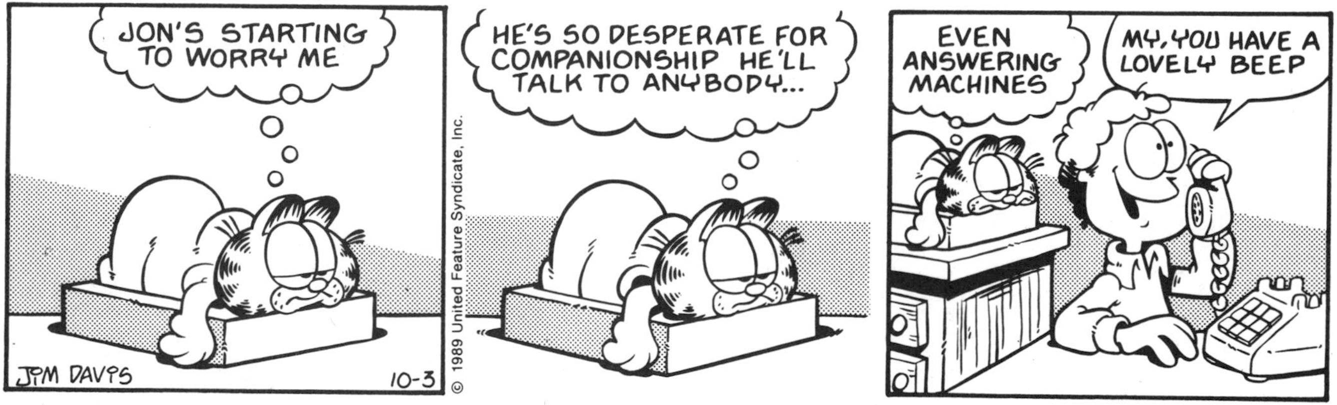
JON'S STARTING TO WORRY ME
HE'S SO DESPERATE FOR COMPANIONSHIP HE'LL TALK TO ANYBODY...
EVEN ANSWERING MACHINES
MY, YOU HAVE A LOVELY BEEP
JIM DAVIS
10-3
© 1989 United Feature Syndicate, Inc.

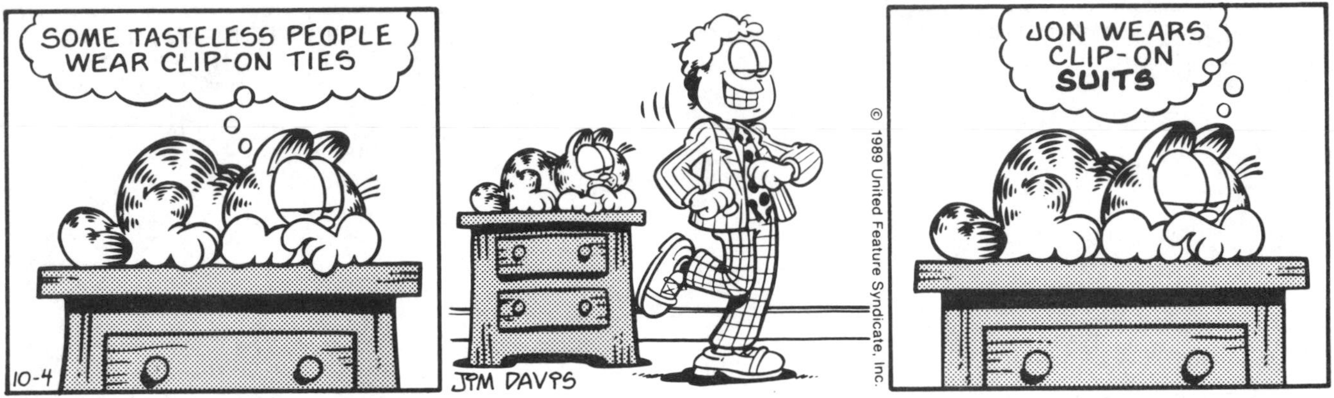
SOME TASTELESS PEOPLE WEAR CLIP-ON TIES
JON WEARS CLIP-ON SUITS
10-4
JIM DAVIS
© 1989 United Feature Syndicate, Inc.

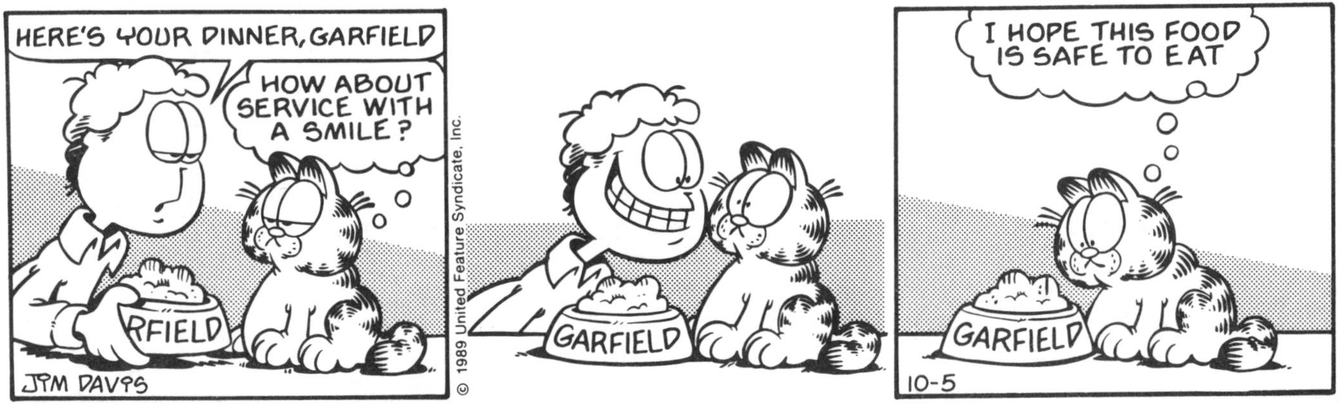
HERE'S YOUR DINNER, GARFIELD
HOW ABOUT SERVICE WITH A SMILE?
RFIELD
JIM DAVIS
© 1989 United Feature Syndicate, Inc.
GARFIELD
I HOPE THIS FOOD IS SAFE TO EAT
GARFIELD
10-5

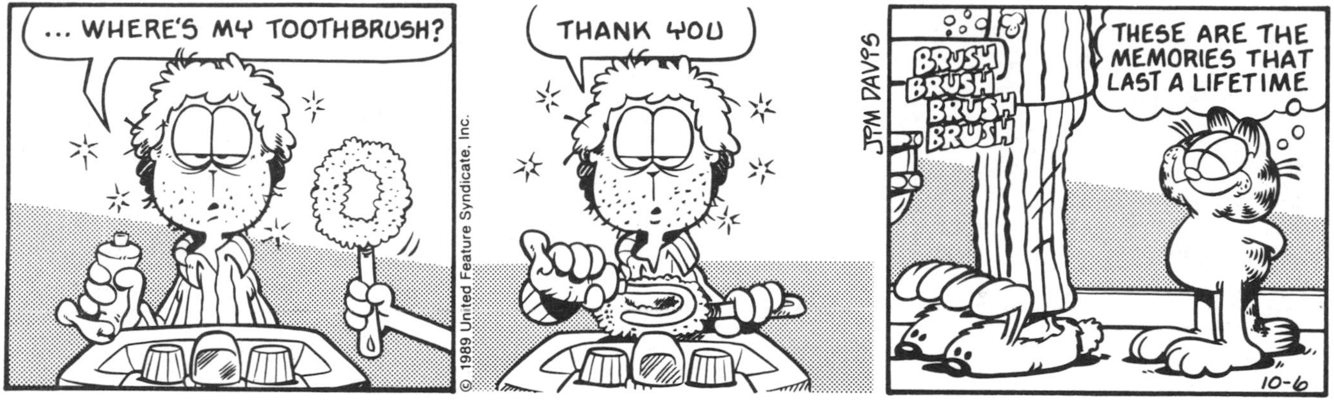
... WHERE'S MY TOOTHBRUSH?
THANK YOU
© 1989 United Feature Syndicate, Inc.
JIM DAVIS
BRUSH BRUSH BRUSH BRUSH
THESE ARE THE MEMORIES THAT LAST A LIFETIME
10-6

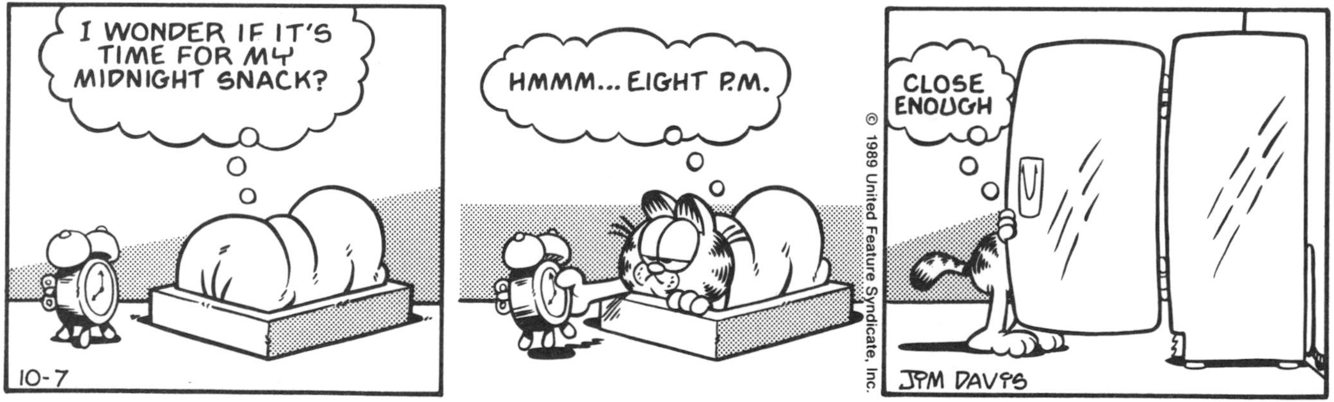
I WONDER IF IT'S TIME FOR MY MIDNIGHT SNACK?
10-7
HMMM... EIGHT P.M.
© 1989 United Feature Syndicate, Inc.
CLOSE ENOUGH
JIM DAVIS

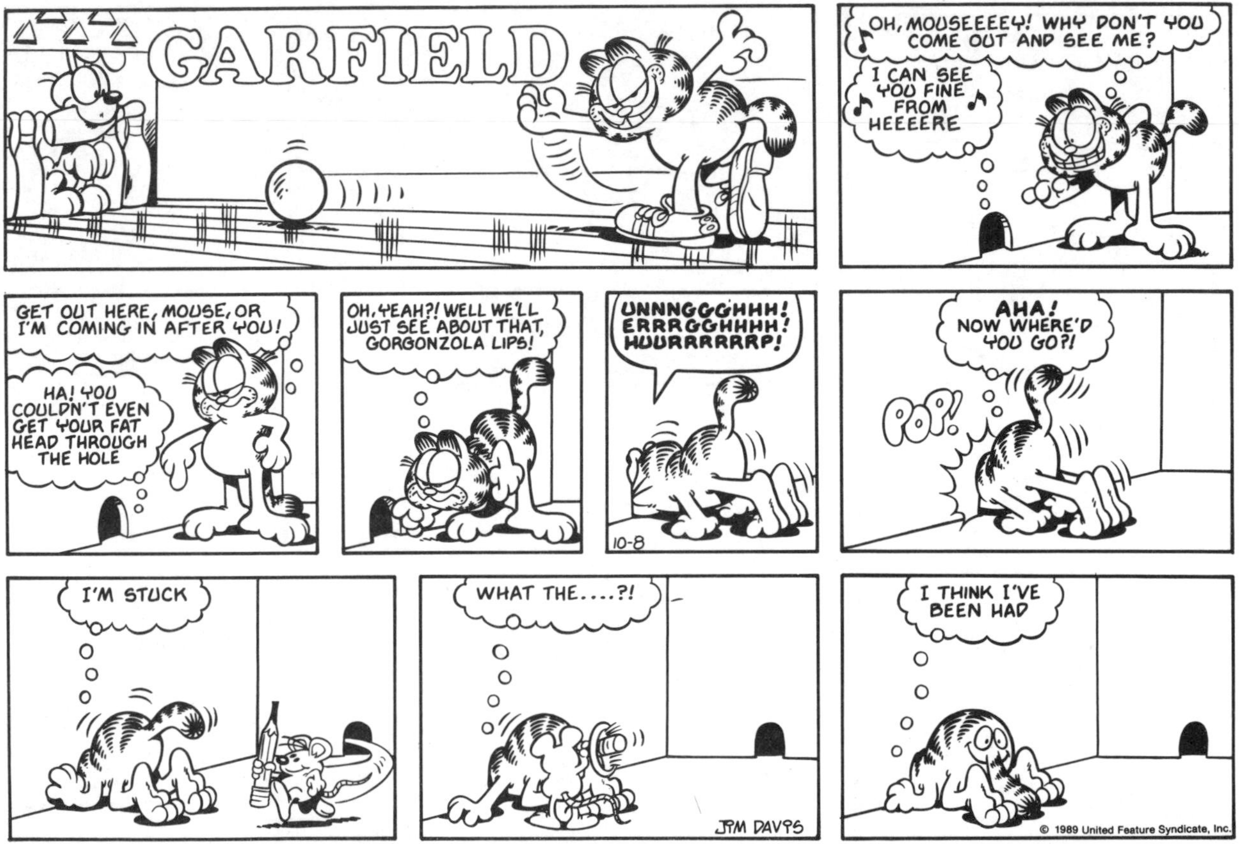
GARFIELD
OH, MOUSEEEEY! WHY DON'T YOU COME OUT AND SEE ME?
I CAN SEE YOU FINE FROM HEEEERE
GET OUT HERE, MOUSE, OR I'M COMING IN AFTER YOU!
HA! YOU COULDN'T EVEN GET YOUR FAT HEAD THROUGH THE HOLE
OH, YEAH?! WELL WE'LL JUST SEE ABOUT THAT, GORGONZOLA LIPS!
UNNNGGGHHH! ERRRGGHHHH! HUURRRRRRP!
10-8
AHA! NOW WHERE'D YOU GO?!
POP!
I'M STUCK
WHAT THE....?!
JIM DAVIS
I THINK I'VE BEEN HAD
© 1989 United Feature Syndicate, Inc.

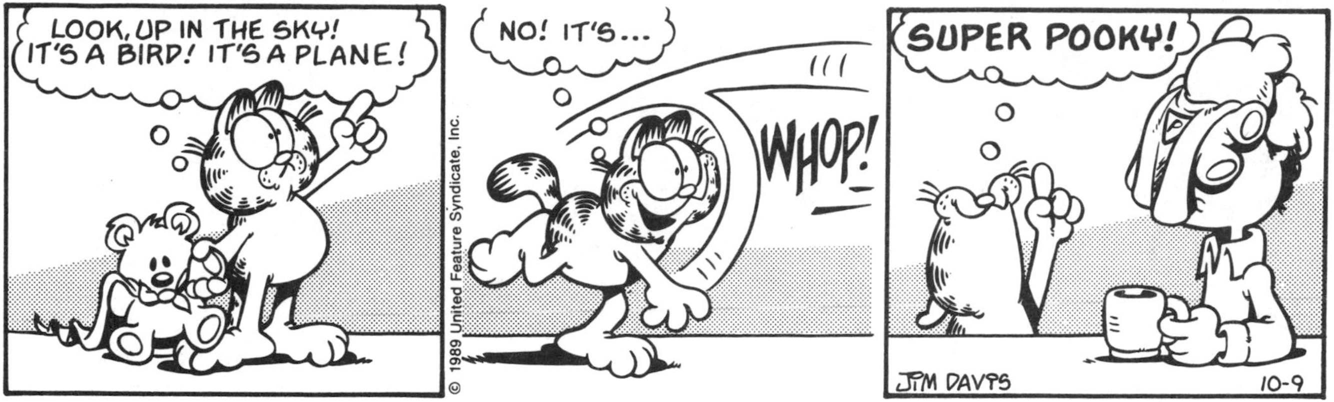
LOOK, UP IN THE SKY! IT'S A BIRD! IT'S A PLANE!
NO! IT'S...
WHOP!
SUPER POOKY!
© 1989 United Feature Syndicate, Inc.
JIM DAVIS
10-9

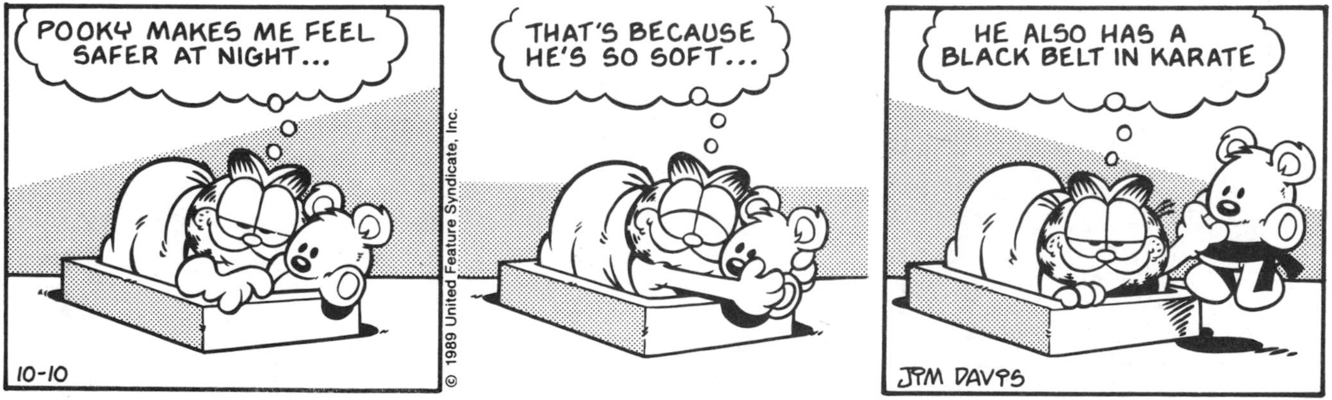
POOKY MAKES ME FEEL SAFER AT NIGHT...
THAT'S BECAUSE HE'S SO SOFT...
HE ALSO HAS A BLACK BELT IN KARATE
© 1989 United Feature Syndicate, Inc.
10-10
JIM DAVIS

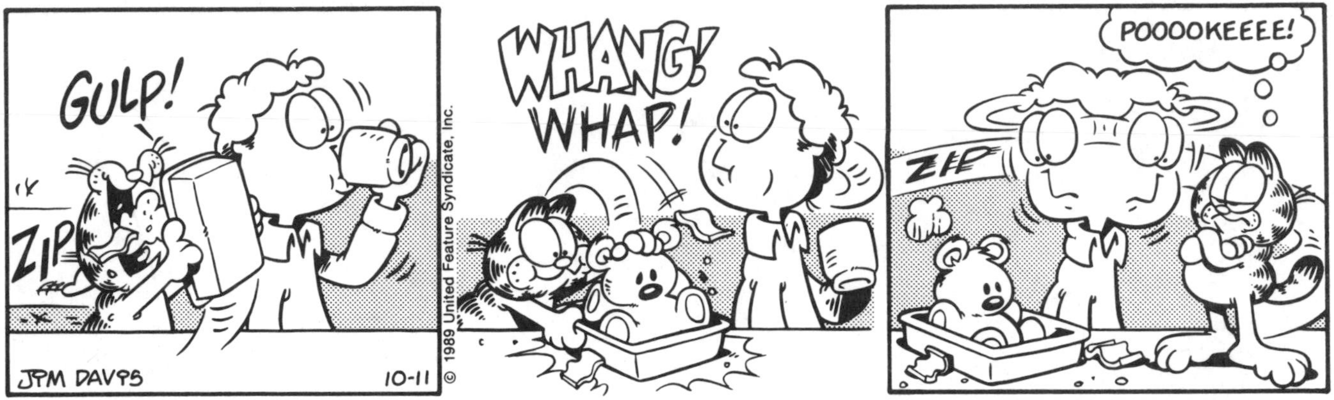
GULP!
ZIP
JIM DAVIS
10-11
© 1989 United Feature Syndicate, Inc.
WHANG!
WHAP!
POOOOKEEEE!
ZIP

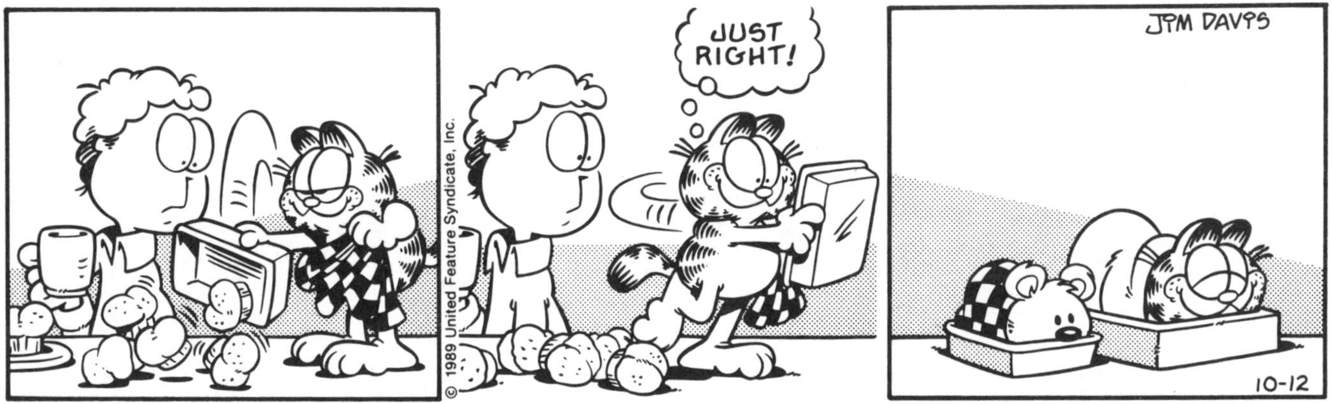
© 1989 United Feature Syndicate, Inc.
JUST RIGHT!
JIM DAVIS
10-12

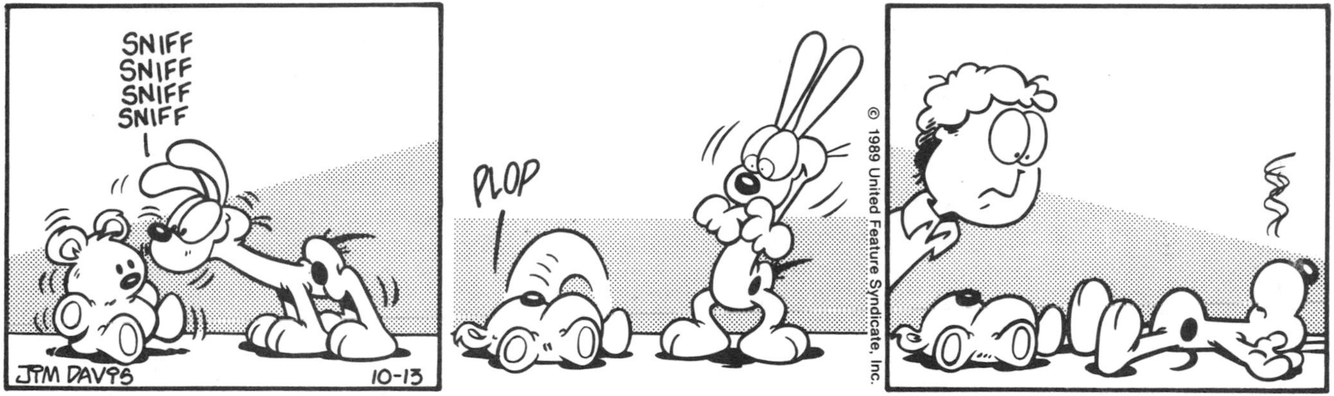
SNIFF
SNIFF
SNIFF
SNIFF
JIM DAVIS
10-13
PLOP
© 1989 United Feature Syndicate, Inc.

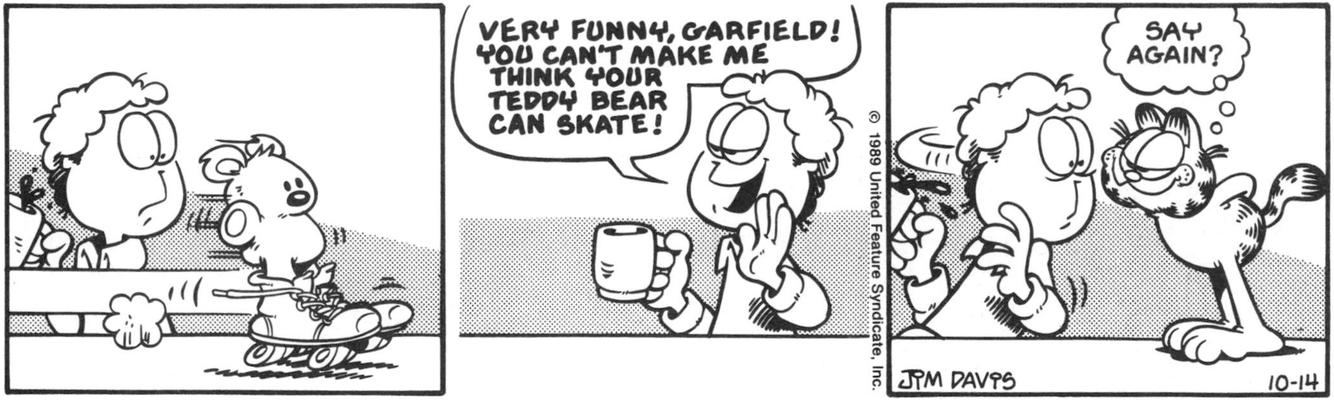
VERY FUNNY, GARFIELD! YOU CAN'T MAKE ME THINK YOUR TEDDY BEAR CAN SKATE!
© 1989 United Feature Syndicate, Inc.
SAY AGAIN?
JIM DAVIS
10-14

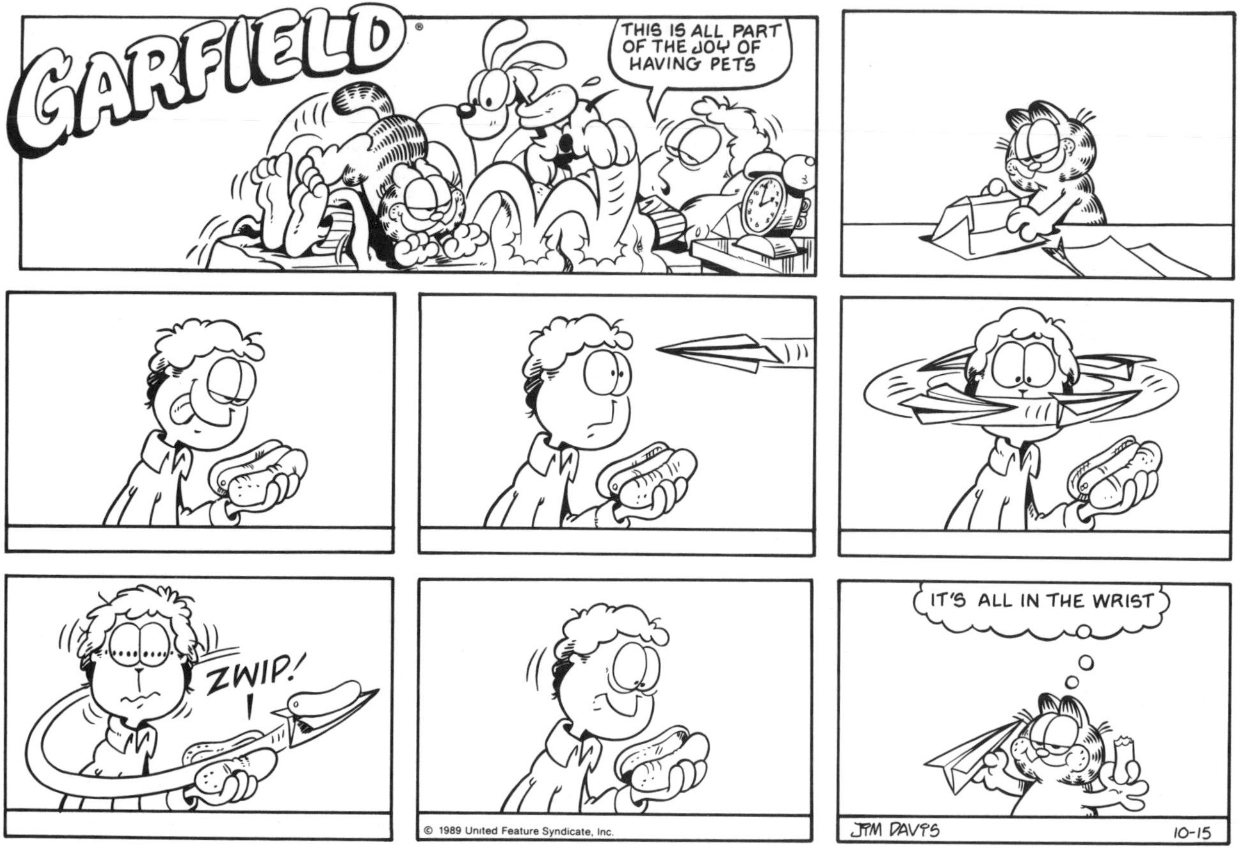
GARFIELD
THIS IS ALL PART OF THE JOY OF HAVING PETS
ZWIP!
IT'S ALL IN THE WRIST
© 1989 United Feature Syndicate, Inc.
JIM DAVIS
10-15

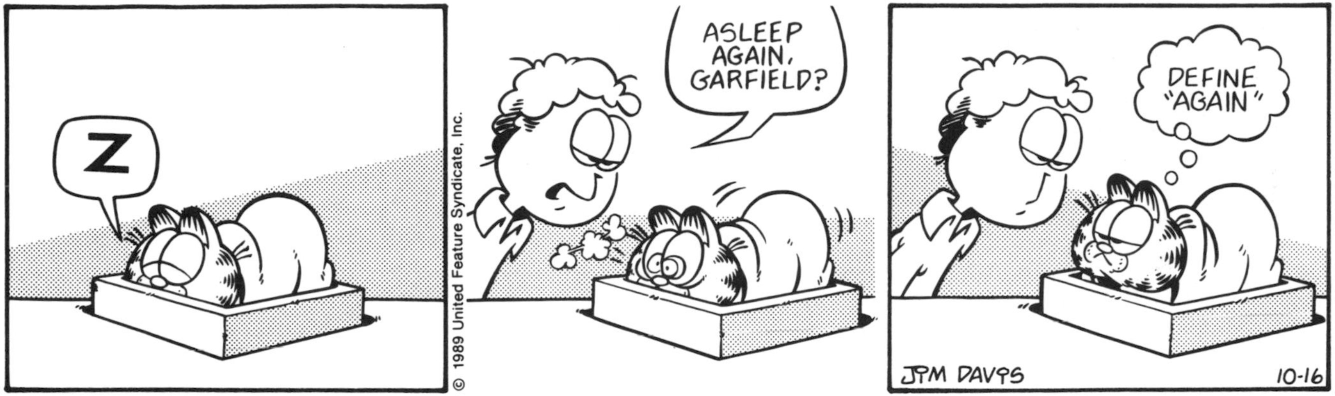
Z
ASLEEP AGAIN, GARFIELD?
DEFINE "AGAIN"
© 1989 United Feature Syndicate, Inc.
JIM DAVIS
10-16

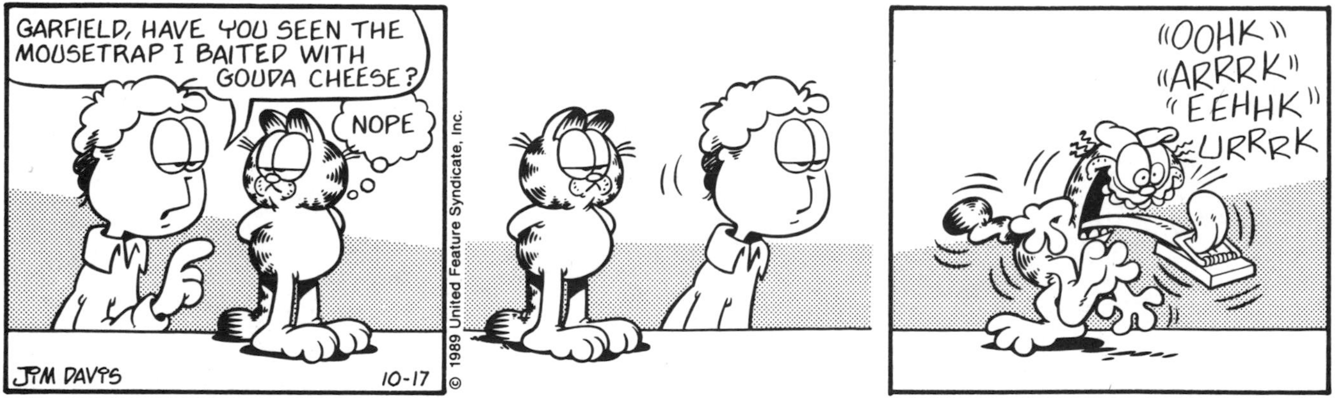
GARFIELD, HAVE YOU SEEN THE MOUSETRAP I BAITED WITH GOUDA CHEESE?
NOPE
"OOHK"
"ARRRK"
"EEHHK"
URRRK
© 1989 United Feature Syndicate, Inc.
JIM DAVIS
10-17

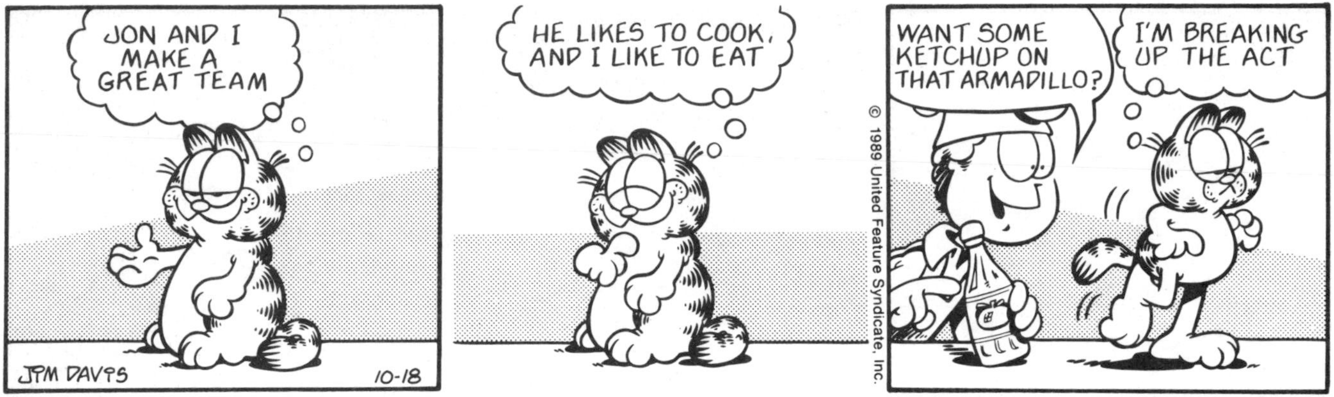
JON AND I MAKE A GREAT TEAM
HE LIKES TO COOK, AND I LIKE TO EAT
WANT SOME KETCHUP ON THAT ARMADILLO?
I'M BREAKING UP THE ACT
JIM DAVIS
10-18
© 1989 United Feature Syndicate, Inc.

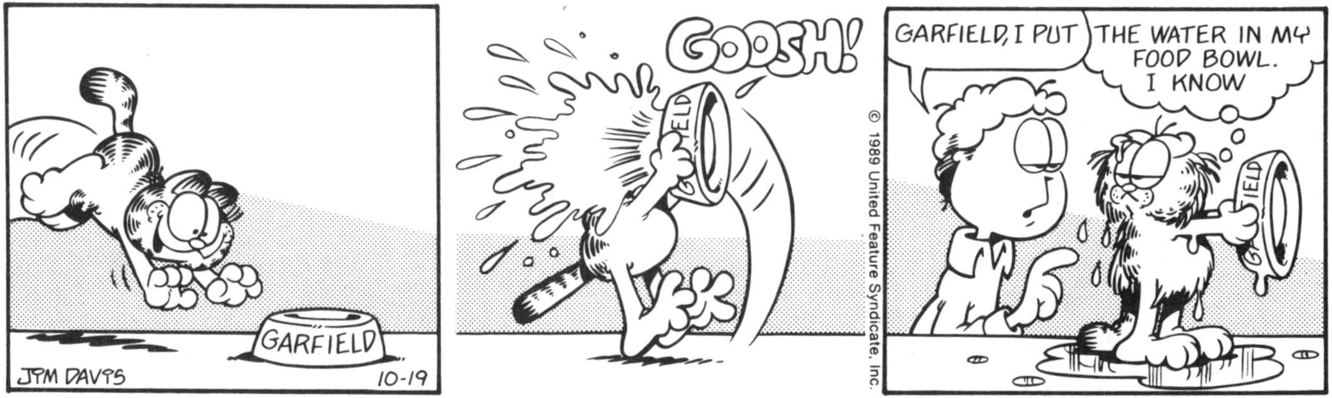
GARFIELD
JIM DAVIS
10-19
GOOSH!
GARFIELD, I PUT
THE WATER IN MY FOOD BOWL. I KNOW
© 1989 United Feature Syndicate, Inc.

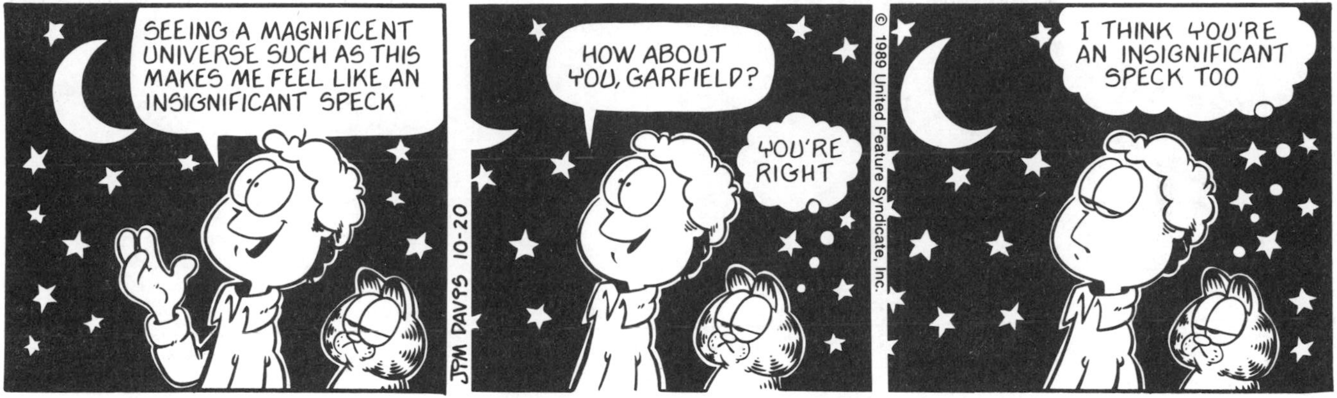
SEEING A MAGNIFICENT UNIVERSE SUCH AS THIS MAKES ME FEEL LIKE AN INSIGNIFICANT SPECK
JIM DAVIS 10-20
HOW ABOUT YOU, GARFIELD?
YOU'RE RIGHT
© 1989 United Feature Syndicate, Inc.
I THINK YOU'RE AN INSIGNIFICANT SPECK TOO

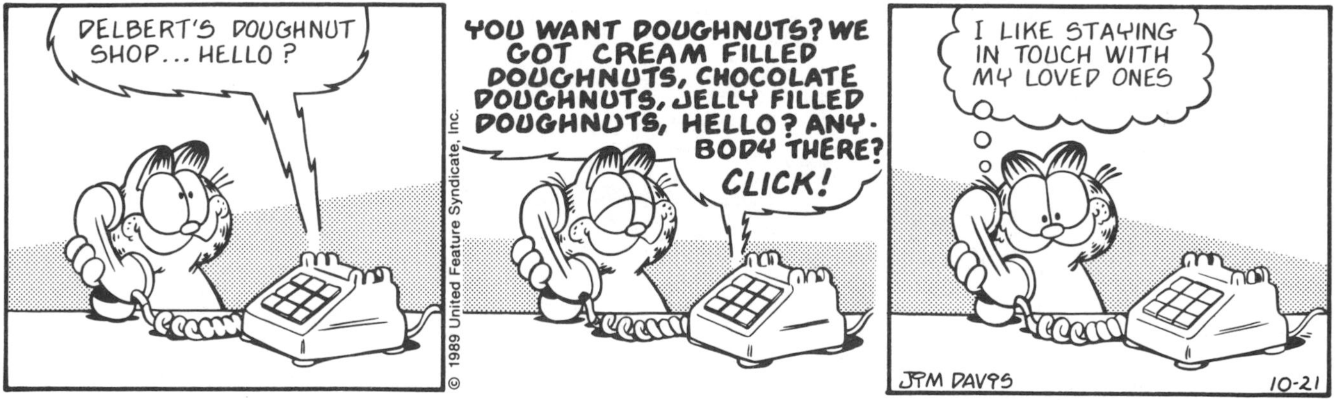
DELBERT'S DOUGHNUT SHOP... HELLO?
© 1989 United Feature Syndicate, Inc.
YOU WANT DOUGHNUTS? WE GOT CREAM FILLED DOUGHNUTS, CHOCOLATE DOUGHNUTS, JELLY FILLED DOUGHNUTS, HELLO? ANY-BODY THERE?
CLICK!
I LIKE STAYING IN TOUCH WITH MY LOVED ONES
JIM DAVIS
10-21

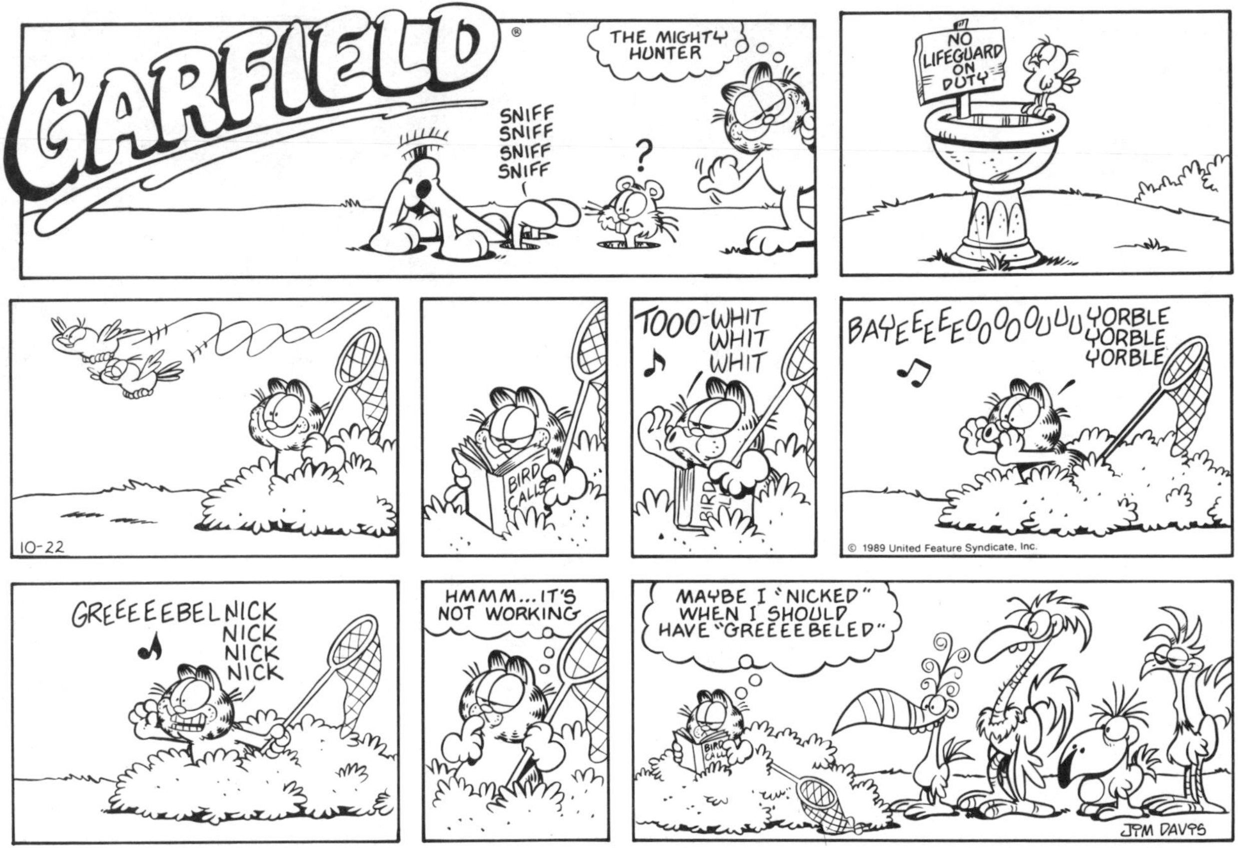
GARFIELD®
SNIFF SNIFF SNIFF SNIFF
?
THE MIGHTY HUNTER
NO LIFEGUARD ON DUTY
10-22
BIRD CALLS
TOOO-WHIT WHIT WHIT
BAYEEEEEOOOOUUU YORBLE YORBLE YORBLE
© 1989 United Feature Syndicate, Inc.
GREEEEEBELNICK NICK NICK NICK
HMMM... IT'S NOT WORKING
MAYBE I "NICKED" WHEN I SHOULD HAVE "GREEEEBELED"
JIM DAVIS

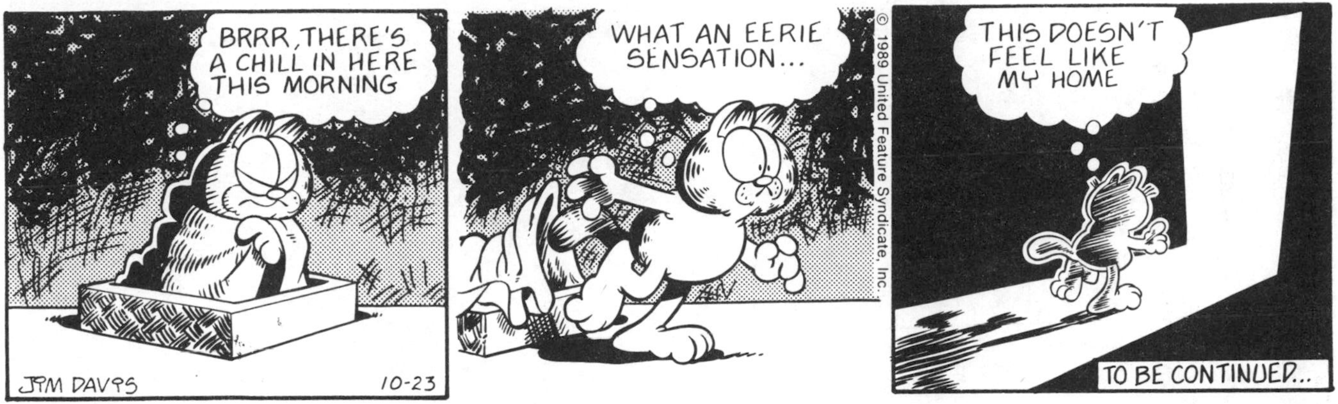
BRRR, THERE'S A CHILL IN HERE THIS MORNING
JIM DAVIS
10-23
WHAT AN EERIE SENSATION...
© 1989 United Feature Syndicate, Inc.
THIS DOESN'T FEEL LIKE MY HOME
TO BE CONTINUED...

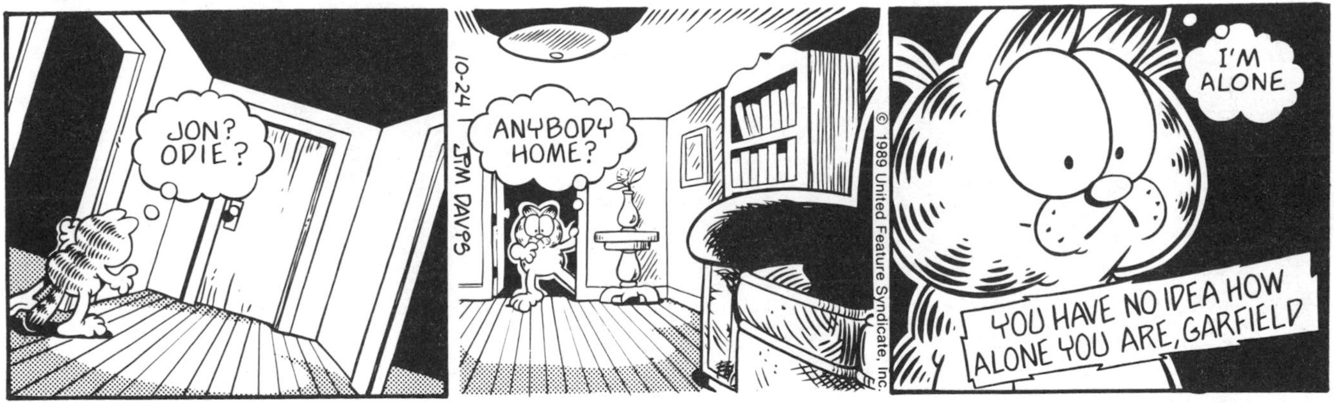
JON? ODIE?
10-24
JIM DAVIS
ANYBODY HOME?
© 1989 United Feature Syndicate, Inc.
I'M ALONE
YOU HAVE NO IDEA HOW ALONE YOU ARE, GARFIELD

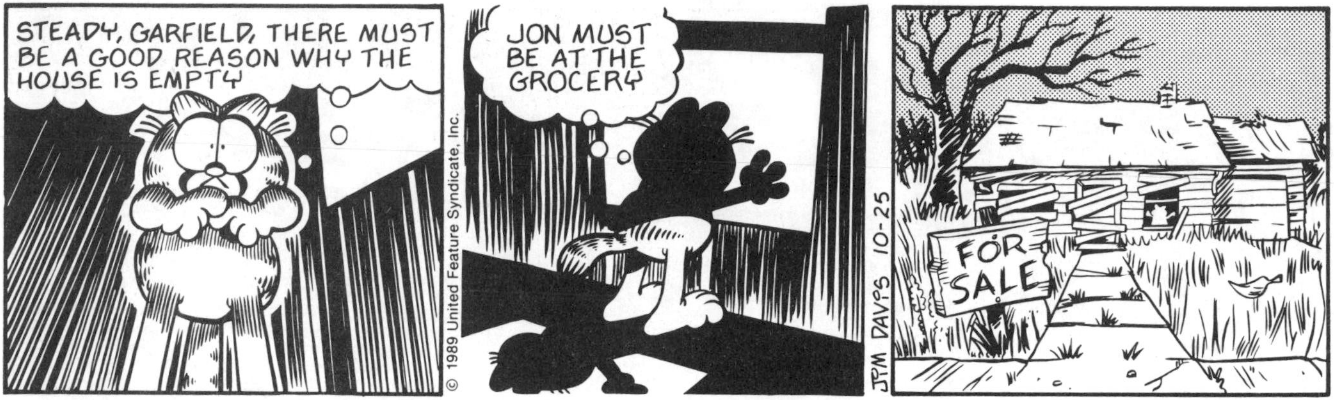
STEADY, GARFIELD, THERE MUST BE A GOOD REASON WHY THE HOUSE IS EMPTY
JON MUST BE AT THE GROCERY
FOR SALE
JIM DAVIS 10-25
© 1989 United Feature Syndicate, Inc.

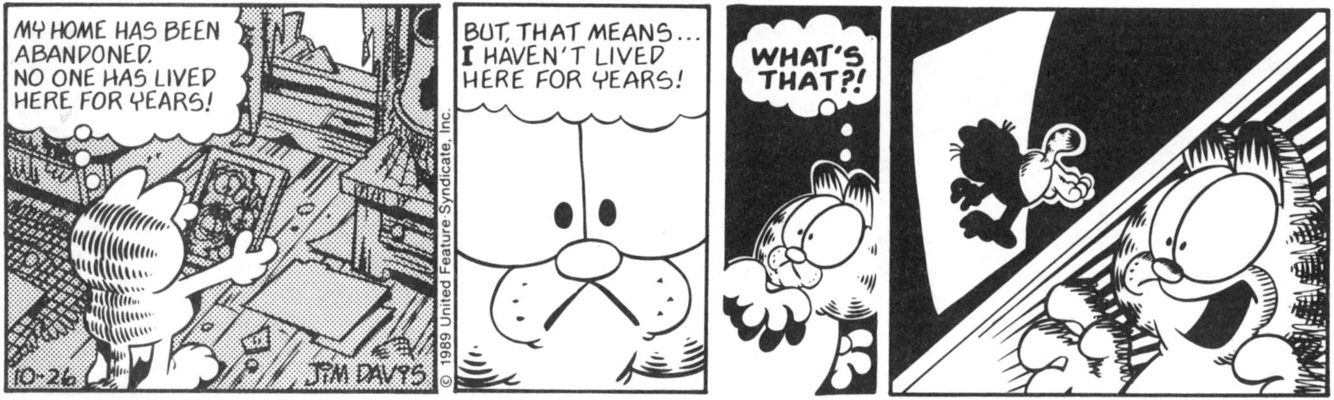
MY HOME HAS BEEN ABANDONED. NO ONE HAS LIVED HERE FOR YEARS!
10-26
JIM DAVIS
© 1989 United Feature Syndicate, Inc.
BUT, THAT MEANS... I HAVEN'T LIVED HERE FOR YEARS!
WHAT'S THAT?!

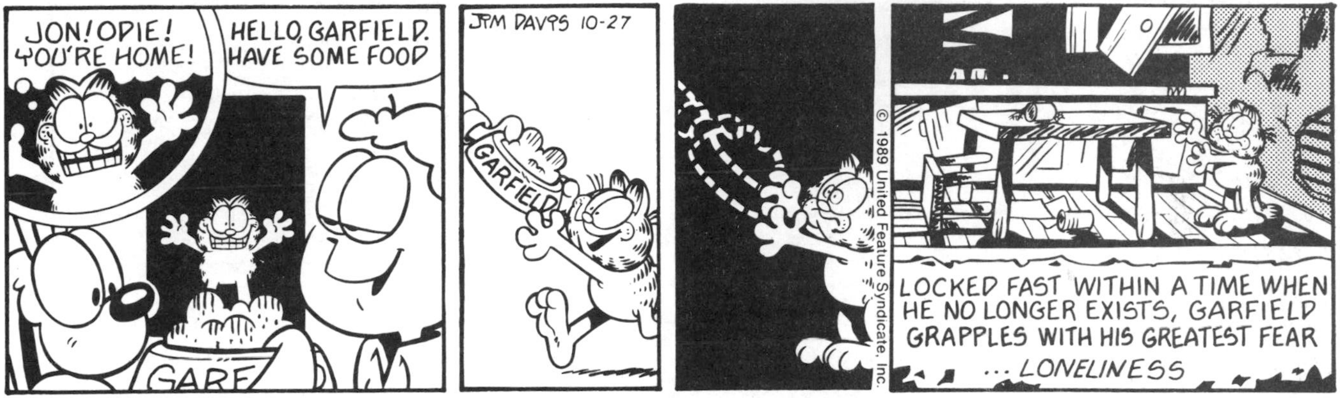
JON! ODIE! YOU'RE HOME!
HELLO, GARFIELD. HAVE SOME FOOD
GARF
JIM DAVIS 10-27
GARFIELD
© 1989 United Feature Syndicate, Inc.
LOCKED FAST WITHIN A TIME WHEN HE NO LONGER EXISTS, GARFIELD GRAPPLES WITH HIS GREATEST FEAR
... LONELINESS

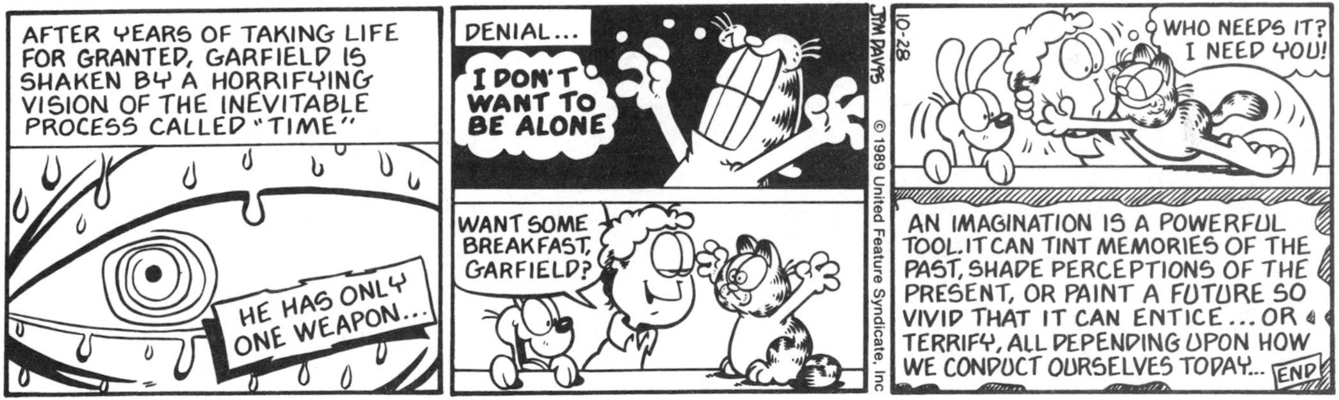
AFTER YEARS OF TAKING LIFE FOR GRANTED, GARFIELD IS SHAKEN BY A HORRIFYING VISION OF THE INEVITABLE PROCESS CALLED "TIME"
HE HAS ONLY ONE WEAPON...
DENIAL...
I DON'T WANT TO BE ALONE
WANT SOME BREAKFAST, GARFIELD?
JIM DAVIS 10-28
© 1989 United Feature Syndicate, Inc
WHO NEEDS IT? I NEED YOU!
AN IMAGINATION IS A POWERFUL TOOL. IT CAN TINT MEMORIES OF THE PAST, SHADE PERCEPTIONS OF THE PRESENT, OR PAINT A FUTURE SO VIVID THAT IT CAN ENTICE... OR TERRIFY, ALL DEPENDING UPON HOW WE CONDUCT OURSELVES TODAY...
END

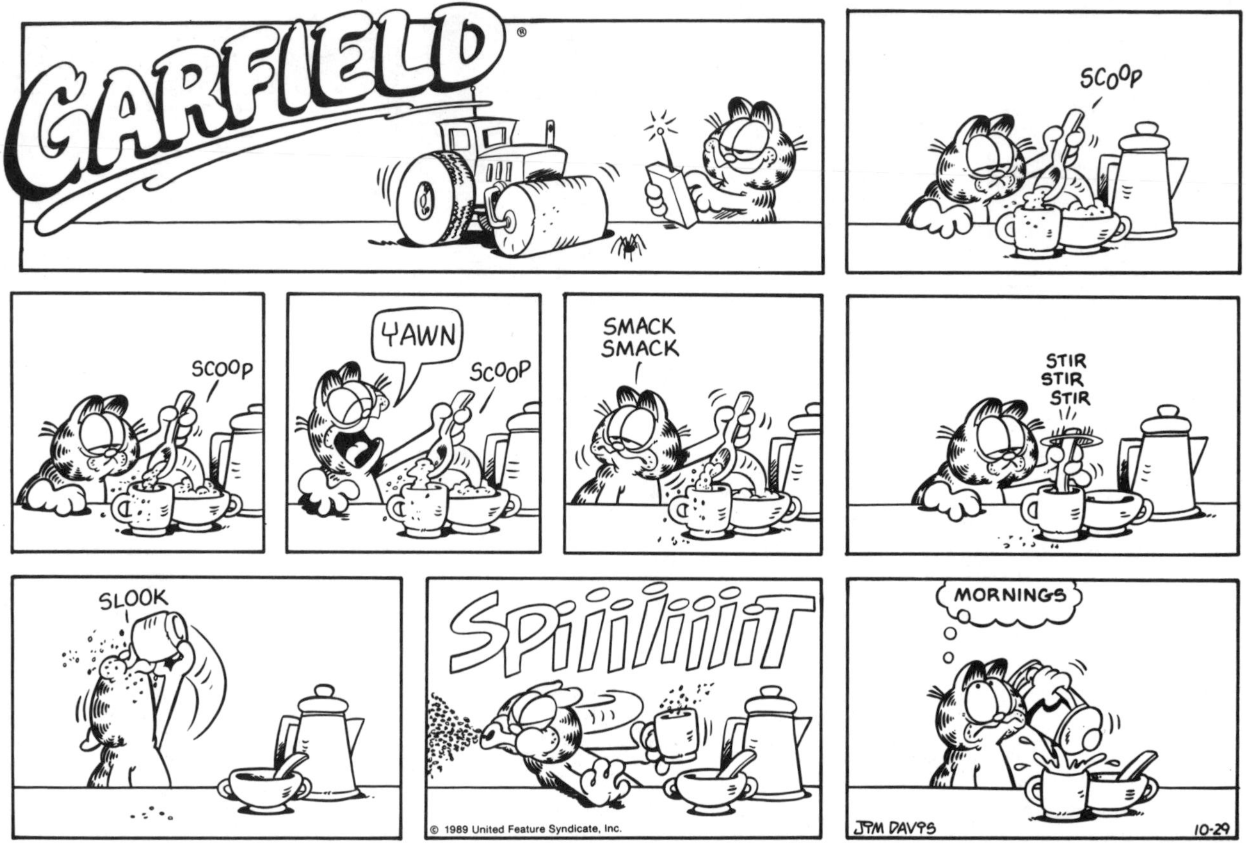
GARFIELD®
SCOOP
SCOOP
YAWN
SCOOP
SMACK SMACK
STIR STIR STIR
SLOOK
SPIIIIIIIT
MORNINGS
© 1989 United Feature Syndicate, Inc.
JIM DAVIS
10-29

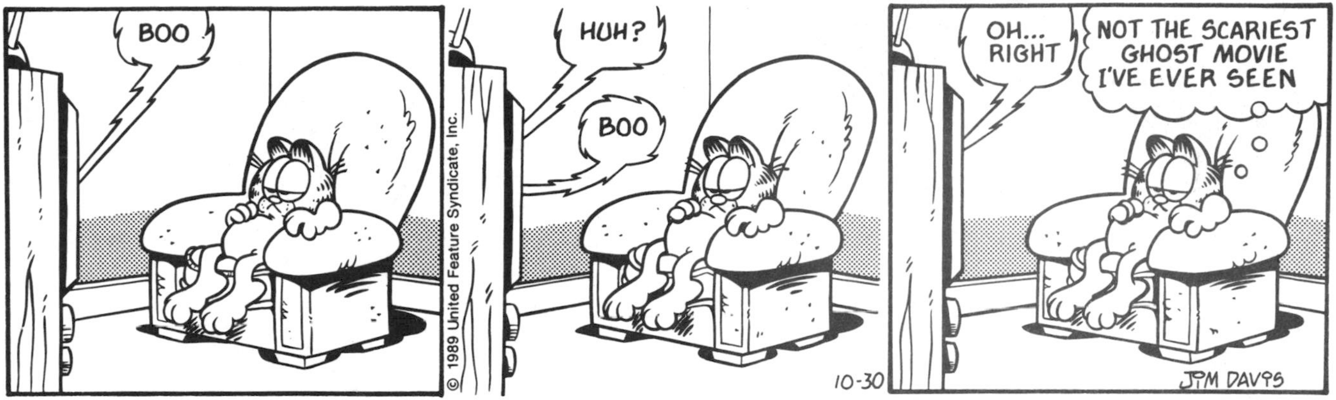
BOO
HUH?
BOO
OH... RIGHT
NOT THE SCARIEST GHOST MOVIE I'VE EVER SEEN
© 1989 United Feature Syndicate, Inc.
10-30
JIM DAVIS

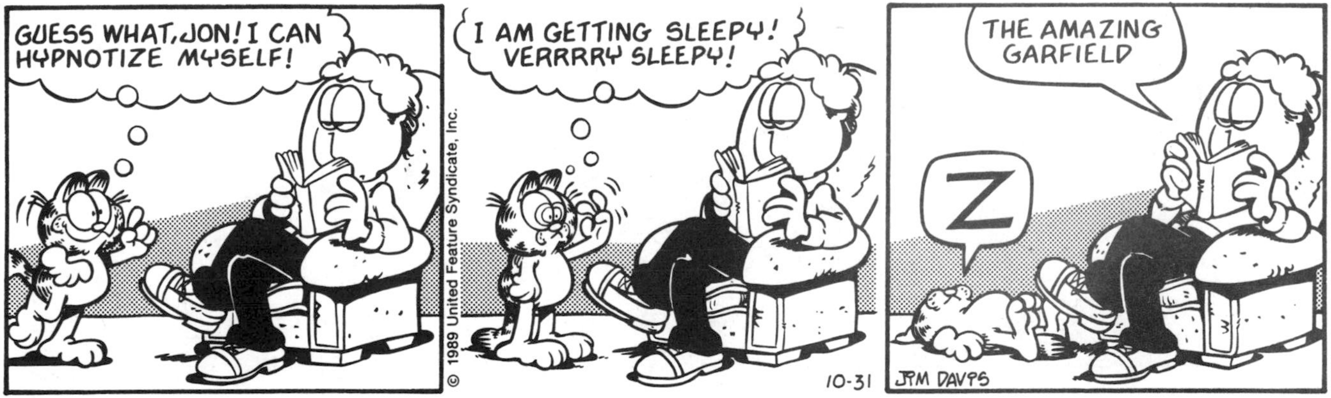
GUESS WHAT, JON! I CAN HYPNOTIZE MYSELF!
I AM GETTING SLEEPY! VERRRRY SLEEPY!
THE AMAZING GARFIELD
Z
© 1989 United Feature Syndicate, Inc.
10-31
JIM DAVIS

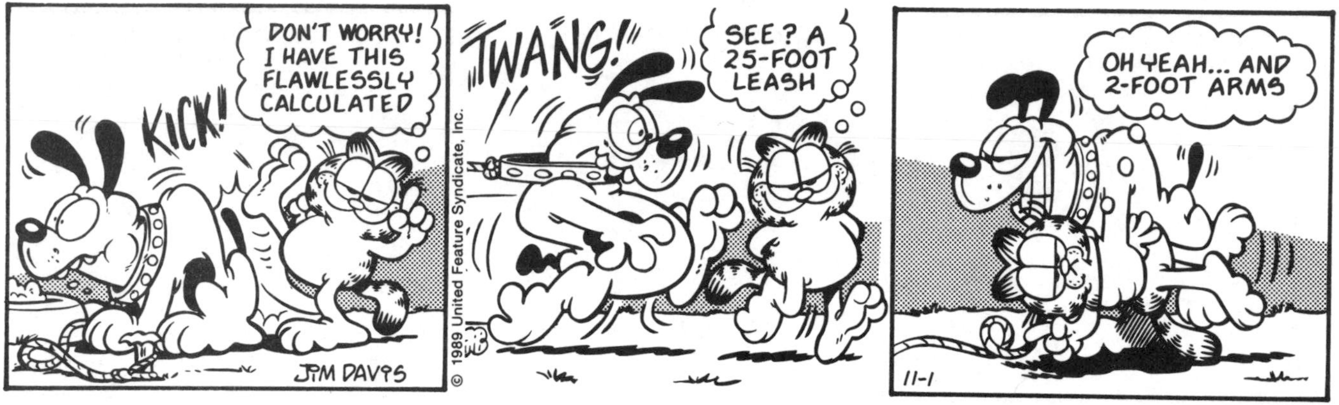
KICK!
DON'T WORRY! I HAVE THIS FLAWLESSLY CALCULATED
JIM DAVIS
© 1989 United Feature Syndicate, Inc.
TWANG!
SEE? A 25-FOOT LEASH
OH YEAH... AND 2-FOOT ARMS
11-1

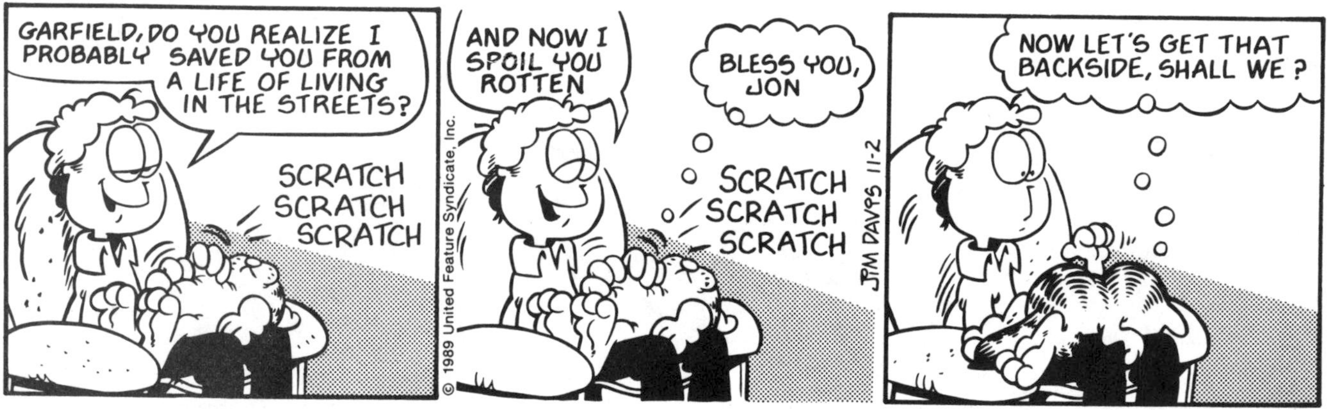
GARFIELD, DO YOU REALIZE I PROBABLY SAVED YOU FROM A LIFE OF LIVING IN THE STREETS?
SCRATCH SCRATCH SCRATCH
© 1989 United Feature Syndicate, Inc.
AND NOW I SPOIL YOU ROTTEN
BLESS YOU, JON
SCRATCH SCRATCH SCRATCH
JIM DAVIS 11-2
NOW LET'S GET THAT BACKSIDE, SHALL WE?

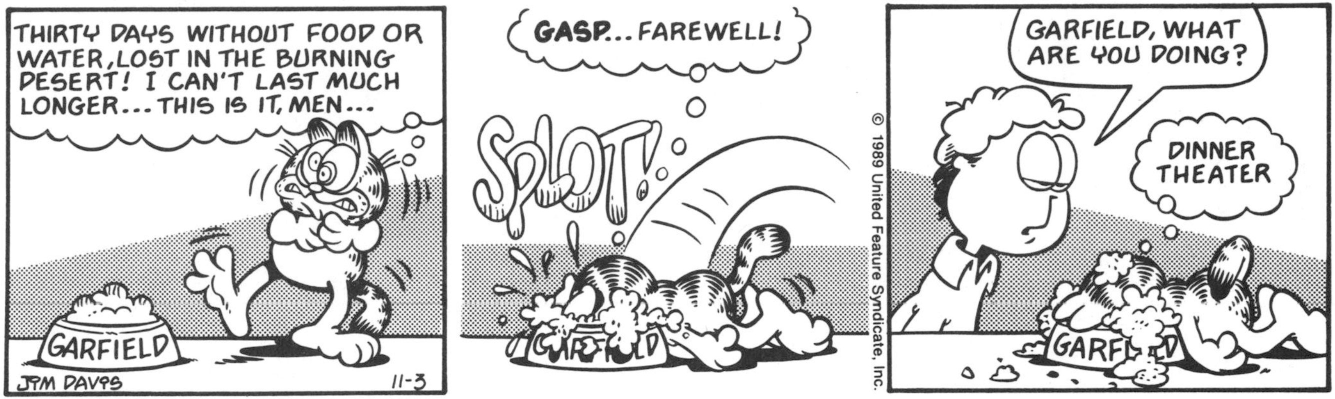
THIRTY DAYS WITHOUT FOOD OR WATER, LOST IN THE BURNING DESERT! I CAN'T LAST MUCH LONGER... THIS IS IT, MEN...
GARFIELD
JIM DAVIS
11-3
GASP... FAREWELL!
SPLOT!
GARFIELD
© 1989 United Feature Syndicate, Inc.
GARFIELD, WHAT ARE YOU DOING?
DINNER THEATER
GARF

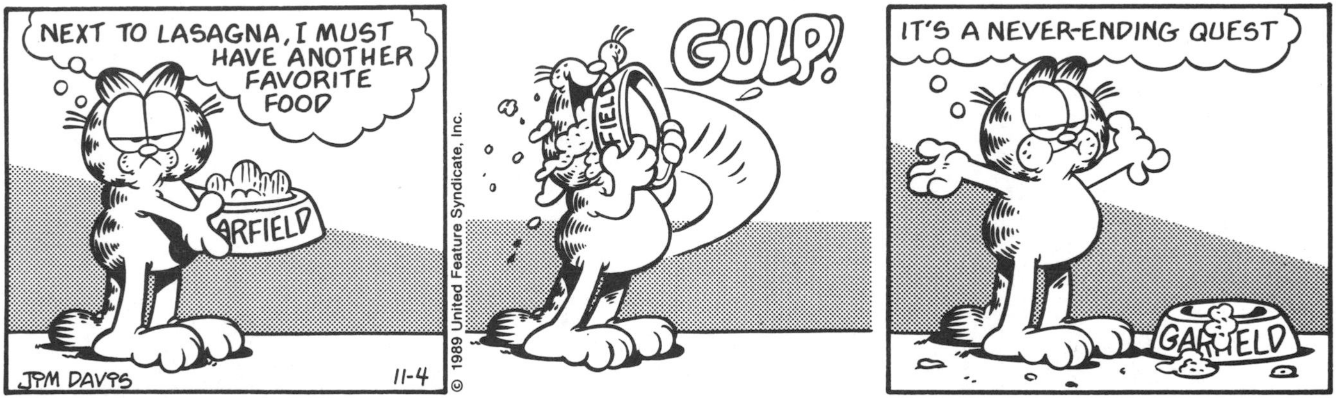
NEXT TO LASAGNA, I MUST HAVE ANOTHER FAVORITE FOOD
ARFIELD
JIM DAVIS
11-4
© 1989 United Feature Syndicate, Inc.
GULP!
FIELD
IT'S A NEVER-ENDING QUEST
GARFIELD

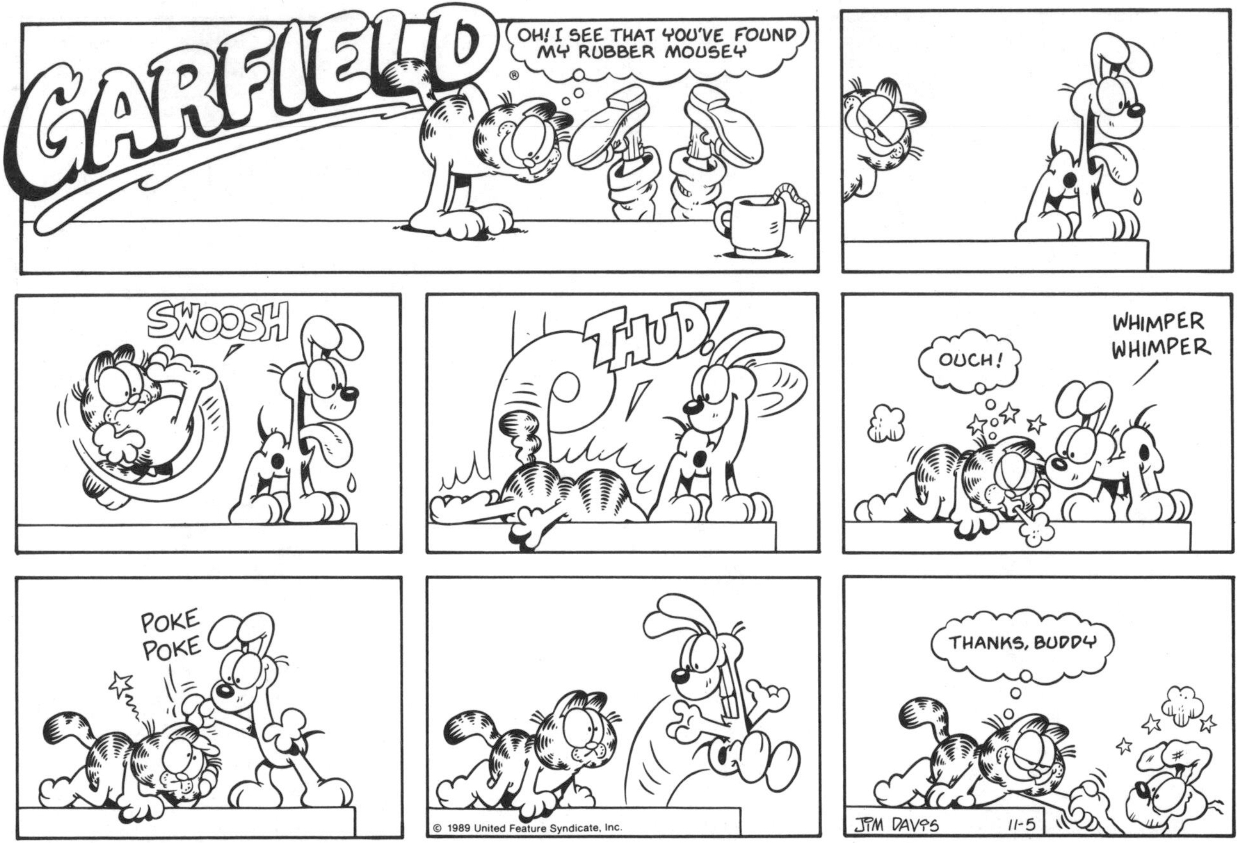
GARFIELD
OH! I SEE THAT YOU'VE FOUND MY RUBBER MOUSEY
SWOOSH
THUD!
OUCH!
WHIMPER WHIMPER
POKE POKE
THANKS, BUDDY
© 1989 United Feature Syndicate, Inc.
JIM DAVIS 11-5

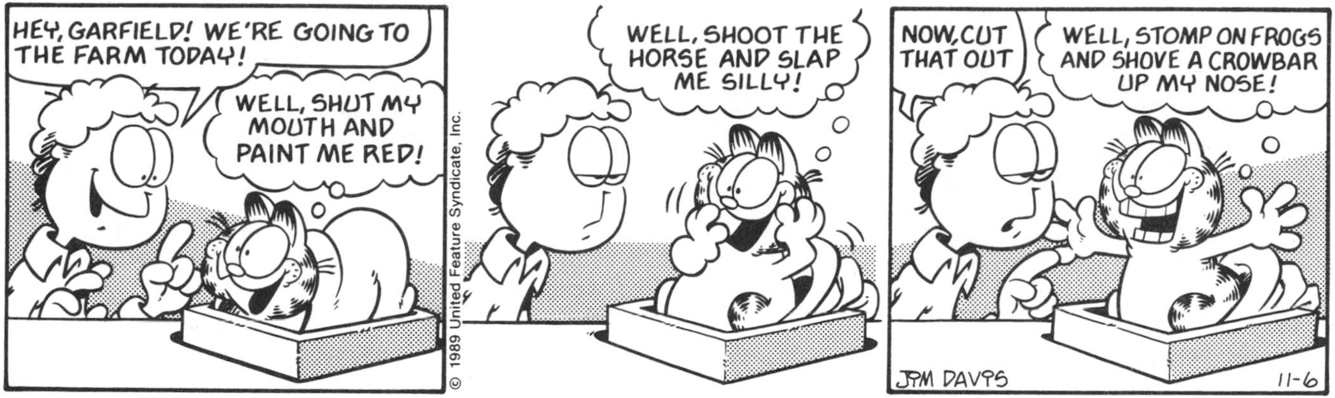
HEY, GARFIELD! WE'RE GOING TO THE FARM TODAY!
WELL, SHUT MY MOUTH AND PAINT ME RED!
© 1989 United Feature Syndicate, Inc.
WELL, SHOOT THE HORSE AND SLAP ME SILLY!
NOW, CUT THAT OUT
WELL, STOMP ON FROGS AND SHOVE A CROWBAR UP MY NOSE!
JIM DAVIS
11-6

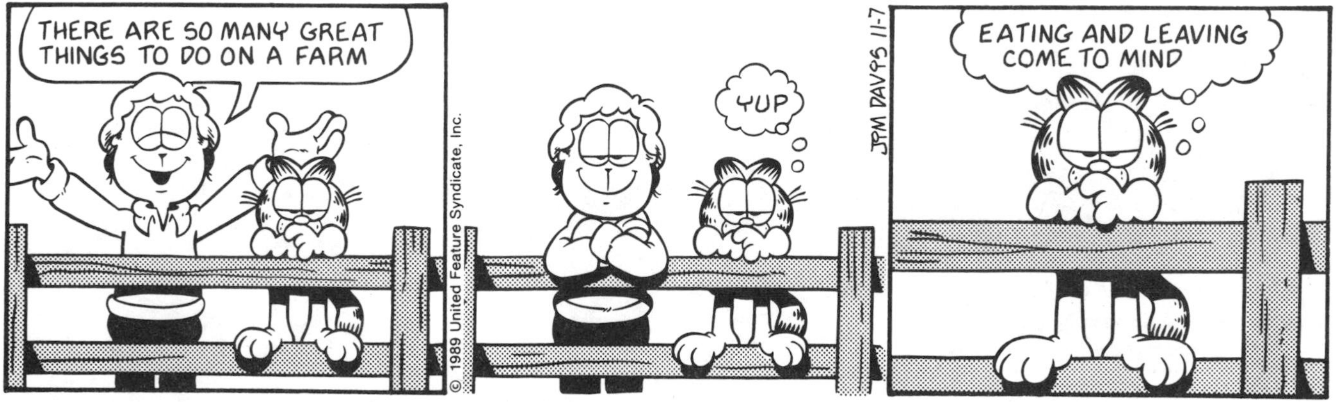
THERE ARE SO MANY GREAT THINGS TO DO ON A FARM
© 1989 United Feature Syndicate, Inc.
YUP
JIM DAVIS 11-7
EATING AND LEAVING COME TO MIND

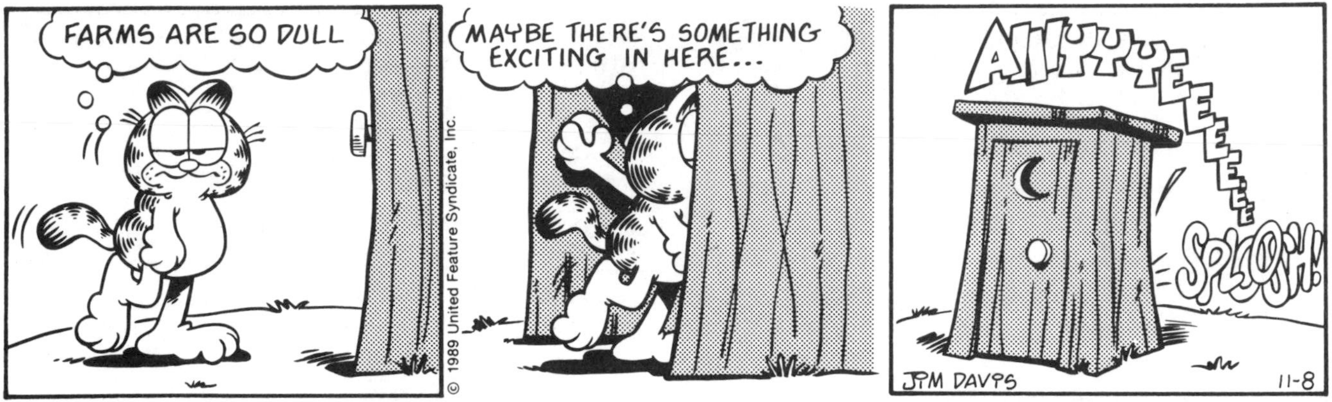
FARMS ARE SO DULL
MAYBE THERE'S SOMETHING EXCITING IN HERE...
AIIYYYEEEEEEE
SPLOOSH!
© 1989 United Feature Syndicate, Inc.
JIM DAVIS
11-8

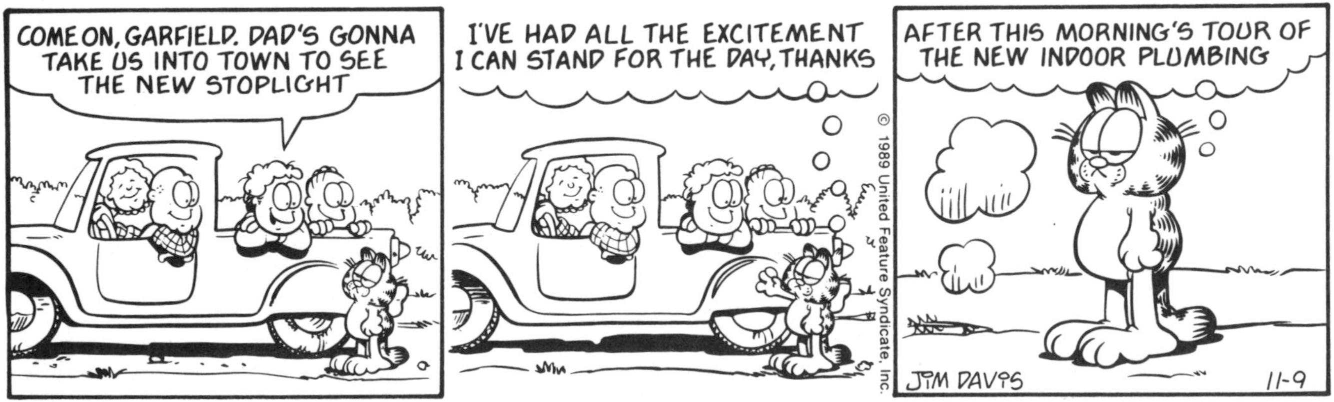
COME ON, GARFIELD. DAD'S GONNA TAKE US INTO TOWN TO SEE THE NEW STOPLIGHT
I'VE HAD ALL THE EXCITEMENT I CAN STAND FOR THE DAY, THANKS
AFTER THIS MORNING'S TOUR OF THE NEW INDOOR PLUMBING
© 1989 United Feature Syndicate, Inc.
JIM DAVIS
11-9

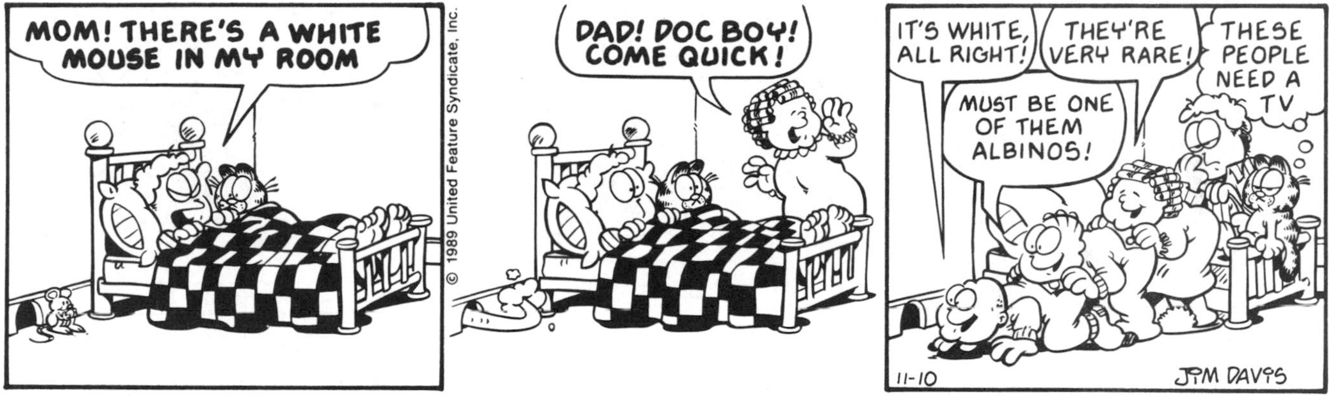
MOM! THERE'S A WHITE MOUSE IN MY ROOM
© 1989 United Feature Syndicate, Inc.
DAD! DOC BOY! COME QUICK!
IT'S WHITE, ALL RIGHT!
THEY'RE VERY RARE!
THESE PEOPLE NEED A TV
MUST BE ONE OF THEM ALBINOS!
11-10
JIM DAVIS

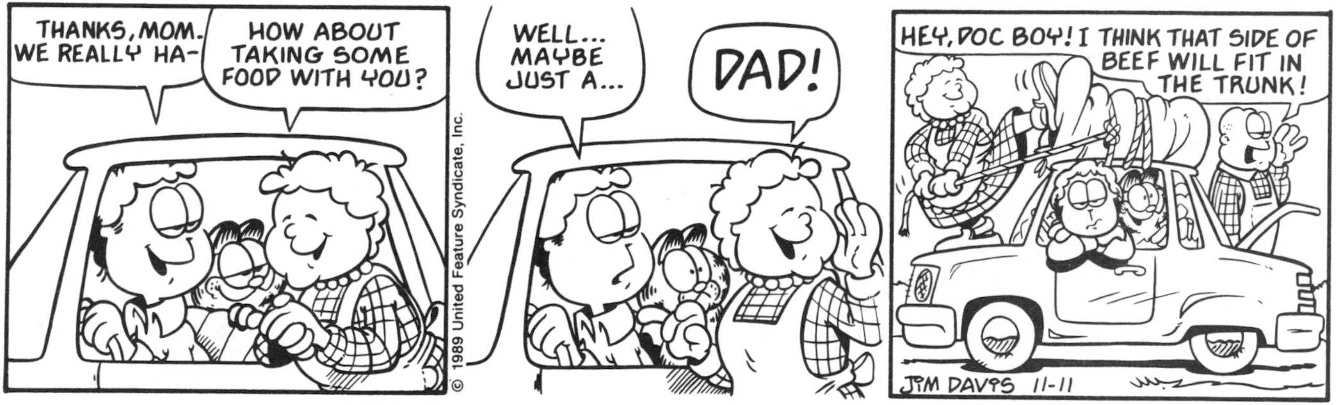
THANKS, MOM. WE REALLY HA-
HOW ABOUT TAKING SOME FOOD WITH YOU?
© 1989 United Feature Syndicate, Inc.
WELL... MAYBE JUST A...
DAD!
HEY, DOC BOY! I THINK THAT SIDE OF BEEF WILL FIT IN THE TRUNK!
JIM DAVIS 11-11

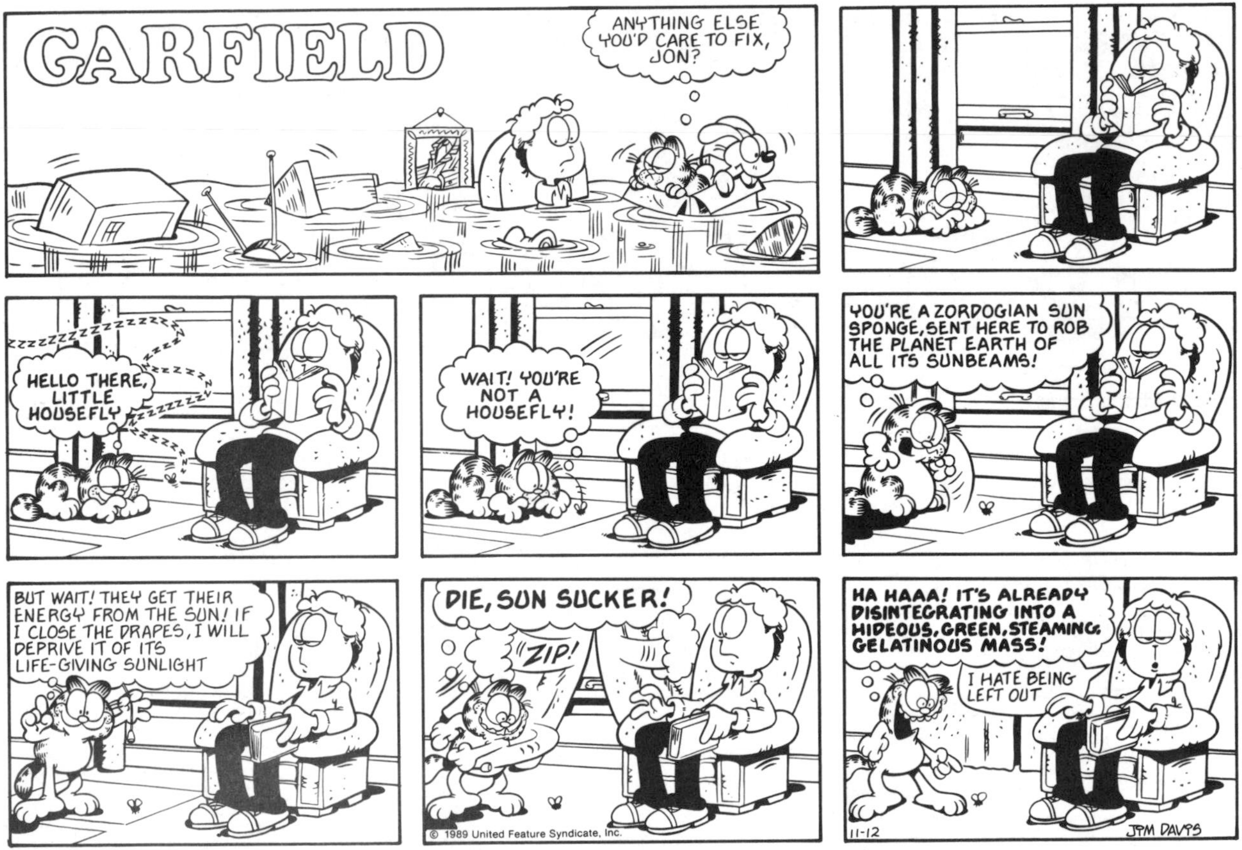
GARFIELD
ANYTHING ELSE YOU'D CARE TO FIX, JON?
HELLO THERE, LITTLE HOUSEFLY
ZZZZZZZZZZZZZZZ
WAIT! YOU'RE NOT A HOUSEFLY!
YOU'RE A ZORDOGIAN SUN SPONGE, SENT HERE TO ROB THE PLANET EARTH OF ALL ITS SUNBEAMS!
BUT WAIT! THEY GET THEIR ENERGY FROM THE SUN! IF I CLOSE THE DRAPES, I WILL DEPRIVE IT OF ITS LIFE-GIVING SUNLIGHT
DIE, SUN SUCKER!
ZIP!
HA HAAA! IT'S ALREADY DISINTEGRATING INTO A HIDEOUS, GREEN, STEAMING, GELATINOUS MASS!
I HATE BEING LEFT OUT
© 1989 United Feature Syndicate, Inc.
11-12
JIM DAVIS

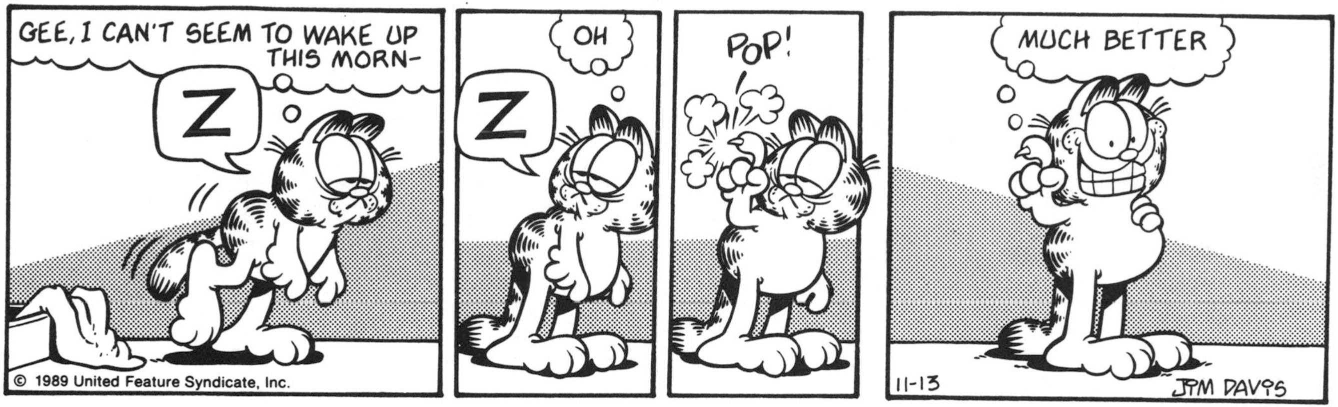
GEE, I CAN'T SEEM TO WAKE UP THIS MORN-
Z
© 1989 United Feature Syndicate, Inc.
OH
Z
POP!
MUCH BETTER
11-13
JIM DAVIS

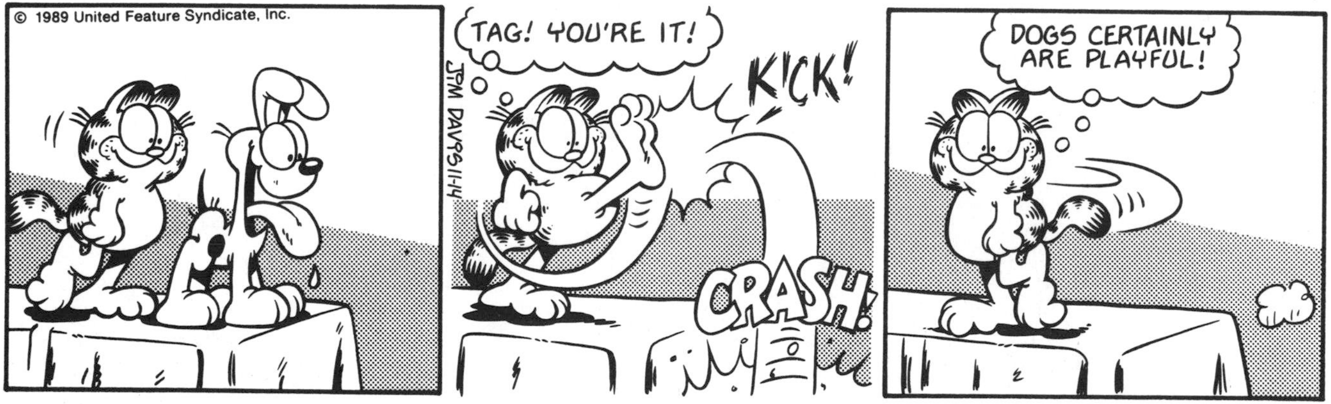
© 1989 United Feature Syndicate, Inc.
JIM DAVIS 11-14
TAG! YOU'RE IT!
KICK!
CRASH!
DOGS CERTAINLY ARE PLAYFUL!

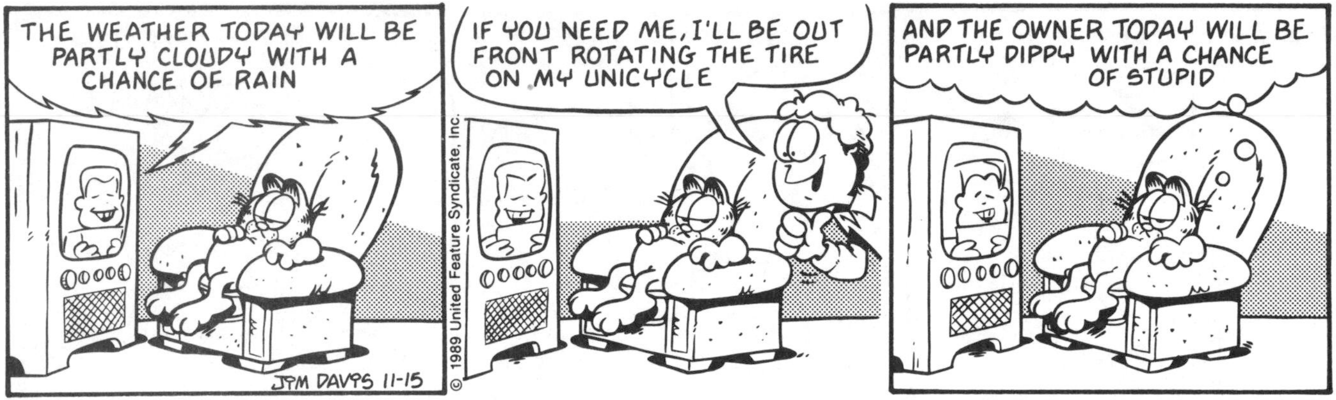
THE WEATHER TODAY WILL BE PARTLY CLOUDY WITH A CHANCE OF RAIN
IF YOU NEED ME, I'LL BE OUT FRONT ROTATING THE TIRE ON MY UNICYCLE
AND THE OWNER TODAY WILL BE PARTLY DIPPY WITH A CHANCE OF STUPID
JIM DAVIS 11-15
© 1989 United Feature Syndicate, Inc.

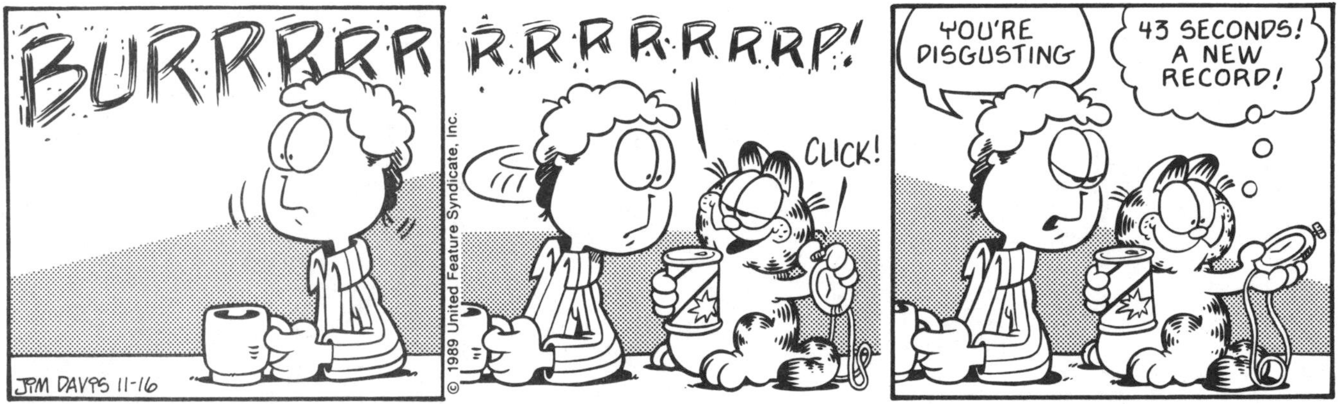
BURRRRRR
RRRRRRRP!
CLICK!
YOU'RE DISGUSTING
43 SECONDS! A NEW RECORD!
JIM DAVIS 11-16
© 1989 United Feature Syndicate, Inc.

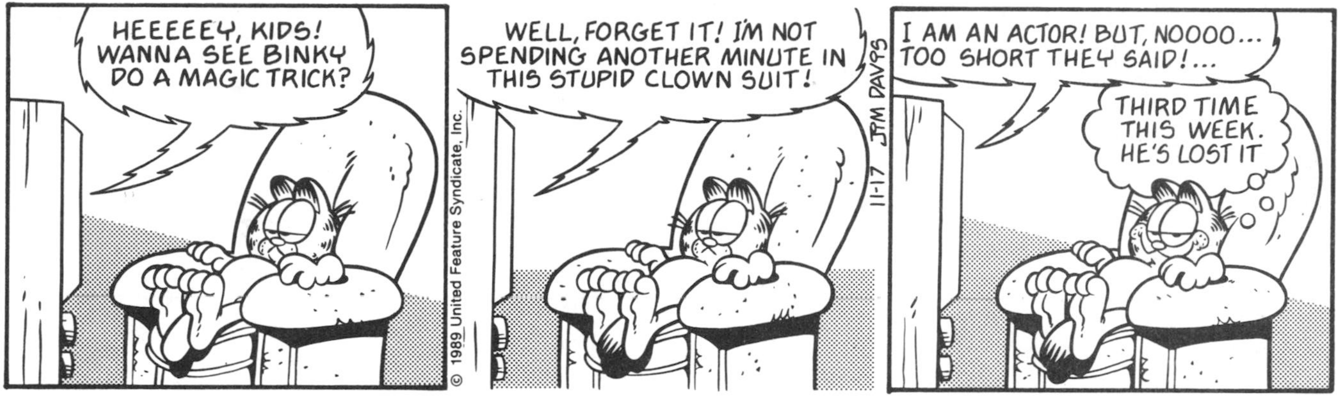
HEEEEEY, KIDS! WANNA SEE BINKY DO A MAGIC TRICK?
© 1989 United Feature Syndicate, Inc.
WELL, FORGET IT! I'M NOT SPENDING ANOTHER MINUTE IN THIS STUPID CLOWN SUIT!
JIM DAVIS 11-17
I AM AN ACTOR! BUT, NOOOO... TOO SHORT THEY SAID!...
THIRD TIME THIS WEEK. HE'S LOST IT

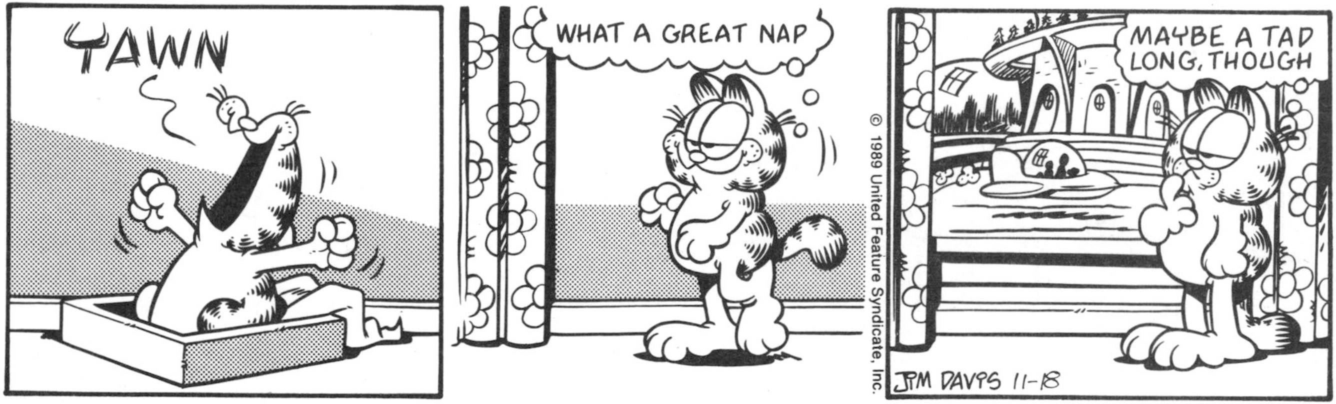
YAWN
WHAT A GREAT NAP
© 1989 United Feature Syndicate, Inc.
MAYBE A TAD LONG, THOUGH
JIM DAVIS 11-18

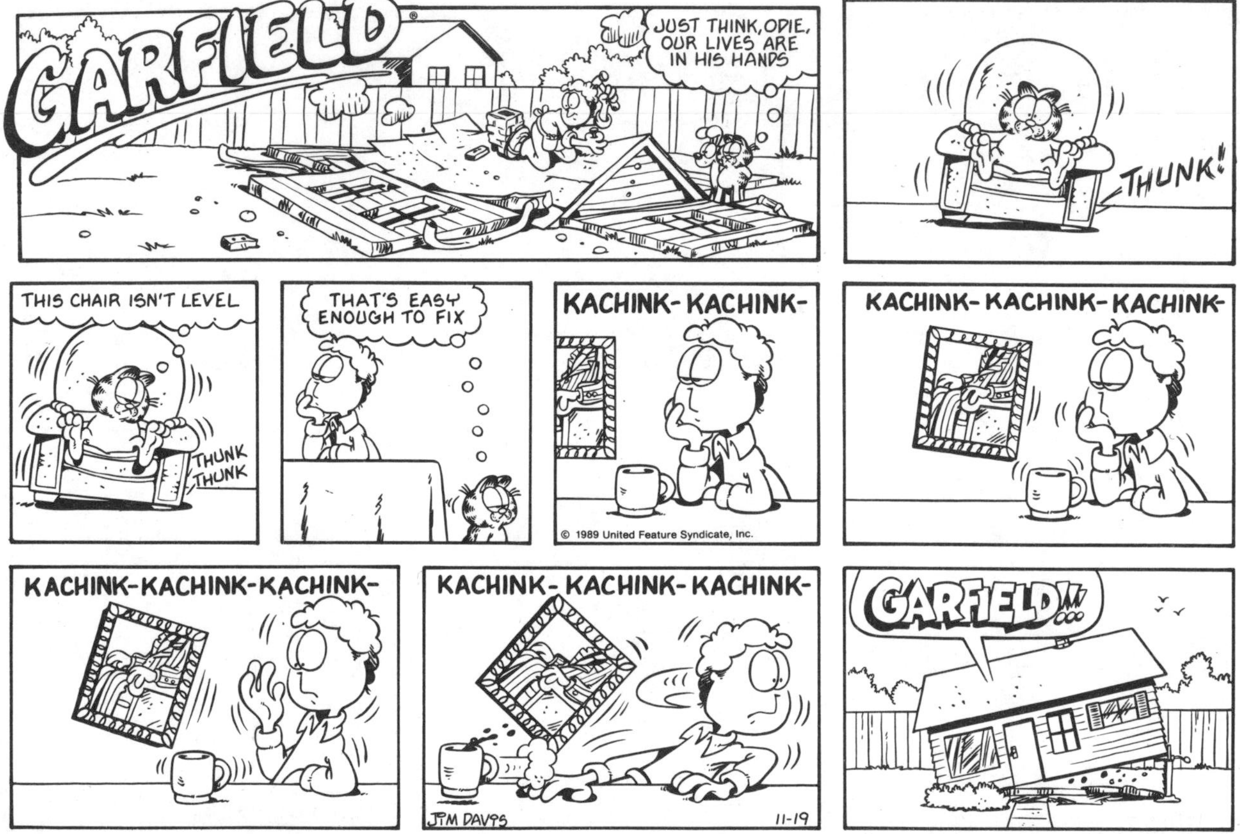

GARFIELD®
JUST THINK, ODIE, OUR LIVES ARE IN HIS HANDS
THUNK!
THIS CHAIR ISN'T LEVEL
THUNK THUNK
THAT'S EASY ENOUGH TO FIX
KACHINK- KACHINK-
© 1989 United Feature Syndicate, Inc.
KACHINK- KACHINK- KACHINK-
KACHINK-KACHINK-KACHINK-
KACHINK- KACHINK- KACHINK-
JIM DAVIS
11-19
GARFIELD!!

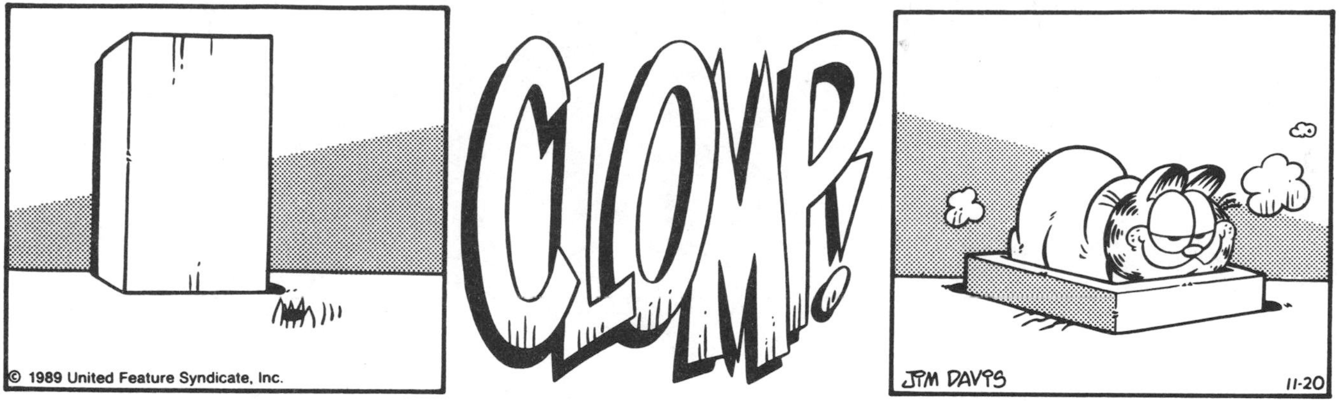
© 1989 United Feature Syndicate, Inc.
CLOMP!
JIM DAVIS
11-20

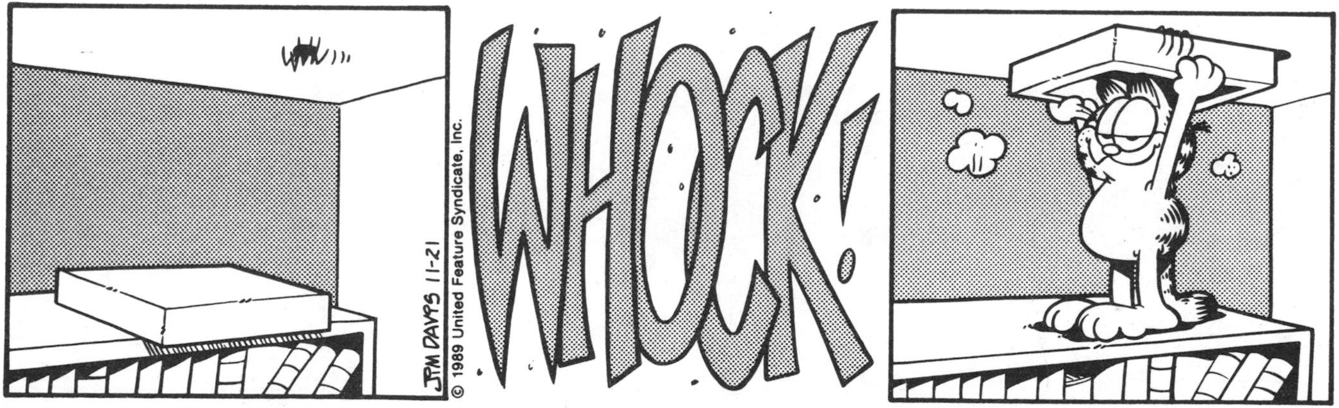
JIM DAVIS 11-21
© 1989 United Feature Syndicate, Inc.
WHOCK!

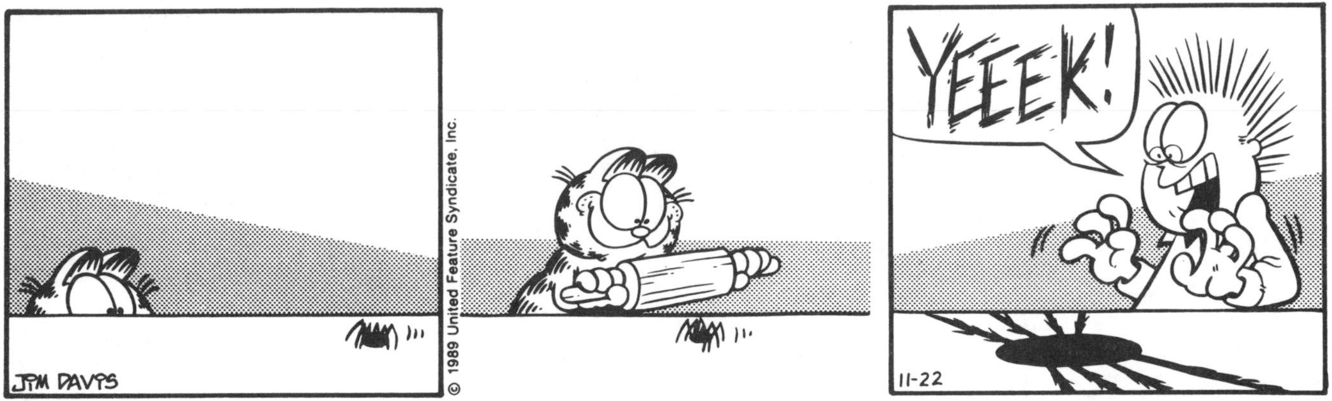
JIM DAVIS
© 1989 United Feature Syndicate, Inc.
YEEEK!
11-22

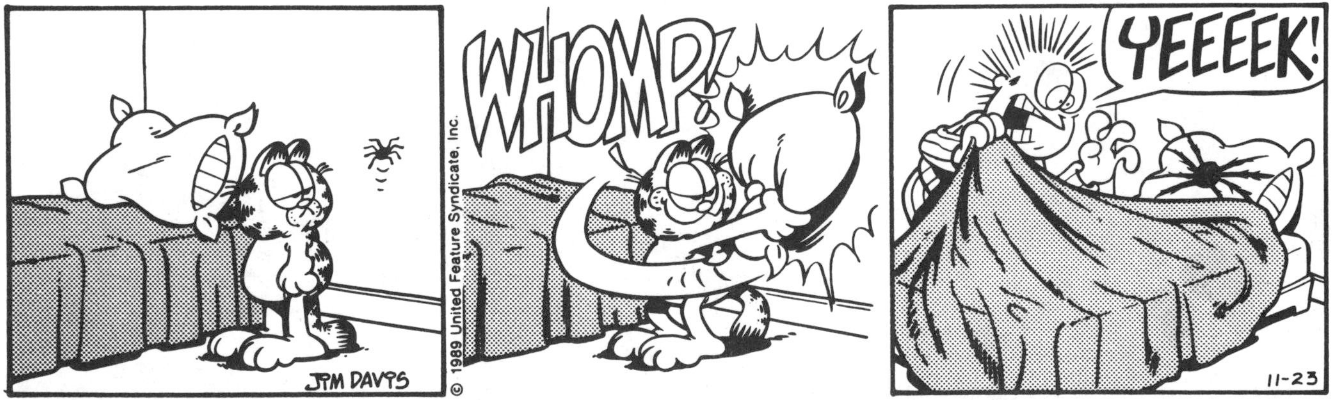
JIM DAVIS
© 1989 United Feature Syndicate, Inc.
WHOMP!
YEEEEK!
11-23

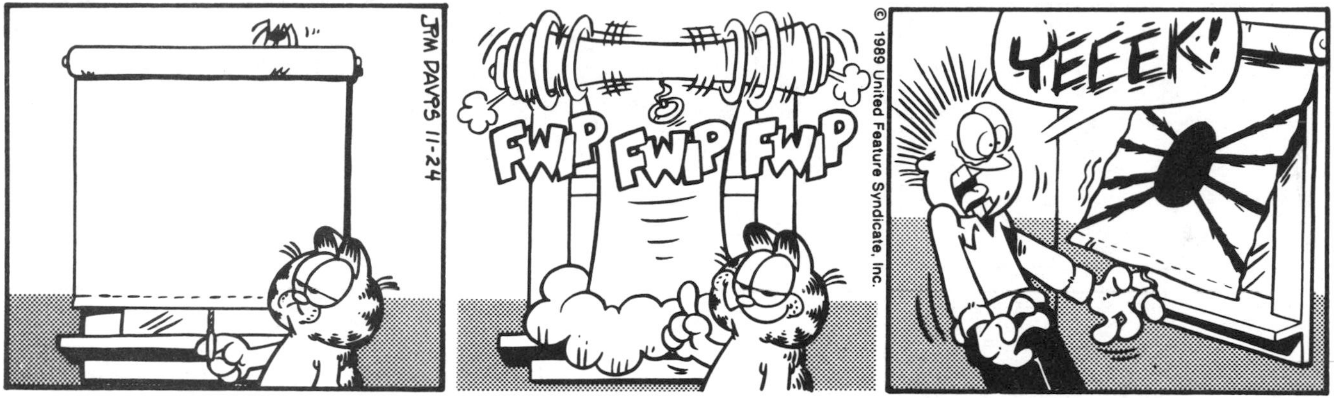
JPM DAVPS 11-24
FWIP FWIP FWIP
© 1989 United Feature Syndicate, Inc.
YEEEK!

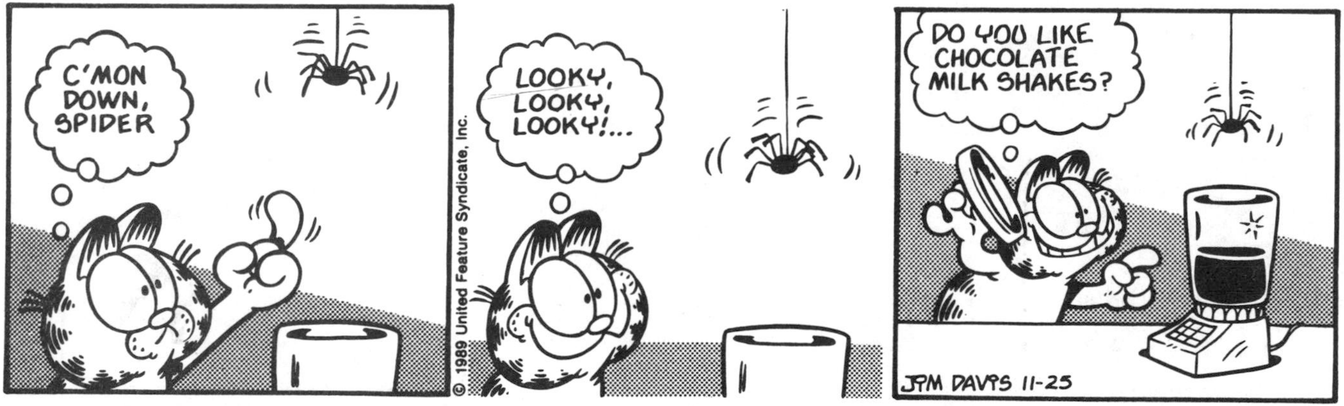
C'MON DOWN, SPIDER
© 1989 United Feature Syndicate, Inc.
LOOKY, LOOKY, LOOKY!...
DO YOU LIKE CHOCOLATE MILK SHAKES?
JPM DAVPS 11-25

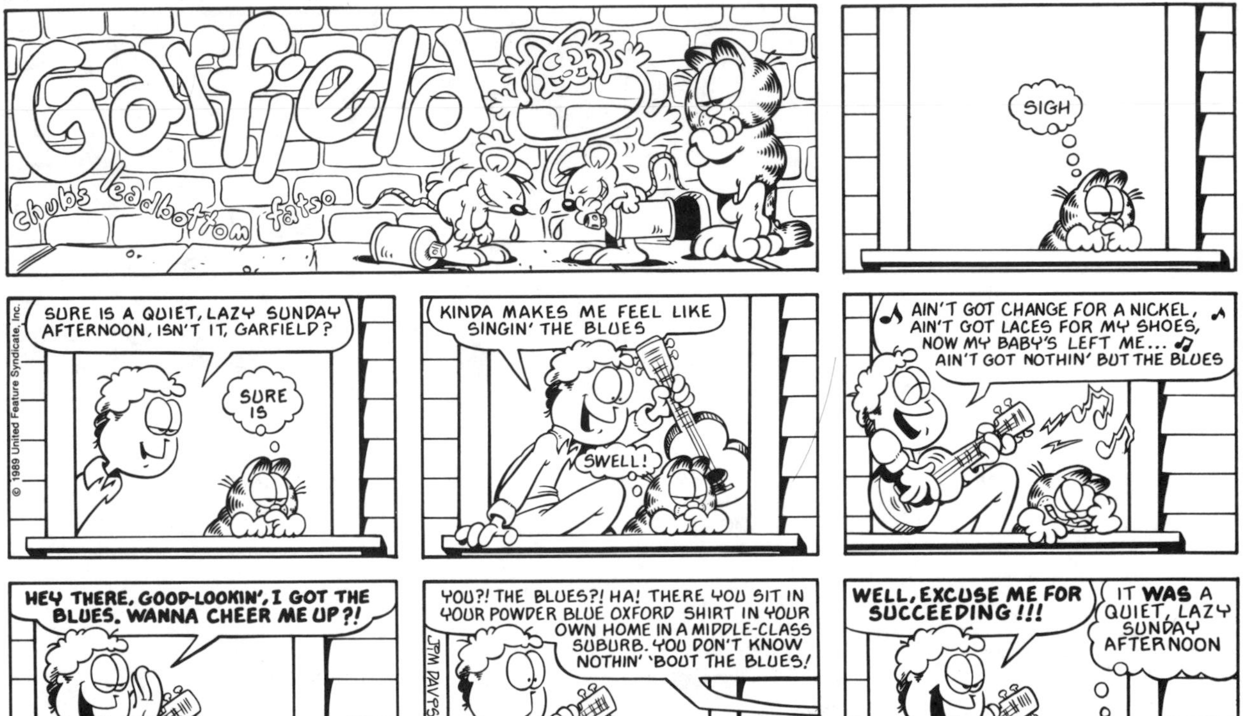
Garfield
chubs leadbottom fatso
SIGH
SURE IS A QUIET, LAZY SUNDAY AFTERNOON, ISN'T IT, GARFIELD?
SURE IS
© 1989 United Feature Syndicate, Inc.
KINDA MAKES ME FEEL LIKE SINGIN' THE BLUES
SWELL!
AIN'T GOT CHANGE FOR A NICKEL, AIN'T GOT LACES FOR MY SHOES, NOW MY BABY'S LEFT ME... AIN'T GOT NOTHIN' BUT THE BLUES
HEY THERE, GOOD-LOOKIN', I GOT THE BLUES. WANNA CHEER ME UP?!
JIM DAVIS
11-26
YOU?! THE BLUES?! HA! THERE YOU SIT IN YOUR POWDER BLUE OXFORD SHIRT IN YOUR OWN HOME IN A MIDDLE-CLASS SUBURB. YOU DON'T KNOW NOTHIN' 'BOUT THE BLUES!
WELL, EXCUSE ME FOR SUCCEEDING!!!
IT WAS A QUIET, LAZY SUNDAY AFTERNOON

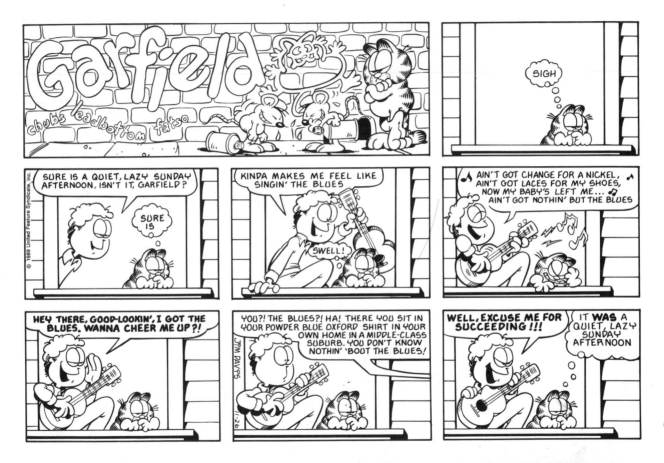

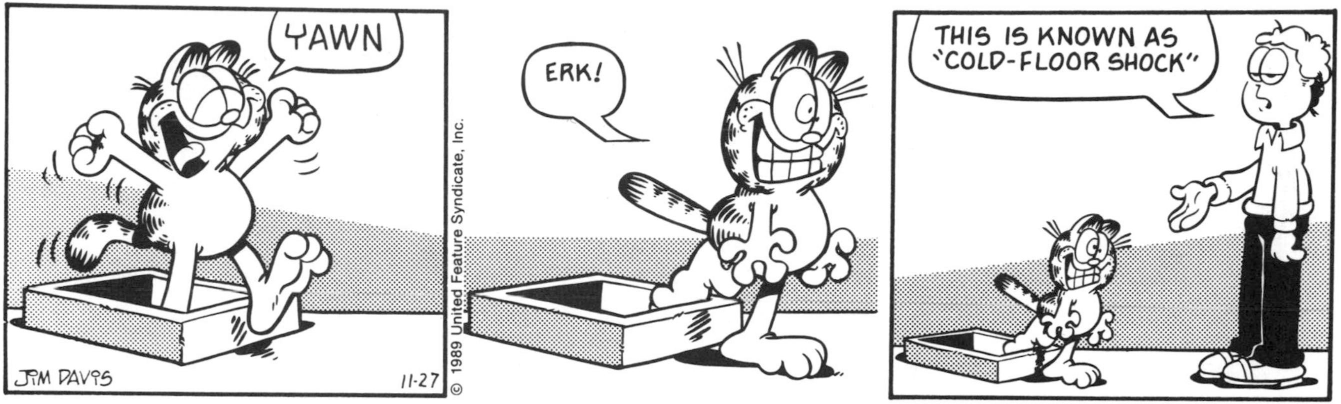
YAWN
ERK!
THIS IS KNOWN AS "COLD-FLOOR SHOCK"
JIM DAVIS
11-27
© 1989 United Feature Syndicate, Inc.

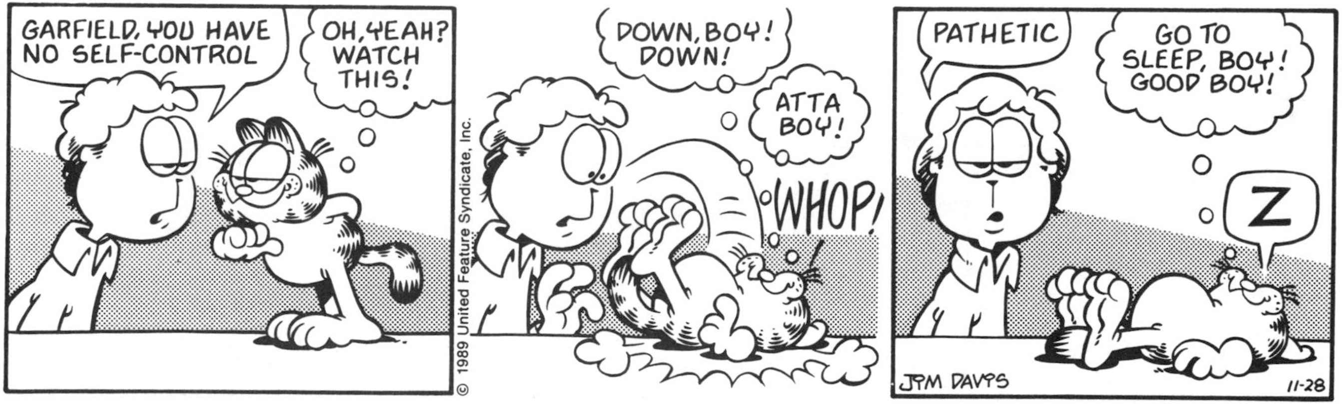
GARFIELD, YOU HAVE NO SELF-CONTROL
OH, YEAH? WATCH THIS!
DOWN, BOY! DOWN!
ATTA BOY!
WHOP!
PATHETIC
GO TO SLEEP, BOY! GOOD BOY!
Z
JIM DAVIS
11-28
© 1989 United Feature Syndicate, Inc.

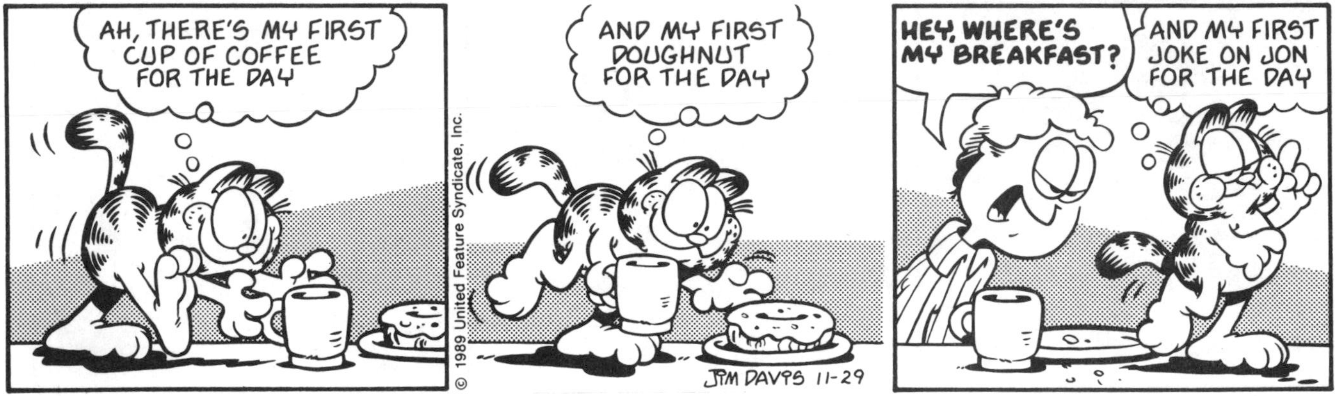
AH, THERE'S MY FIRST CUP OF COFFEE FOR THE DAY
AND MY FIRST DOUGHNUT FOR THE DAY
HEY, WHERE'S MY BREAKFAST?
AND MY FIRST JOKE ON JON FOR THE DAY
© 1989 United Feature Syndicate, Inc.
JIM DAVIS 11-29

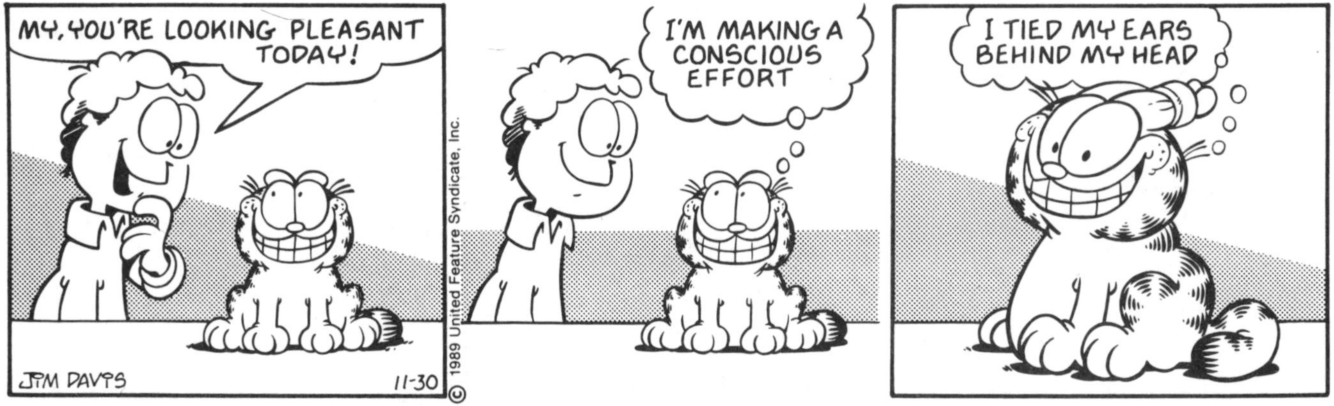
MY, YOU'RE LOOKING PLEASANT TODAY!
I'M MAKING A CONSCIOUS EFFORT
I TIED MY EARS BEHIND MY HEAD
© 1989 United Feature Syndicate, Inc.
JIM DAVIS
11-30

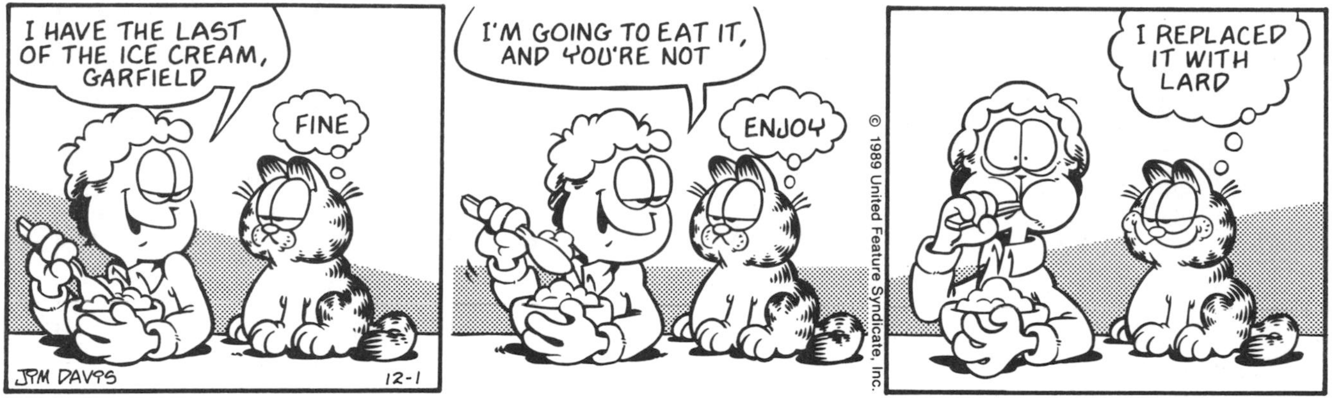
I HAVE THE LAST OF THE ICE CREAM, GARFIELD
FINE
JIM DAVIS
12-1
I'M GOING TO EAT IT, AND YOU'RE NOT
ENJOY
© 1989 United Feature Syndicate, Inc.
I REPLACED IT WITH LARD

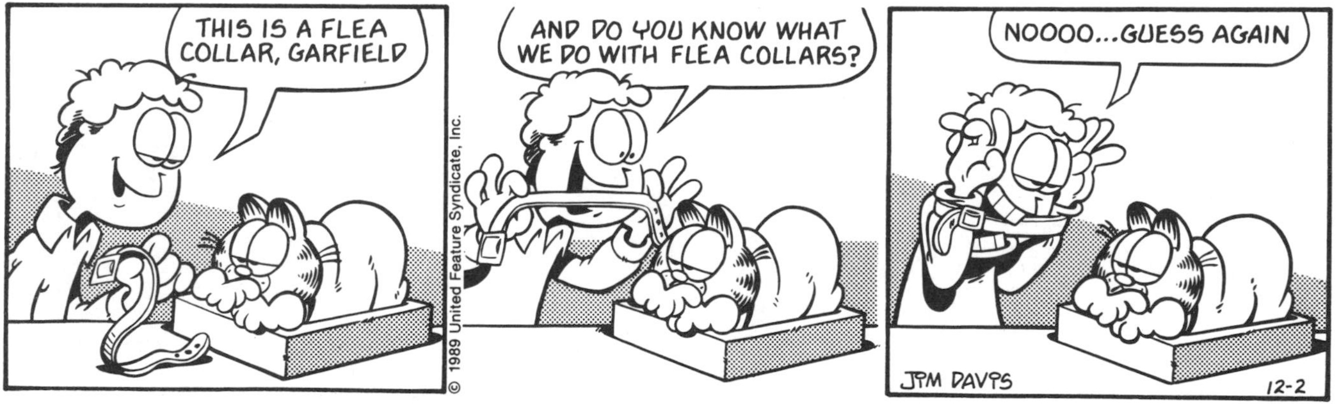
THIS IS A FLEA COLLAR, GARFIELD
© 1989 United Feature Syndicate, Inc.
AND DO YOU KNOW WHAT WE DO WITH FLEA COLLARS?
NOOOO...GUESS AGAIN
JIM DAVIS
12-2

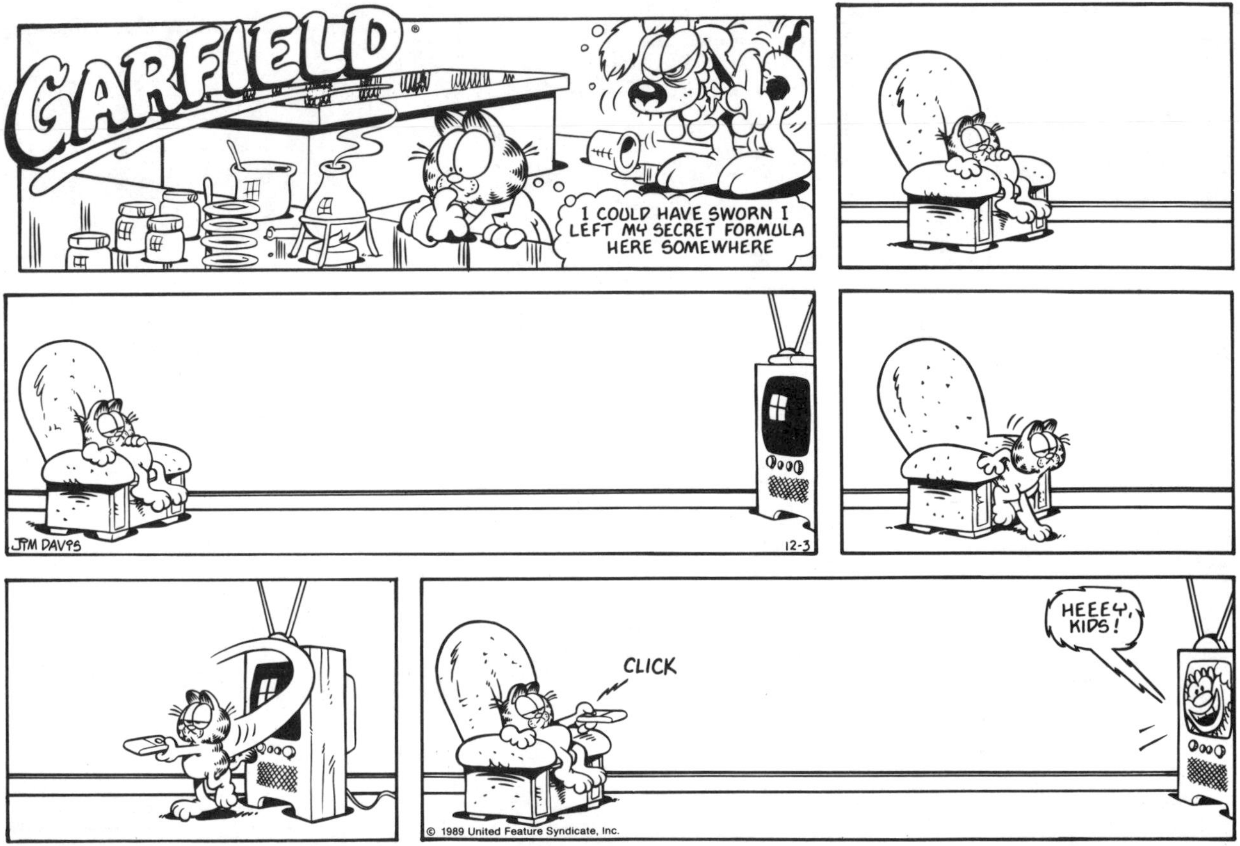
GARFIELD®
I COULD HAVE SWORN I LEFT MY SECRET FORMULA HERE SOMEWHERE
JIM DAVIS
12-3
CLICK
HEEEY, KIDS!
© 1989 United Feature Syndicate, Inc.

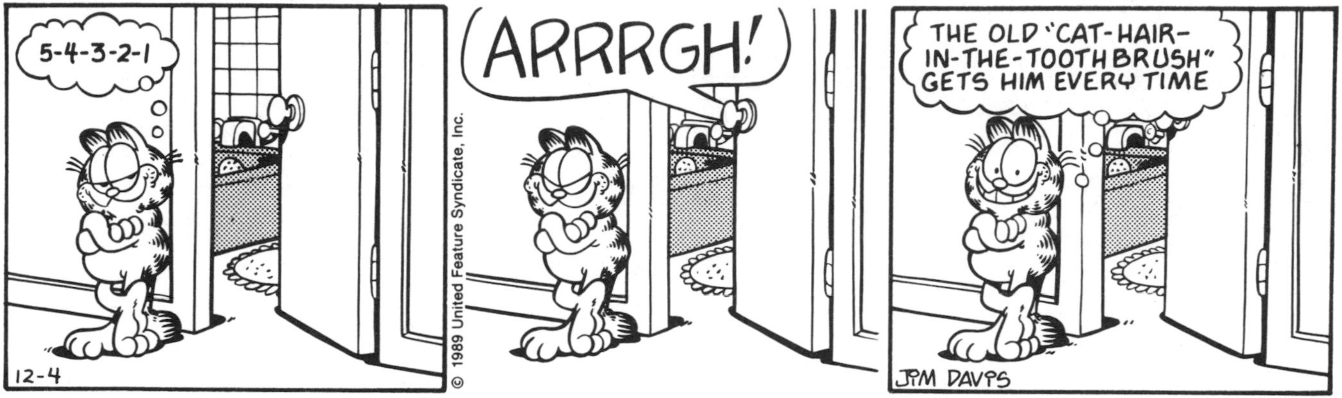
5-4-3-2-1
ARRRGH!
THE OLD "CAT-HAIR-IN-THE-TOOTHBRUSH" GETS HIM EVERY TIME
12-4
© 1989 United Feature Syndicate, Inc.
JIM DAVIS

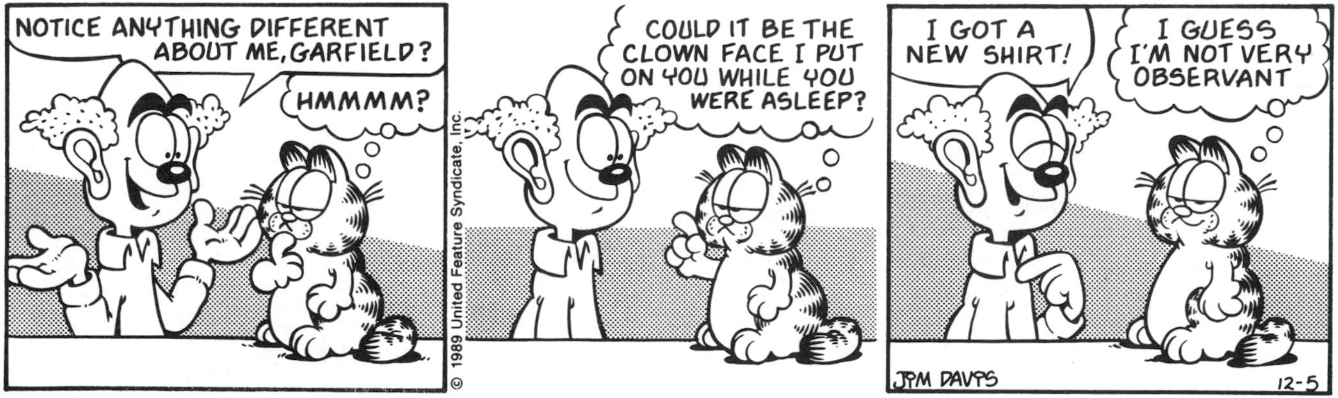
NOTICE ANYTHING DIFFERENT ABOUT ME, GARFIELD?
HMMMM?
COULD IT BE THE CLOWN FACE I PUT ON YOU WHILE YOU WERE ASLEEP?
I GOT A NEW SHIRT!
I GUESS I'M NOT VERY OBSERVANT
© 1989 United Feature Syndicate, Inc.
JIM DAVIS
12-5

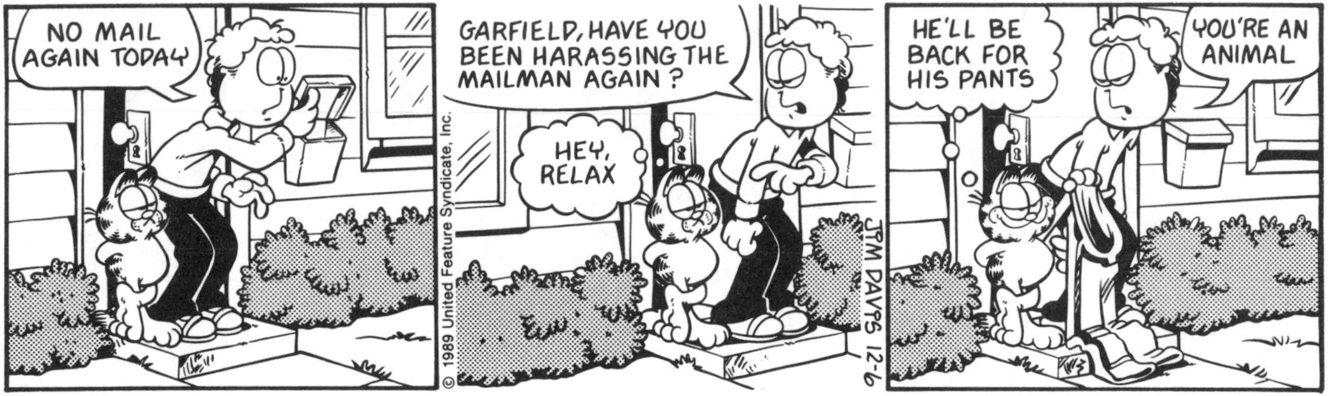
NO MAIL AGAIN TODAY
GARFIELD, HAVE YOU BEEN HARASSING THE MAILMAN AGAIN ?
HEY, RELAX
HE'LL BE BACK FOR HIS PANTS
YOU'RE AN ANIMAL
© 1989 United Feature Syndicate, Inc.
JIM DAVIS 12-6

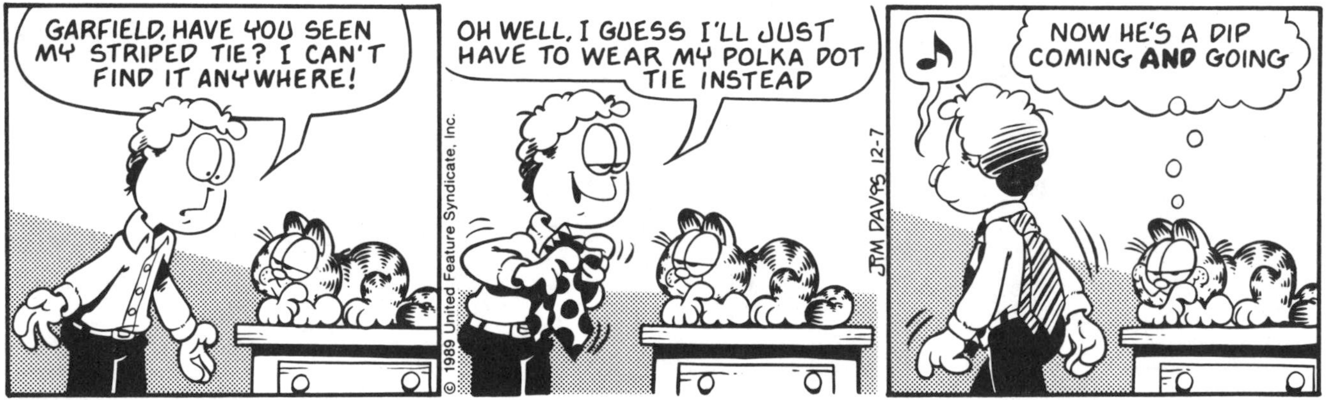
GARFIELD, HAVE YOU SEEN MY STRIPED TIE? I CAN'T FIND IT ANYWHERE!
OH WELL, I GUESS I'LL JUST HAVE TO WEAR MY POLKA DOT TIE INSTEAD
NOW HE'S A DIP COMING **AND** GOING
© 1989 United Feature Syndicate, Inc.
JIM DAVIS 12-7

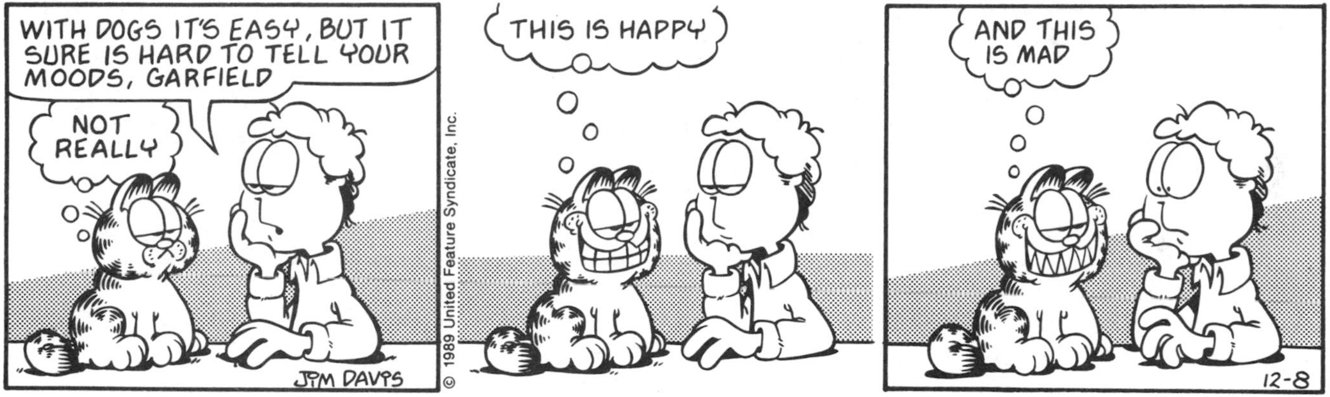
WITH DOGS IT'S EASY, BUT IT SURE IS HARD TO TELL YOUR MOODS, GARFIELD
NOT REALLY
THIS IS HAPPY
AND THIS IS MAD
JIM DAVIS
12-8
© 1989 United Feature Syndicate, Inc.

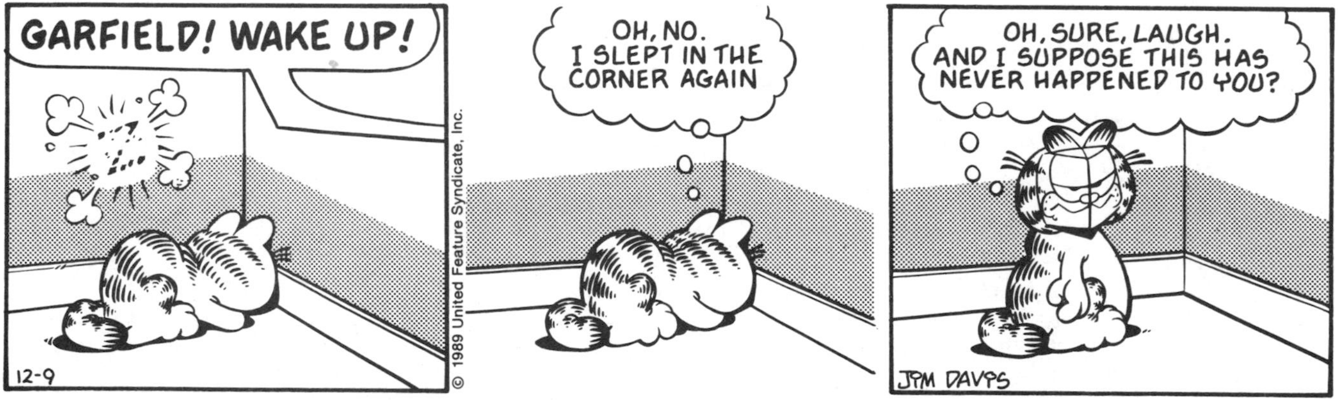
GARFIELD! WAKE UP!
OH, NO. I SLEPT IN THE CORNER AGAIN
OH, SURE, LAUGH. AND I SUPPOSE THIS HAS NEVER HAPPENED TO YOU?
12-9
JIM DAVIS
© 1989 United Feature Syndicate, Inc.

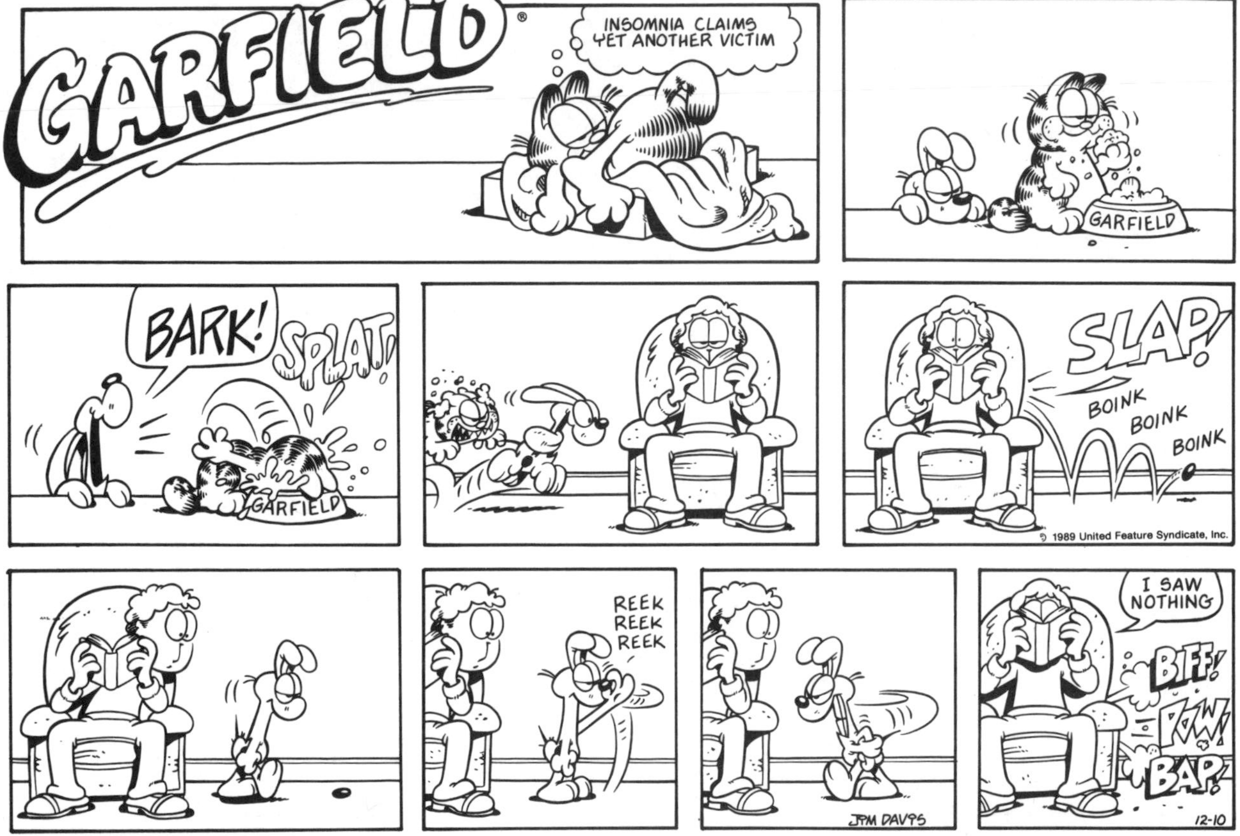
GARFIELD®
INSOMNIA CLAIMS YET ANOTHER VICTIM
GARFIELD
BARK!
SPLAT!
GARFIELD
SLAP!
BOINK
BOINK
BOINK
© 1989 United Feature Syndicate, Inc.
REEK
REEK
REEK
JPM DAVIS
I SAW NOTHING
BIFF!
POW!
BAP!
12-10

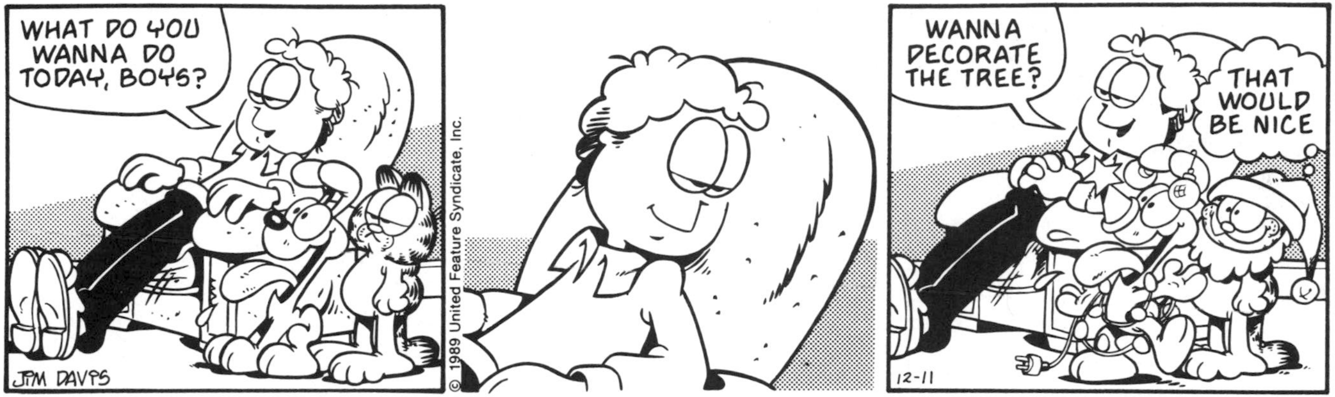
WHAT DO YOU WANNA DO TODAY, BOYS?
JIM DAVIS
WANNA DECORATE THE TREE?
THAT WOULD BE NICE
12-11

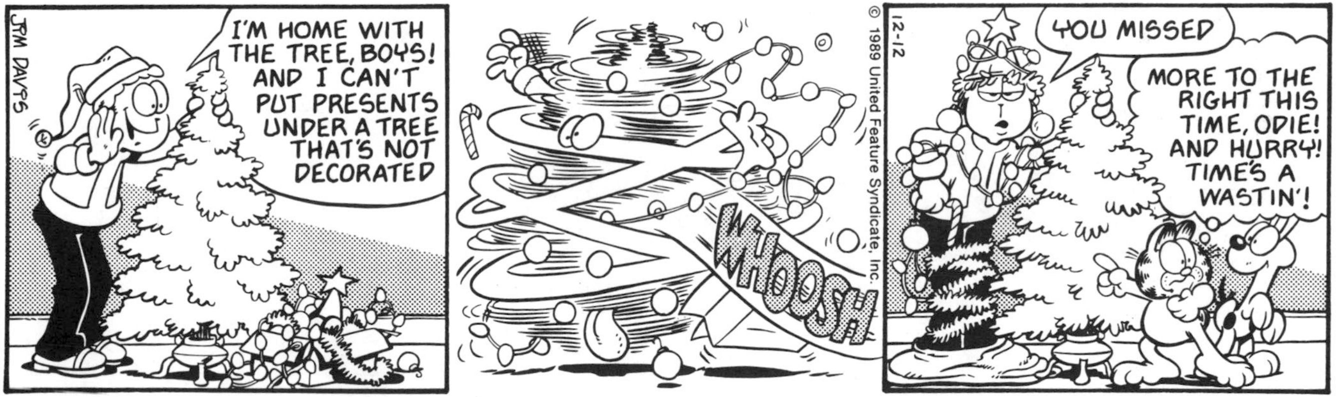
JIM DAVIS
I'M HOME WITH THE TREE, BOYS! AND I CAN'T PUT PRESENTS UNDER A TREE THAT'S NOT DECORATED
WHOOSH
12-12
YOU MISSED
MORE TO THE RIGHT THIS TIME, ODIE! AND HURRY! TIME'S A WASTIN'!

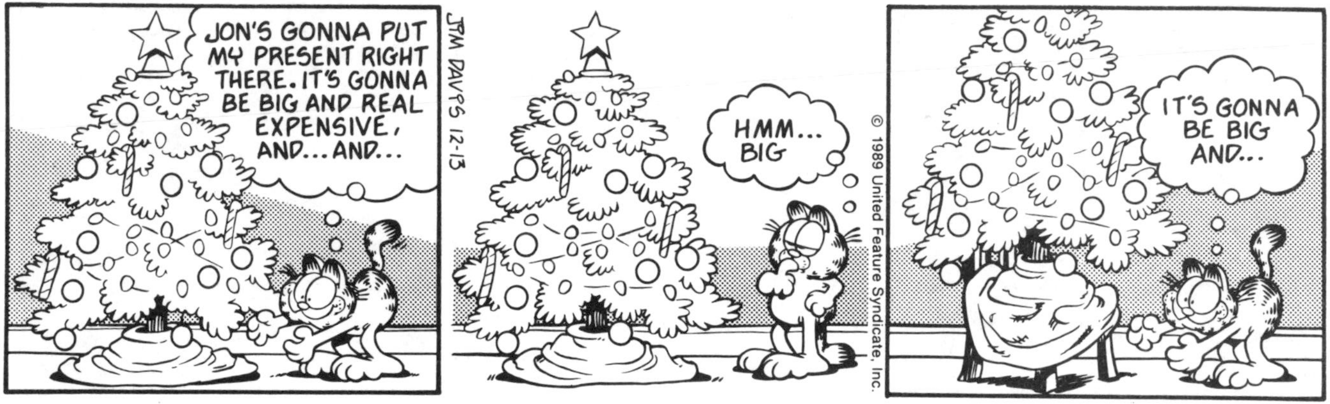
JON'S GONNA PUT MY PRESENT RIGHT THERE. IT'S GONNA BE BIG AND REAL EXPENSIVE, AND... AND...
JIM DAVIS 12-13
HMM... BIG
© 1989 United Feature Syndicate, Inc.
IT'S GONNA BE BIG AND...

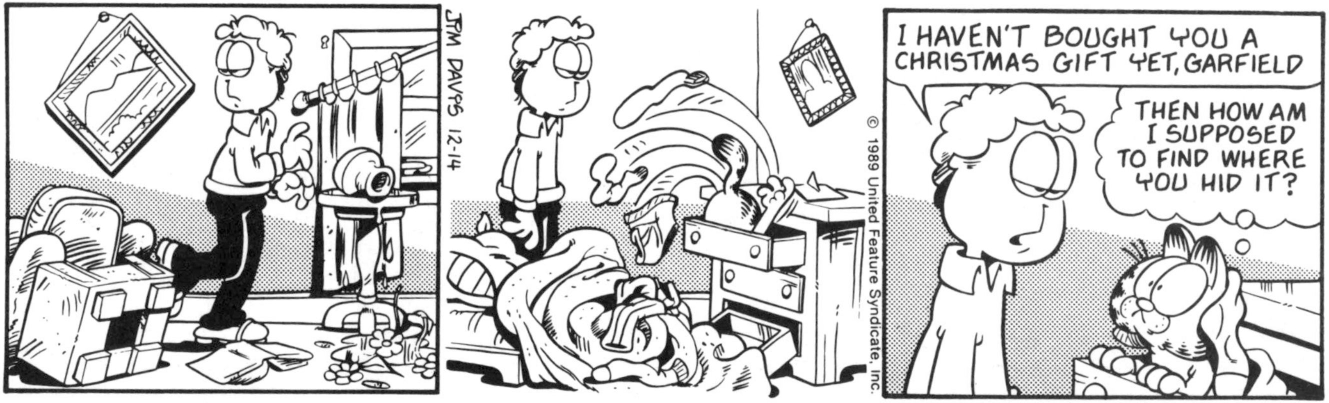
JIM DAVIS 12-14
© 1989 United Feature Syndicate, Inc.
I HAVEN'T BOUGHT YOU A CHRISTMAS GIFT YET, GARFIELD
THEN HOW AM I SUPPOSED TO FIND WHERE YOU HID IT?

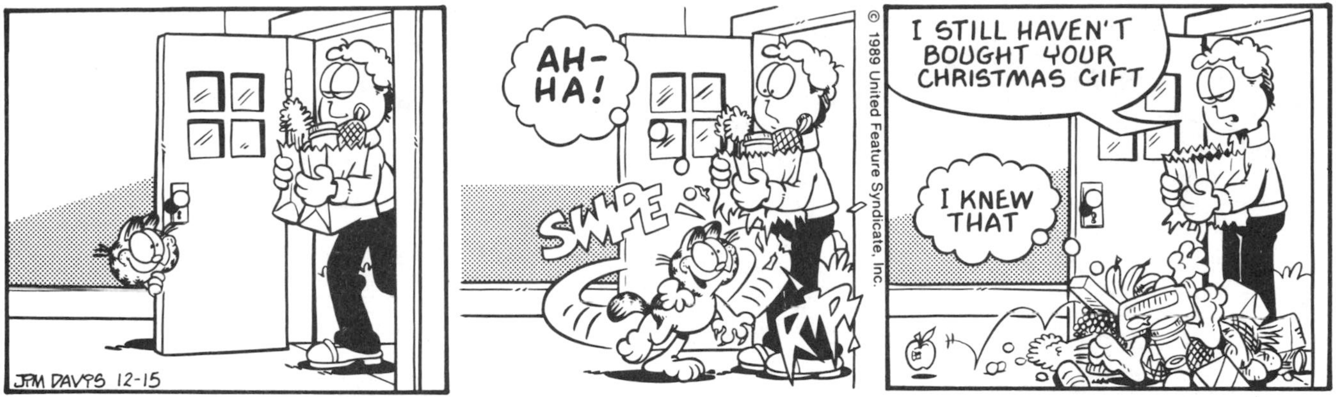
AH-HA!
SWIPE
RIP
I STILL HAVEN'T BOUGHT YOUR CHRISTMAS GIFT
I KNEW THAT
© 1989 United Feature Syndicate, Inc.
JIM DAVIS 12-15

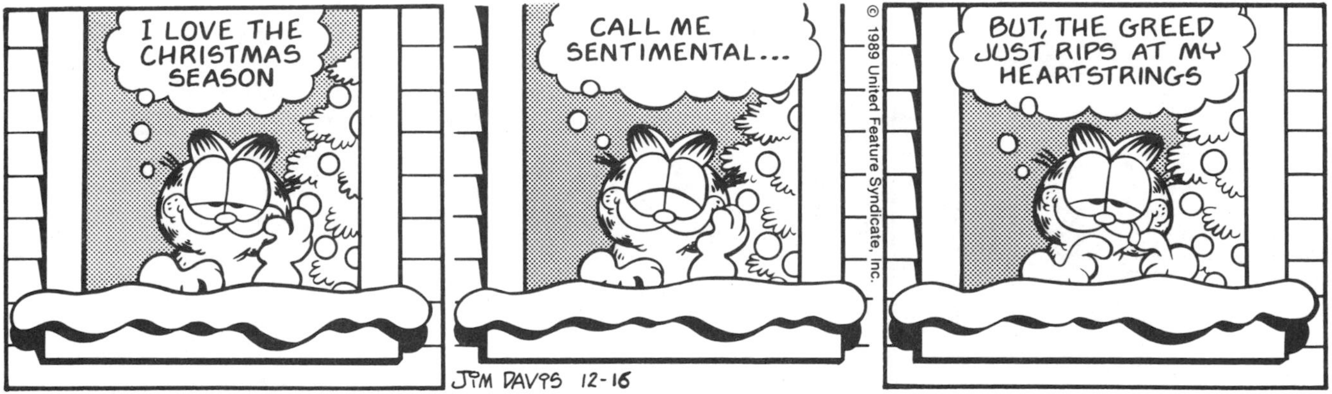
I LOVE THE CHRISTMAS SEASON
CALL ME SENTIMENTAL...
BUT, THE GREED JUST RIPS AT MY HEARTSTRINGS
© 1989 United Feature Syndicate, Inc.
JIM DAVIS 12-16

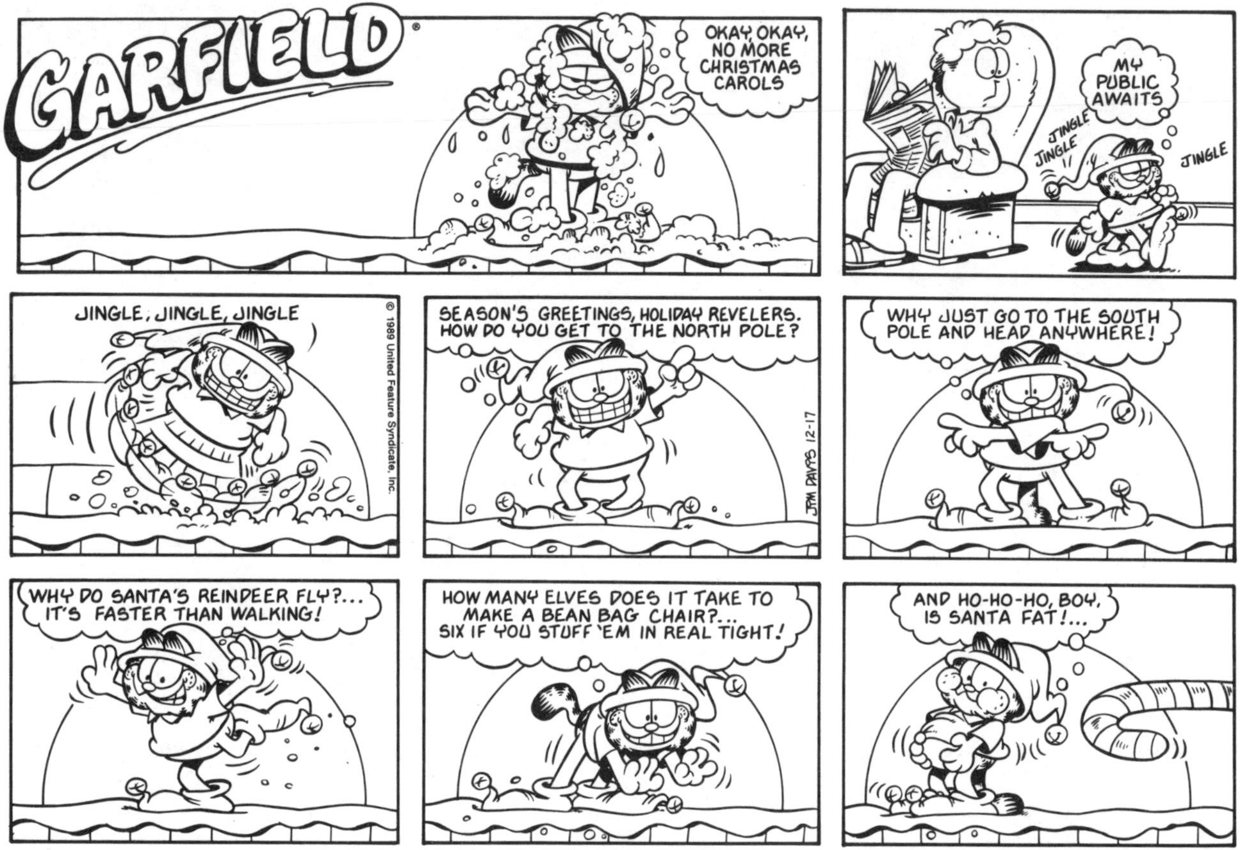

GARFIELD
OKAY, OKAY, NO MORE CHRISTMAS CAROLS
MY PUBLIC AWAITS
JINGLE JINGLE
JINGLE
JINGLE, JINGLE, JINGLE
© 1989 United Feature Syndicate, Inc.
SEASON'S GREETINGS, HOLIDAY REVELERS. HOW DO YOU GET TO THE NORTH POLE?
JPM DAVIS 12-17
WHY JUST GO TO THE SOUTH POLE AND HEAD ANYWHERE!
WHY DO SANTA'S REINDEER FLY?... IT'S FASTER THAN WALKING!
HOW MANY ELVES DOES IT TAKE TO MAKE A BEAN BAG CHAIR?... SIX IF YOU STUFF 'EM IN REAL TIGHT!
AND HO-HO-HO, BOY, IS SANTA FAT!...

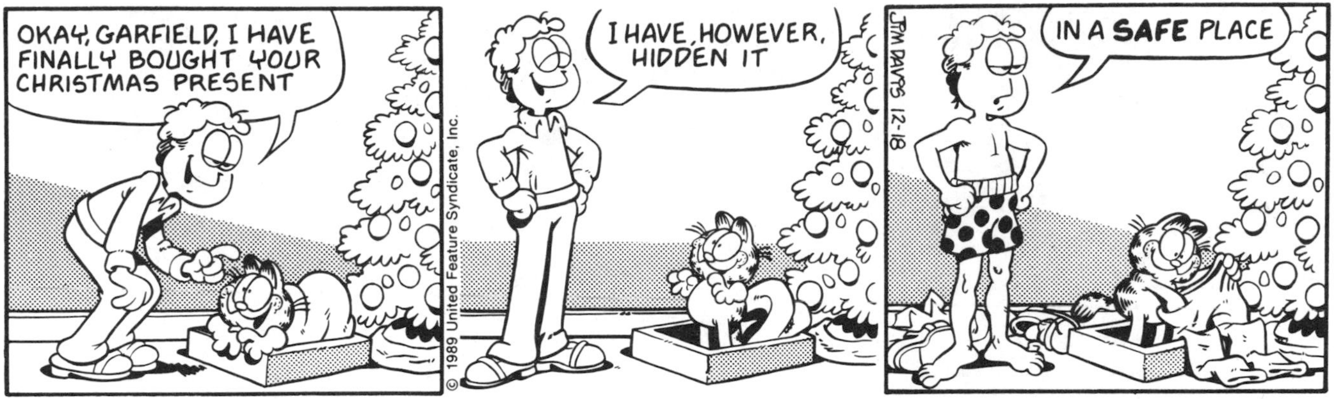

OKAY, GARFIELD, I HAVE FINALLY BOUGHT YOUR CHRISTMAS PRESENT
© 1989 United Feature Syndicate, Inc.
I HAVE, HOWEVER, HIDDEN IT
JIM DAVIS 12-18
IN A **SAFE** PLACE

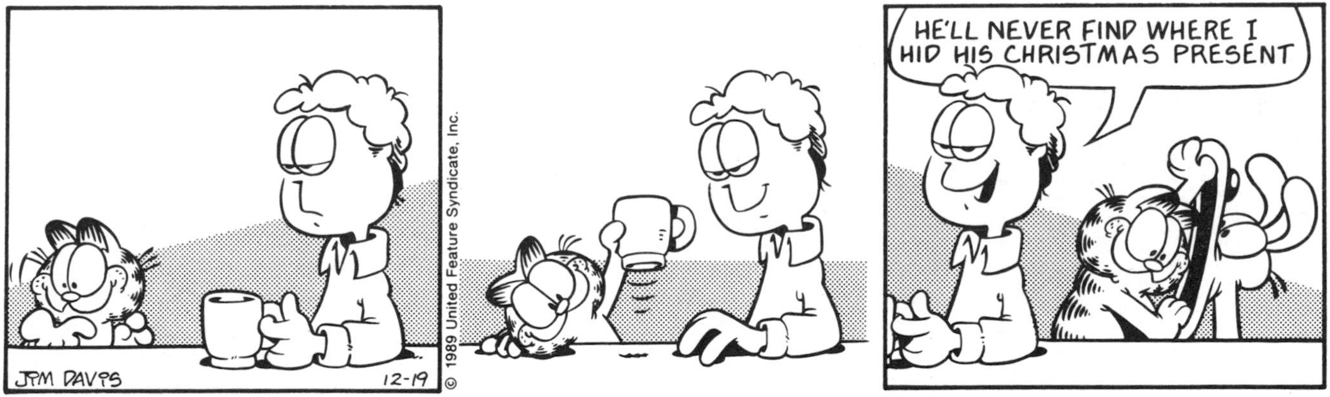

JIM DAVIS
12-19
© 1989 United Feature Syndicate, Inc.
HE'LL NEVER FIND WHERE I HID HIS CHRISTMAS PRESENT

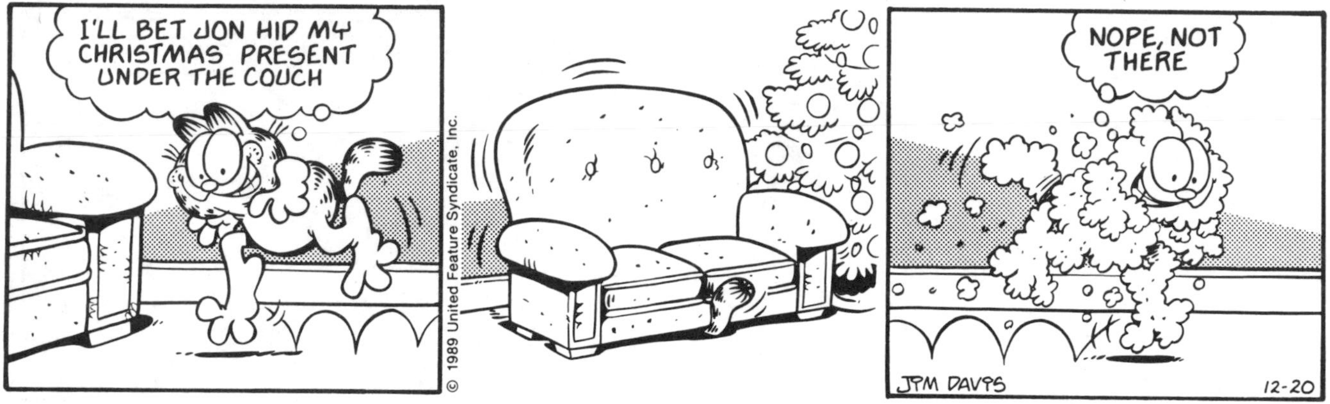
I'LL BET JON HID MY CHRISTMAS PRESENT UNDER THE COUCH
© 1989 United Feature Syndicate, Inc.
NOPE, NOT THERE
JIM DAVIS
12-20

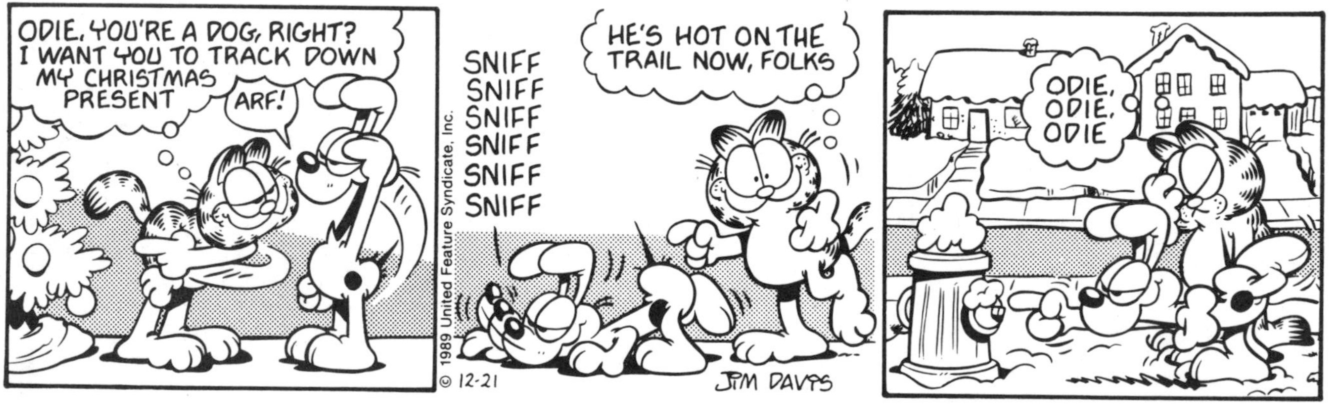
ODIE, YOU'RE A DOG, RIGHT? I WANT YOU TO TRACK DOWN MY CHRISTMAS PRESENT
ARF!
© 1989 United Feature Syndicate, Inc.
© 12-21
SNIFF SNIFF SNIFF SNIFF SNIFF SNIFF
HE'S HOT ON THE TRAIL NOW, FOLKS
JIM DAVIS
ODIE, ODIE, ODIE

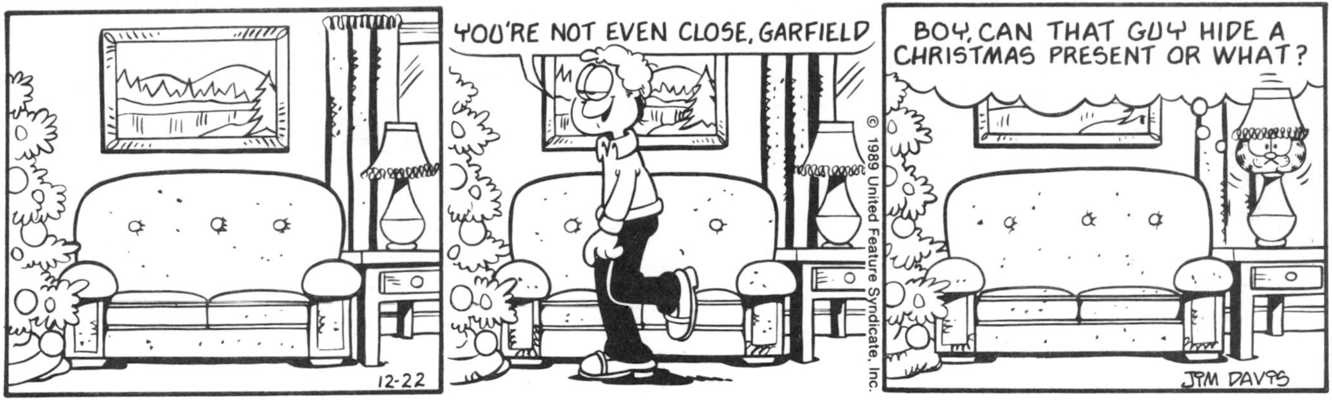
YOU'RE NOT EVEN CLOSE, GARFIELD
BOY, CAN THAT GUY HIDE A CHRISTMAS PRESENT OR WHAT?
12-22
© 1989 United Feature Syndicate, Inc.
JIM DAVIS

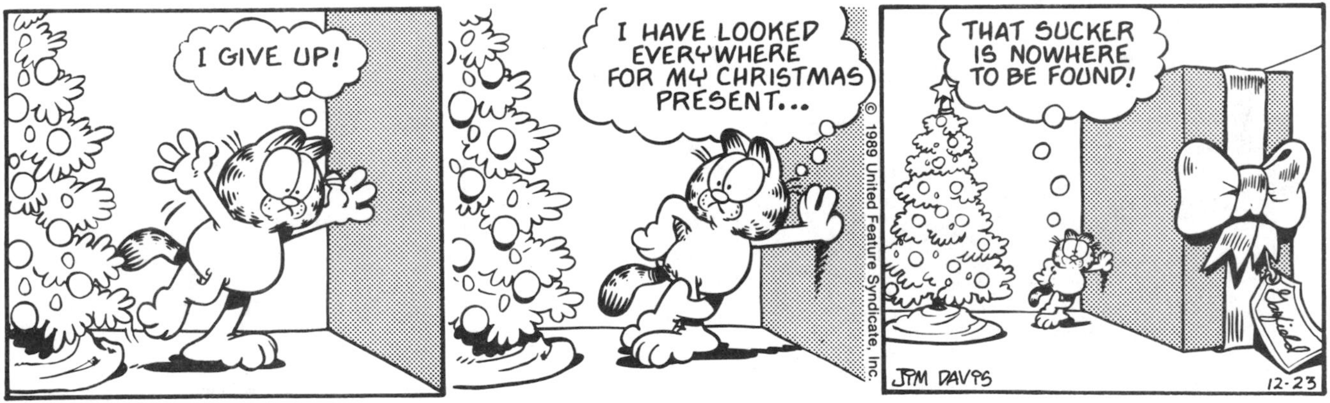
I GIVE UP!
I HAVE LOOKED EVERYWHERE FOR MY CHRISTMAS PRESENT...
THAT SUCKER IS NOWHERE TO BE FOUND!
Garfield
© 1989 United Feature Syndicate, Inc.
JIM DAVIS
12-23

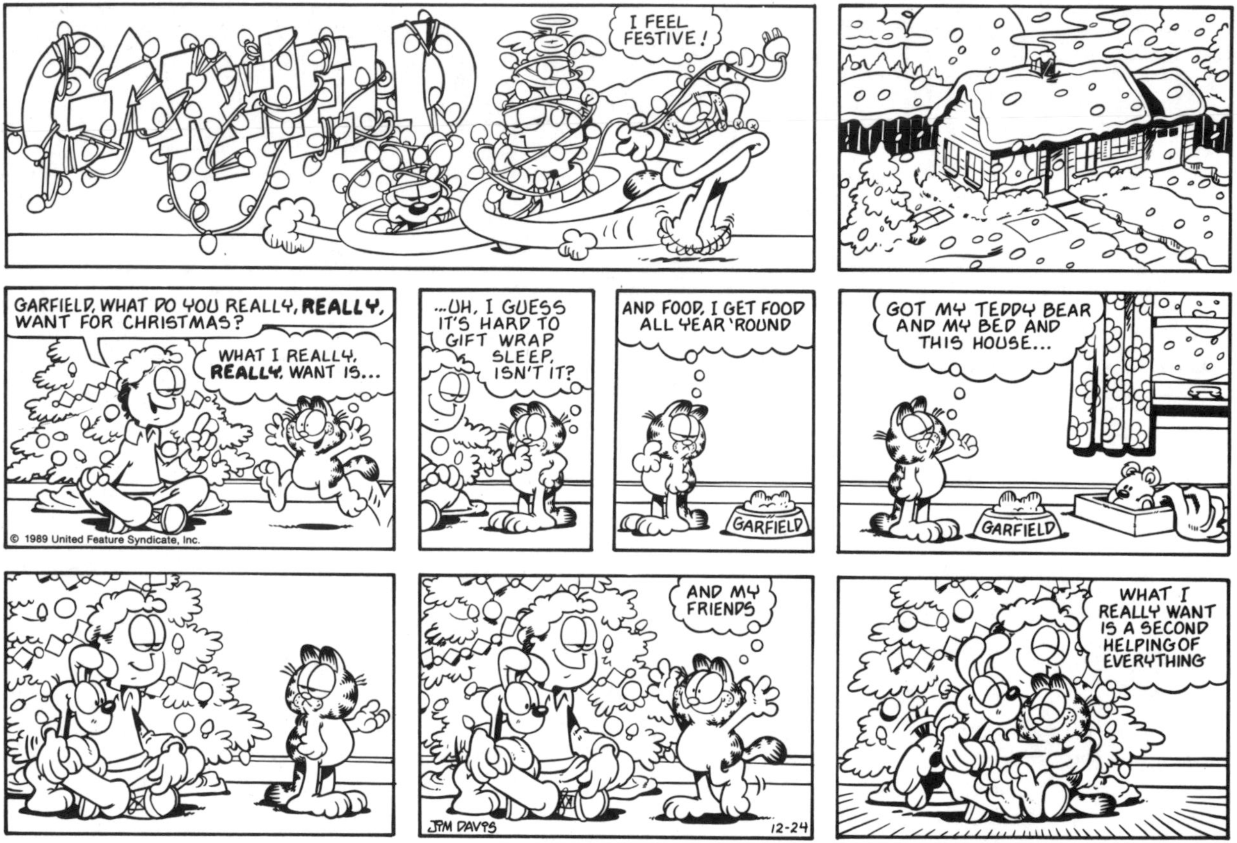
GARFIELD
I FEEL FESTIVE!
GARFIELD, WHAT DO YOU REALLY, REALLY, WANT FOR CHRISTMAS?
WHAT I REALLY, REALLY, WANT IS...
© 1989 United Feature Syndicate, Inc.
...UH, I GUESS IT'S HARD TO GIFT WRAP SLEEP, ISN'T IT?
AND FOOD, I GET FOOD ALL YEAR 'ROUND
GARFIELD
GOT MY TEDDY BEAR AND MY BED AND THIS HOUSE...
GARFIELD
AND MY FRIENDS
JIM DAVIS
12-24
WHAT I REALLY WANT IS A SECOND HELPING OF EVERYTHING

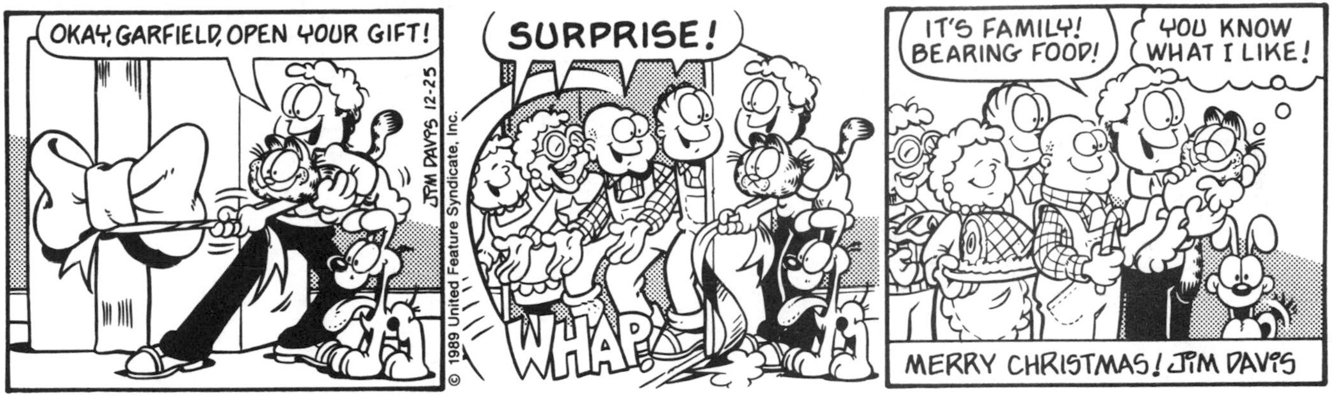
OKAY, GARFIELD, OPEN YOUR GIFT!
JIM DAVIS 12-25
© 1989 United Feature Syndicate, Inc.
SURPRISE!
WHAP!
IT'S FAMILY! BEARING FOOD!
YOU KNOW WHAT I LIKE!
MERRY CHRISTMAS! JIM DAVIS

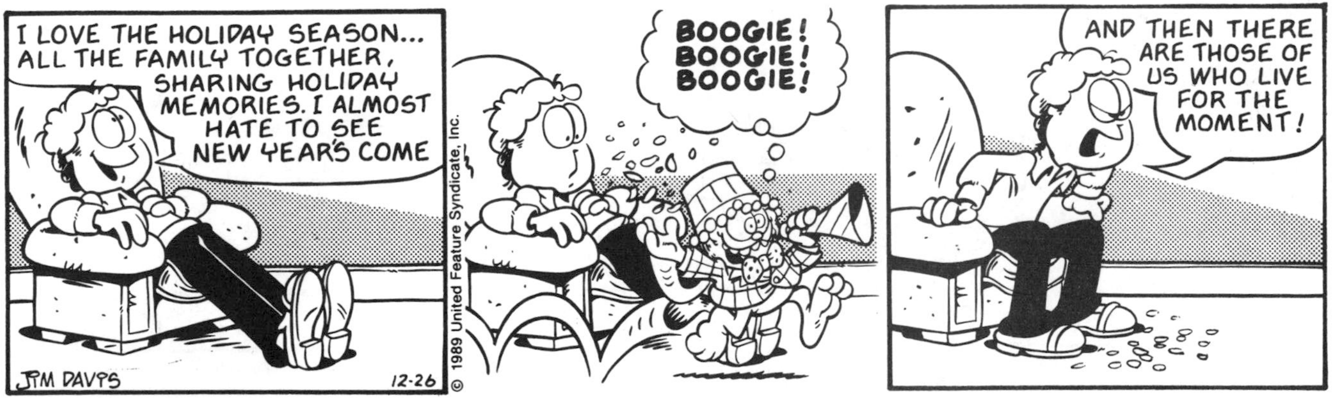
I LOVE THE HOLIDAY SEASON... ALL THE FAMILY TOGETHER, SHARING HOLIDAY MEMORIES. I ALMOST HATE TO SEE NEW YEAR'S COME
JIM DAVIS
12-26
© 1989 United Feature Syndicate, Inc.
BOOGIE! BOOGIE! BOOGIE!
AND THEN THERE ARE THOSE OF US WHO LIVE FOR THE MOMENT!

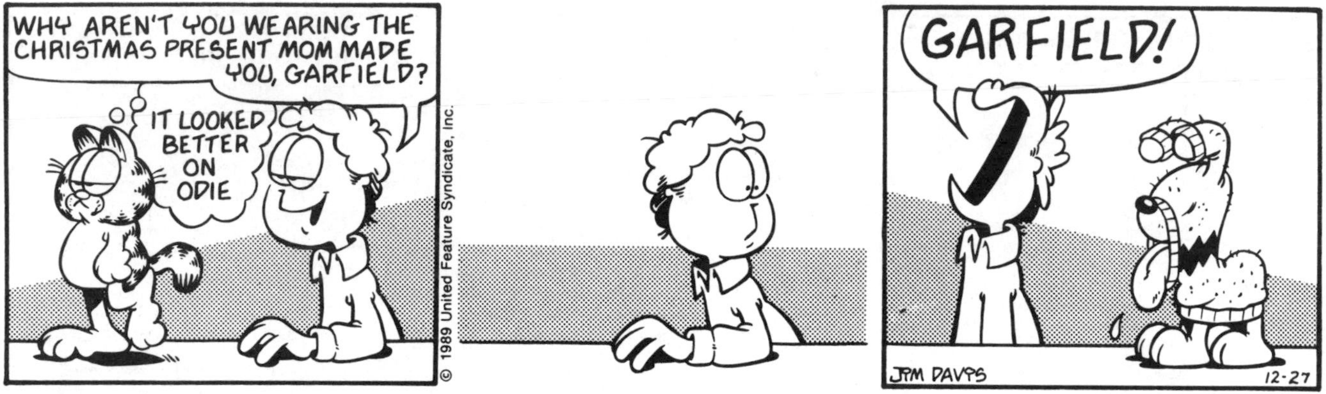
WHY AREN'T YOU WEARING THE CHRISTMAS PRESENT MOM MADE YOU, GARFIELD?
IT LOOKED BETTER ON ODIE
© 1989 United Feature Syndicate, Inc.
GARFIELD!
JIM DAVIS
12-27

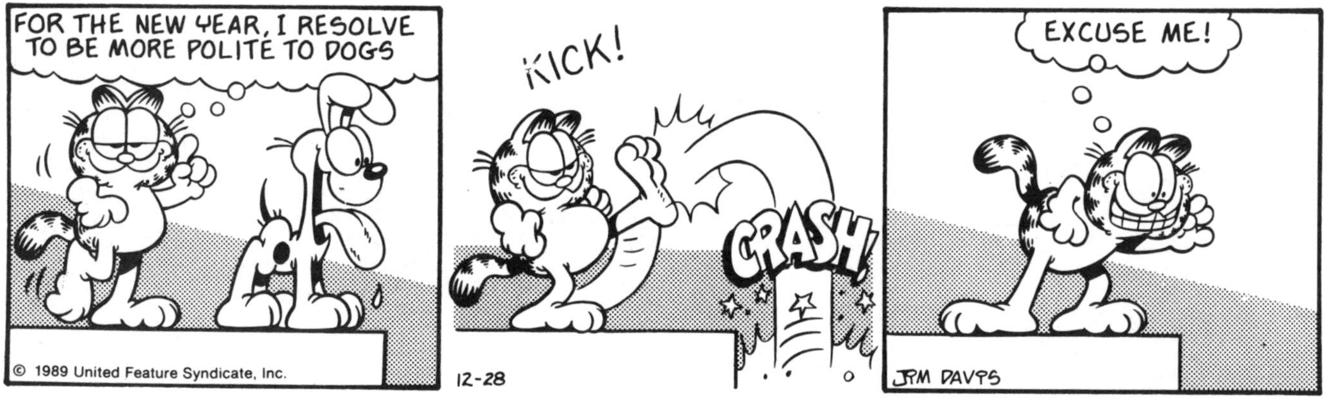
FOR THE NEW YEAR, I RESOLVE TO BE MORE POLITE TO DOGS
© 1989 United Feature Syndicate, Inc.
KICK!
CRASH!
12-28
EXCUSE ME!
JIM DAVIS

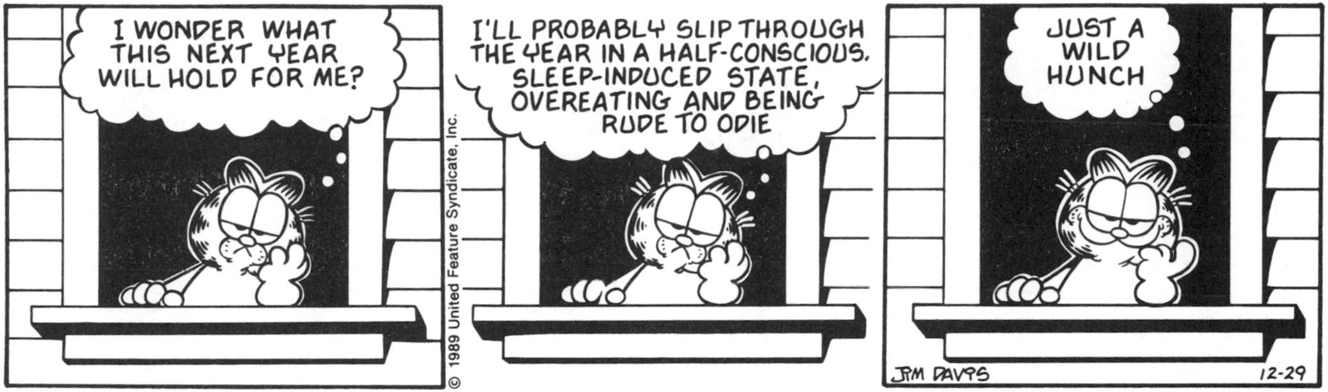
I WONDER WHAT THIS NEXT YEAR WILL HOLD FOR ME?
I'LL PROBABLY SLIP THROUGH THE YEAR IN A HALF-CONSCIOUS, SLEEP-INDUCED STATE, OVEREATING AND BEING RUDE TO ODIE
JUST A WILD HUNCH
© 1989 United Feature Syndicate, Inc.
JIM DAVIS
12-29

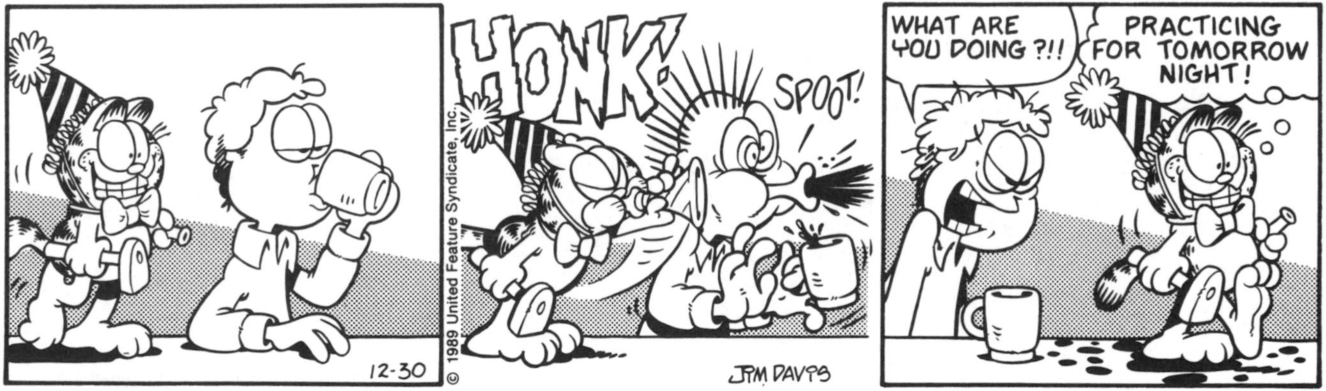
12-30
HONK!
SPOOT!
WHAT ARE YOU DOING ?!!
PRACTICING FOR TOMORROW NIGHT!
© 1989 United Feature Syndicate, Inc.
JIM DAVIS

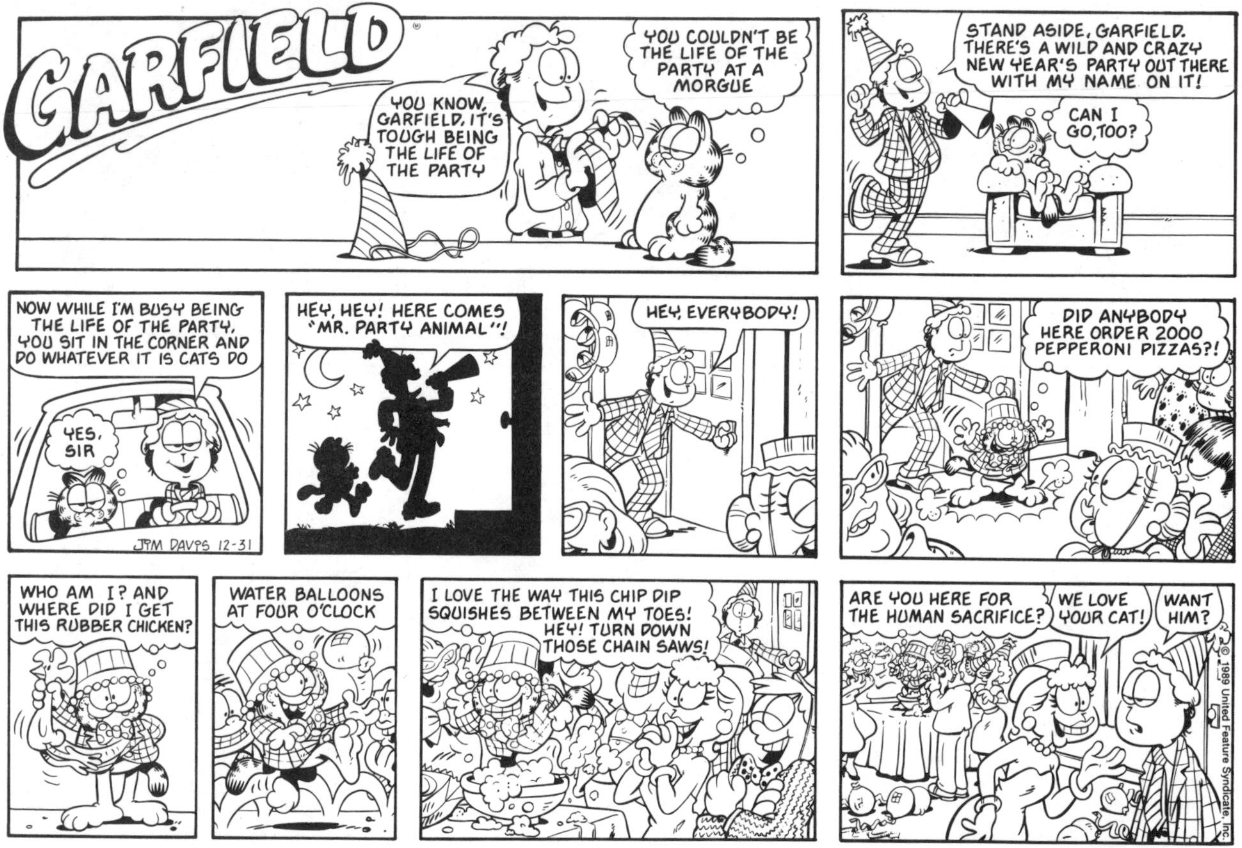
GARFIELD
YOU KNOW, GARFIELD, IT'S TOUGH BEING THE LIFE OF THE PARTY
YOU COULDN'T BE THE LIFE OF THE PARTY AT A MORGUE
STAND ASIDE, GARFIELD. THERE'S A WILD AND CRAZY NEW YEAR'S PARTY OUT THERE WITH MY NAME ON IT!
CAN I GO, TOO?
NOW WHILE I'M BUSY BEING THE LIFE OF THE PARTY, YOU SIT IN THE CORNER AND DO WHATEVER IT IS CATS DO
YES, SIR
JIM DAVIS 12-31
HEY, HEY! HERE COMES "MR. PARTY ANIMAL"!
HEY, EVERYBODY!
DID ANYBODY HERE ORDER 2000 PEPPERONI PIZZAS?!
WHO AM I? AND WHERE DID I GET THIS RUBBER CHICKEN?
WATER BALLOONS AT FOUR O'CLOCK
I LOVE THE WAY THIS CHIP DIP SQUISHES BETWEEN MY TOES!
HEY! TURN DOWN THOSE CHAIN SAWS!
ARE YOU HERE FOR THE HUMAN SACRIFICE?
WE LOVE YOUR CAT!
WANT HIM?
© 1989 United Feature Syndicate, Inc.

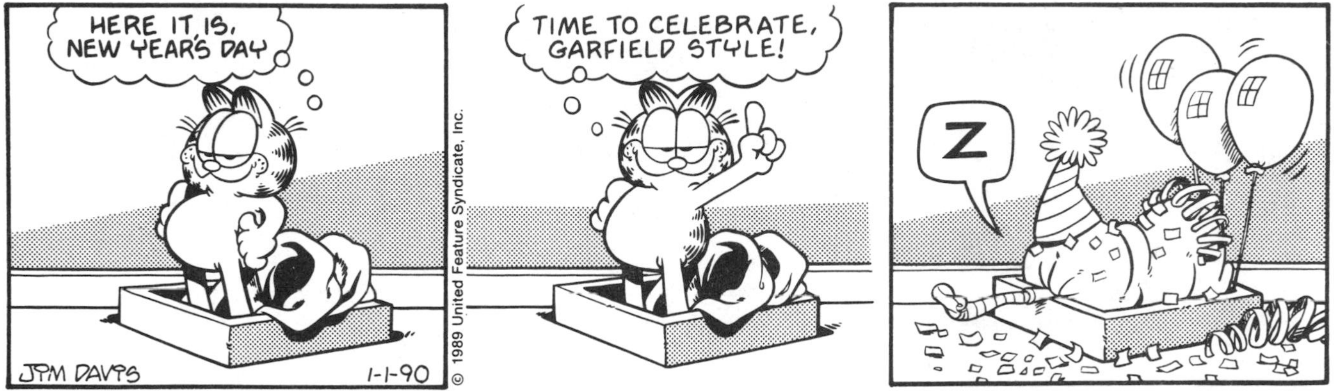
HERE IT IS, NEW YEAR'S DAY
JIM DAVIS
1-1-90
© 1989 United Feature Syndicate, Inc.
TIME TO CELEBRATE, GARFIELD STYLE!
Z

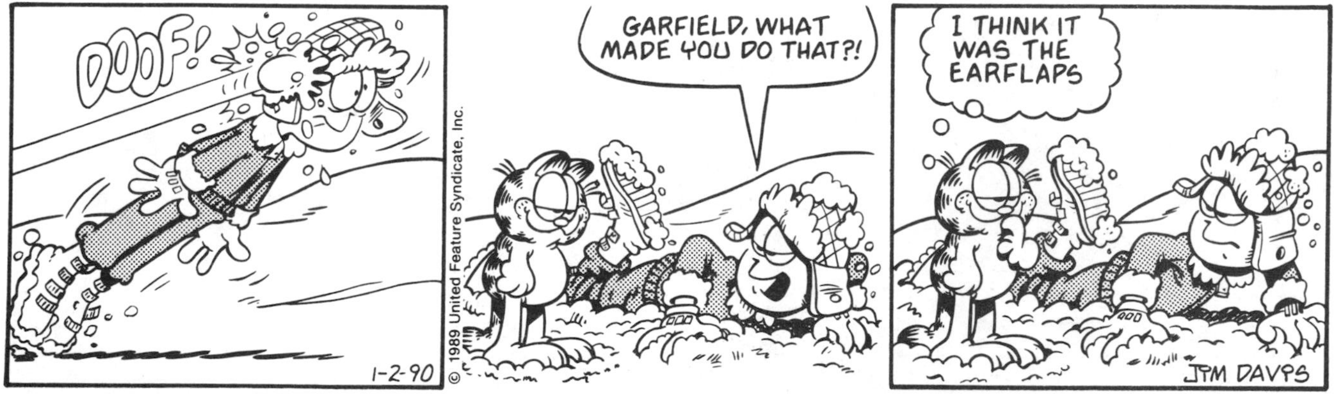
DOOF!
1-2-90
© 1989 United Feature Syndicate, Inc.
GARFIELD, WHAT MADE YOU DO THAT?!
I THINK IT WAS THE EARFLAPS
JIM DAVIS

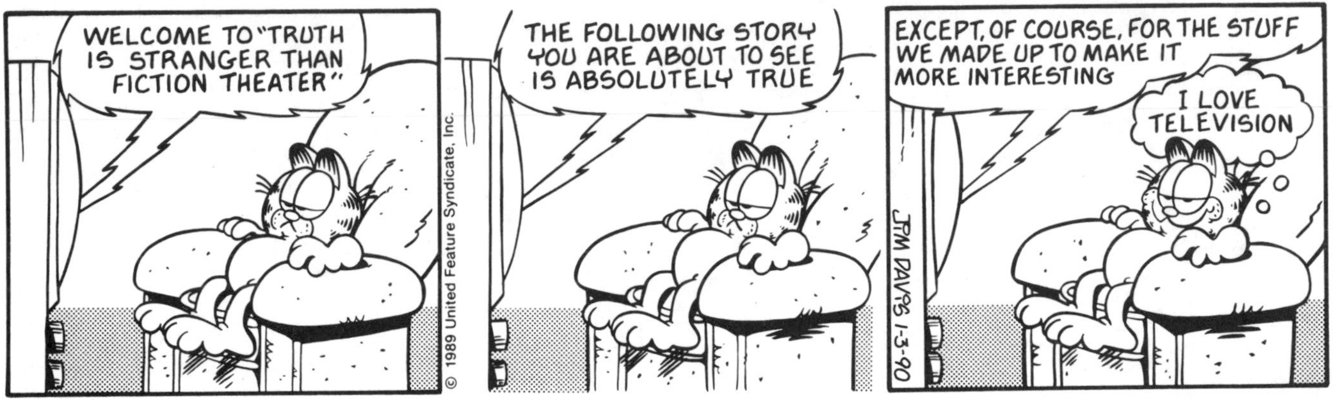
WELCOME TO "TRUTH IS STRANGER THAN FICTION THEATER"
© 1989 United Feature Syndicate, Inc.
THE FOLLOWING STORY YOU ARE ABOUT TO SEE IS ABSOLUTELY TRUE
EXCEPT, OF COURSE, FOR THE STUFF WE MADE UP TO MAKE IT MORE INTERESTING
I LOVE TELEVISION
JIM DAVIS 1-3-90

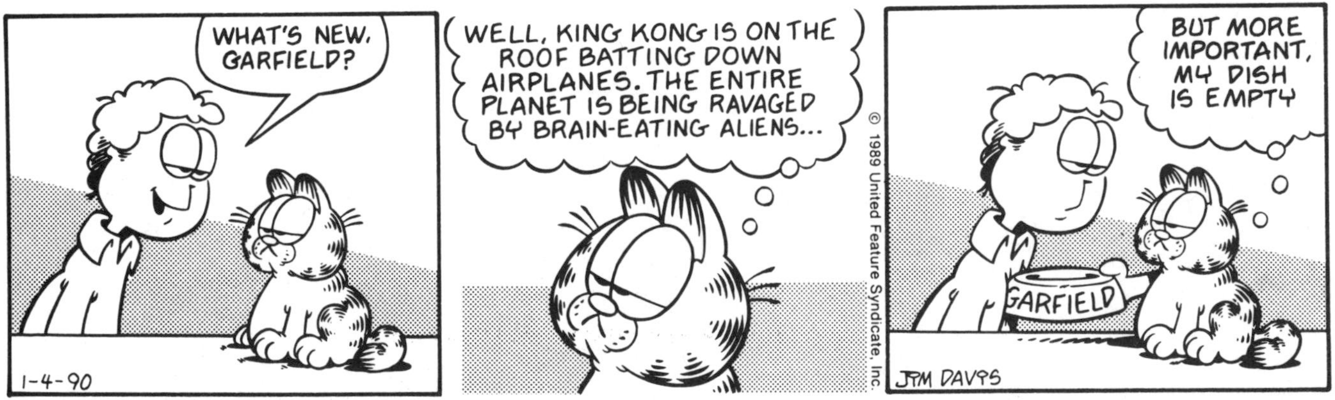
WHAT'S NEW, GARFIELD?
1-4-90
WELL, KING KONG IS ON THE ROOF BATTING DOWN AIRPLANES. THE ENTIRE PLANET IS BEING RAVAGED BY BRAIN-EATING ALIENS...
© 1989 United Feature Syndicate, Inc.
BUT MORE IMPORTANT, MY DISH IS EMPTY
GARFIELD
JIM DAVIS

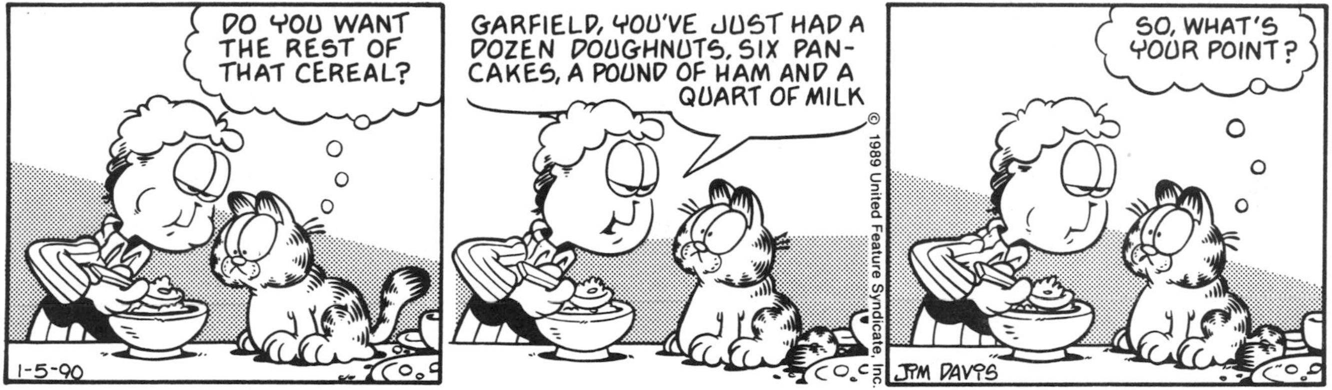
DO YOU WANT THE REST OF THAT CEREAL?
1-5-90
GARFIELD, YOU'VE JUST HAD A DOZEN DOUGHNUTS, SIX PANCAKES, A POUND OF HAM AND A QUART OF MILK
© 1989 United Feature Syndicate, Inc.
SO, WHAT'S YOUR POINT?
JIM DAVIS

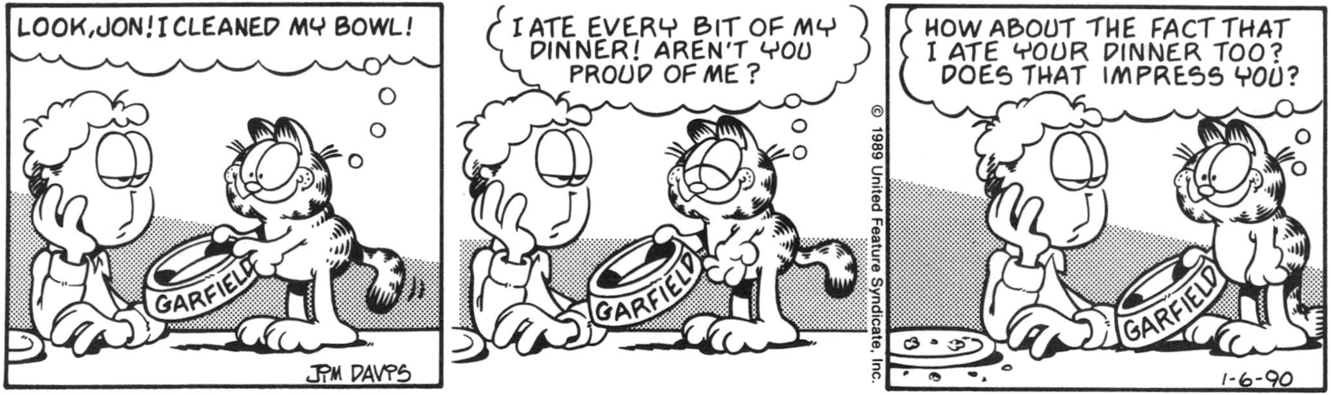
LOOK, JON! I CLEANED MY BOWL!
GARFIELD
JIM DAVIS
I ATE EVERY BIT OF MY DINNER! AREN'T YOU PROUD OF ME?
GARFIELD
© 1989 United Feature Syndicate, Inc.
HOW ABOUT THE FACT THAT I ATE YOUR DINNER TOO? DOES THAT IMPRESS YOU?
GARFIELD
1-6-90

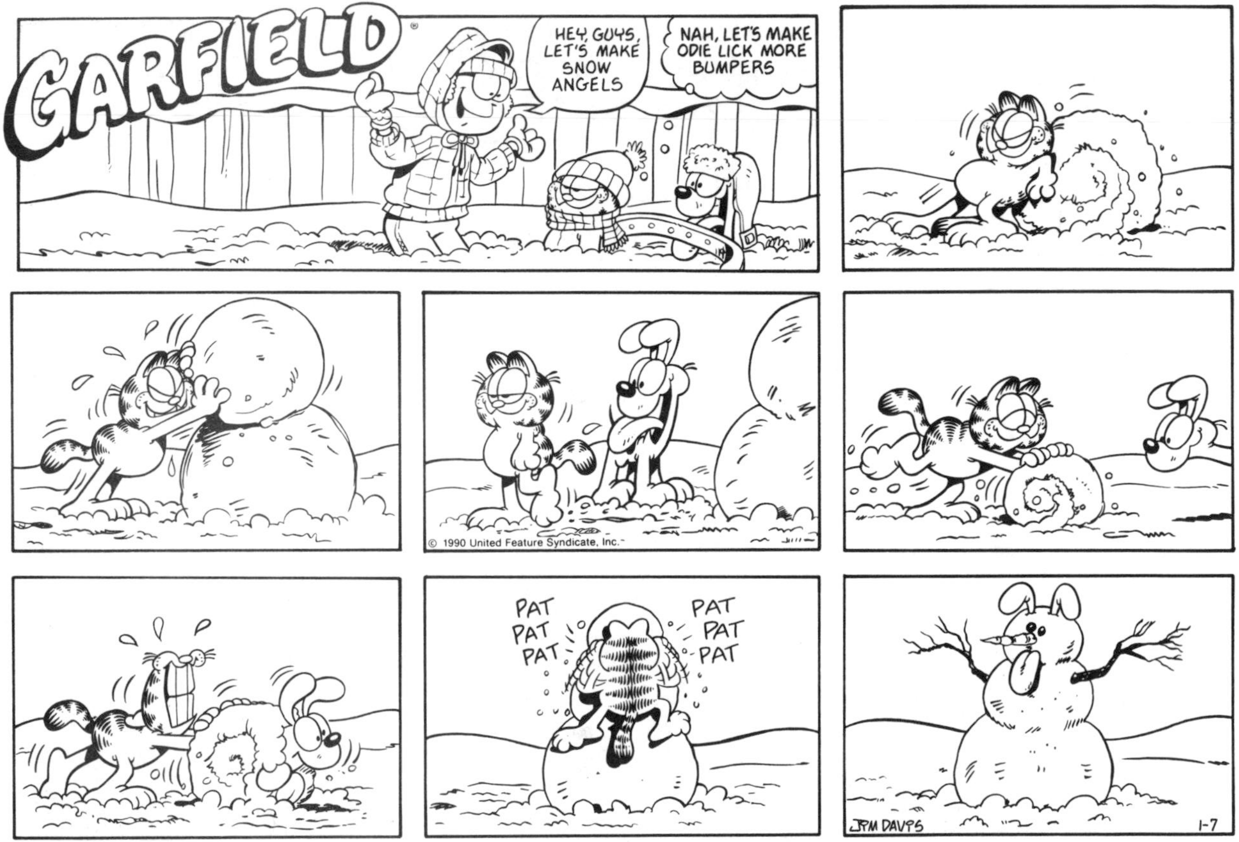
GARFIELD®
HEY, GUYS, LET'S MAKE SNOW ANGELS
NAH, LET'S MAKE ODIE LICK MORE BUMPERS
© 1990 United Feature Syndicate, Inc.
PAT PAT PAT
PAT PAT PAT
JIM DAVIS
1-7

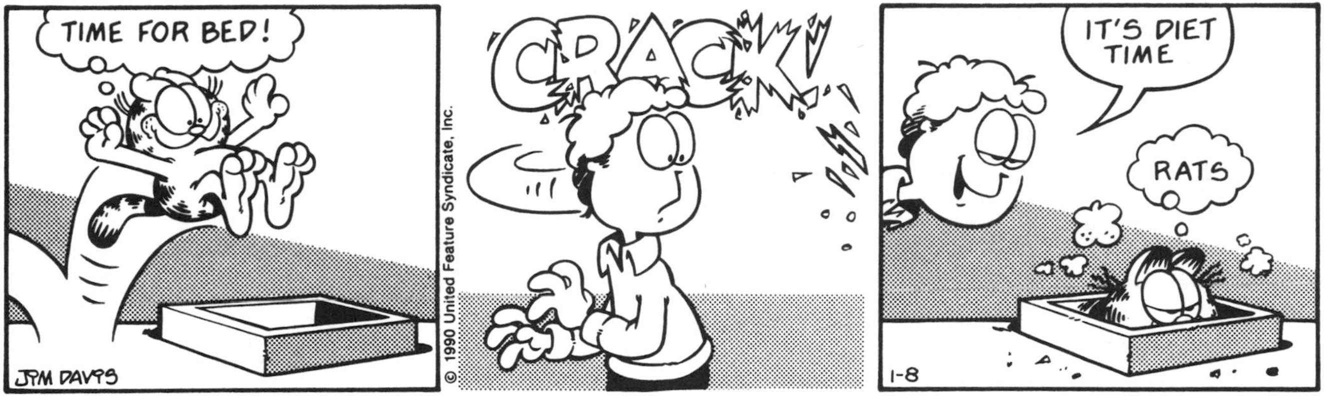
TIME FOR BED!
CRACK!
IT'S DIET TIME
RATS
JIM DAVIS
© 1990 United Feature Syndicate, Inc.
1-8

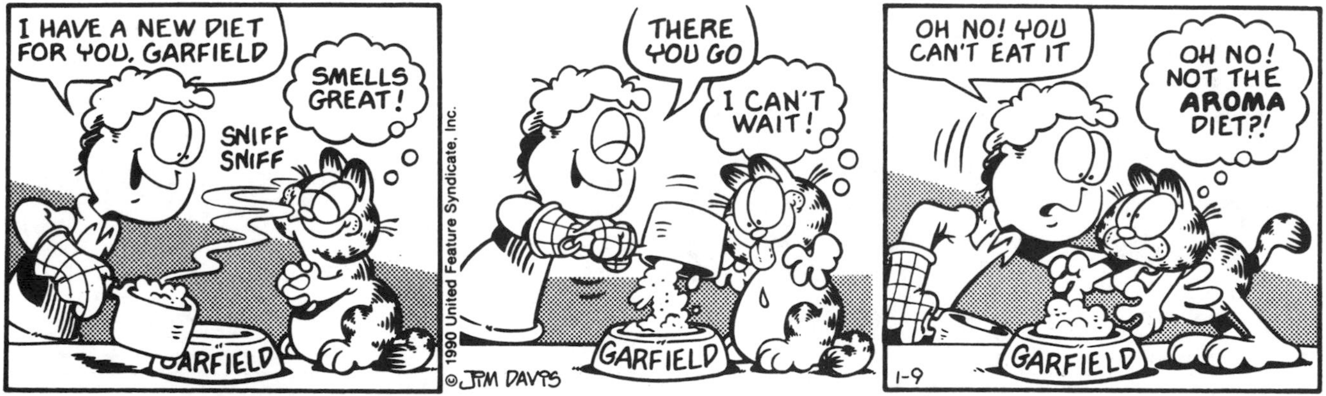
I HAVE A NEW DIET FOR YOU, GARFIELD
SNIFF SNIFF
SMELLS GREAT!
GARFIELD
THERE YOU GO
I CAN'T WAIT!
GARFIELD
OH NO! YOU CAN'T EAT IT
OH NO! NOT THE **AROMA** DIET?!
GARFIELD
© 1990 United Feature Syndicate, Inc.
© JIM DAVIS
1-9

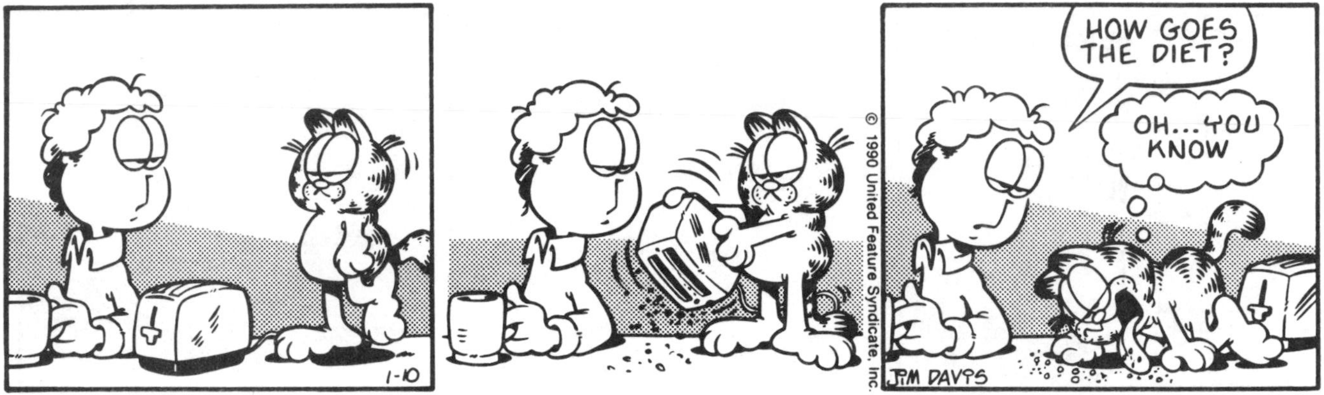
HOW GOES THE DIET?
OH... YOU KNOW
1-10
© 1990 United Feature Syndicate, Inc.
JIM DAVIS

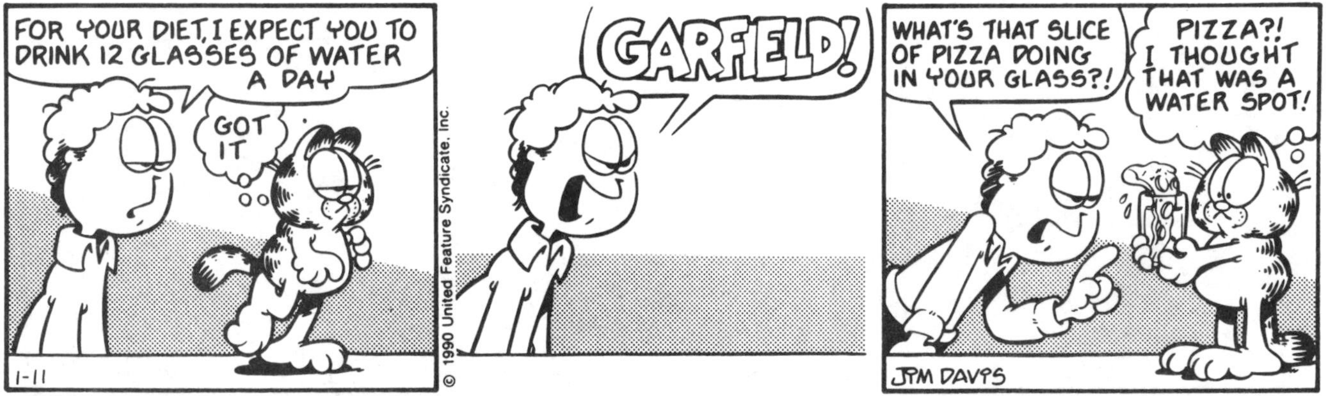
FOR YOUR DIET, I EXPECT YOU TO DRINK 12 GLASSES OF WATER A DAY
GOT IT
GARFIELD!
WHAT'S THAT SLICE OF PIZZA DOING IN YOUR GLASS?!
PIZZA?! I THOUGHT THAT WAS A WATER SPOT!
1-11
© 1990 United Feature Syndicate, Inc.
JIM DAVIS

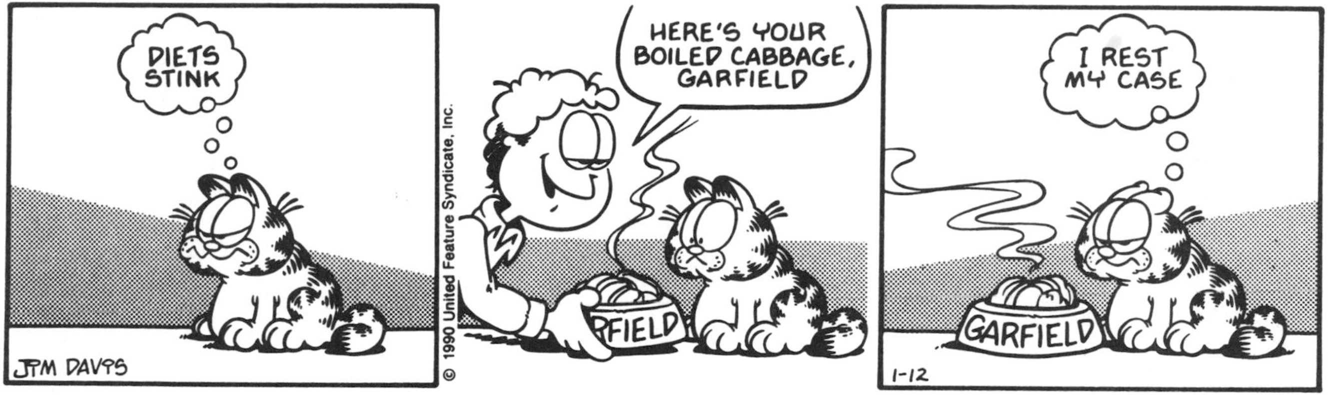
DIETS STINK
JIM DAVIS
HERE'S YOUR BOILED CABBAGE, GARFIELD
RFIELD
I REST MY CASE
GARFIELD
1-12

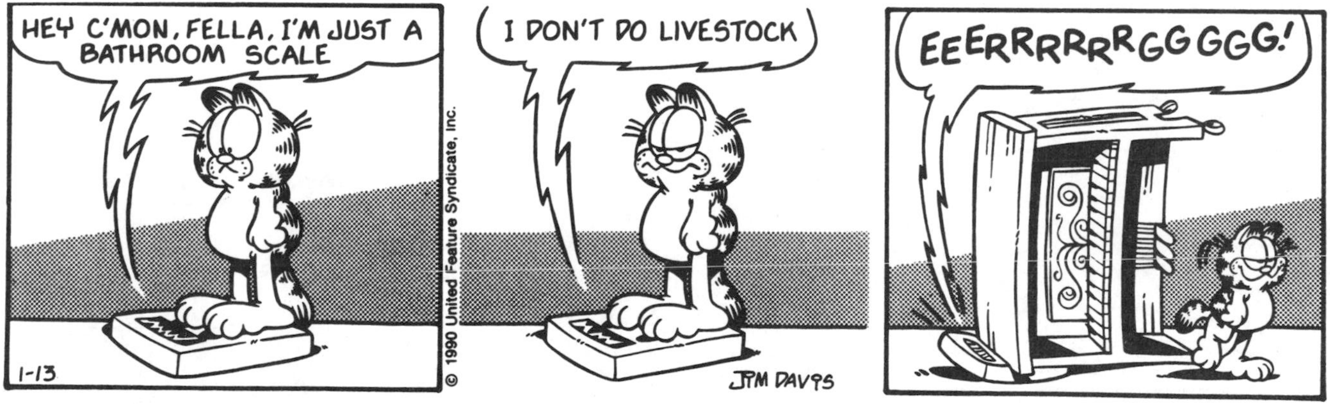
HEY C'MON, FELLA, I'M JUST A BATHROOM SCALE
1-13
I DON'T DO LIVESTOCK
JIM DAVIS
EEERRRRRRRGGGGG!

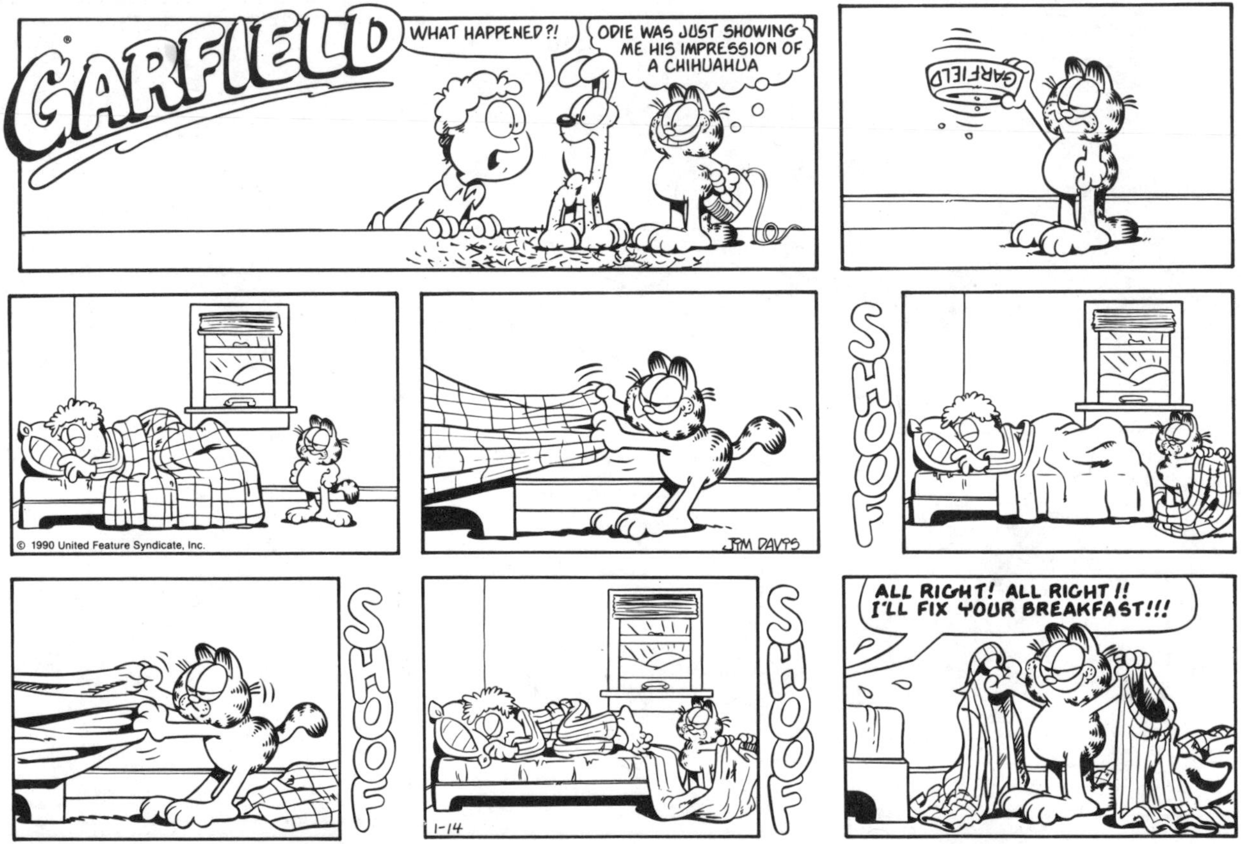
GARFIELD®
WHAT HAPPENED?!
ODIE WAS JUST SHOWING ME HIS IMPRESSION OF A CHIHUAHUA
GARFIELD
© 1990 United Feature Syndicate, Inc.
JPM DAVPS
SHOOF
SHOOF
1-14
SHOOF
ALL RIGHT! ALL RIGHT!! I'LL FIX YOUR BREAKFAST!!!

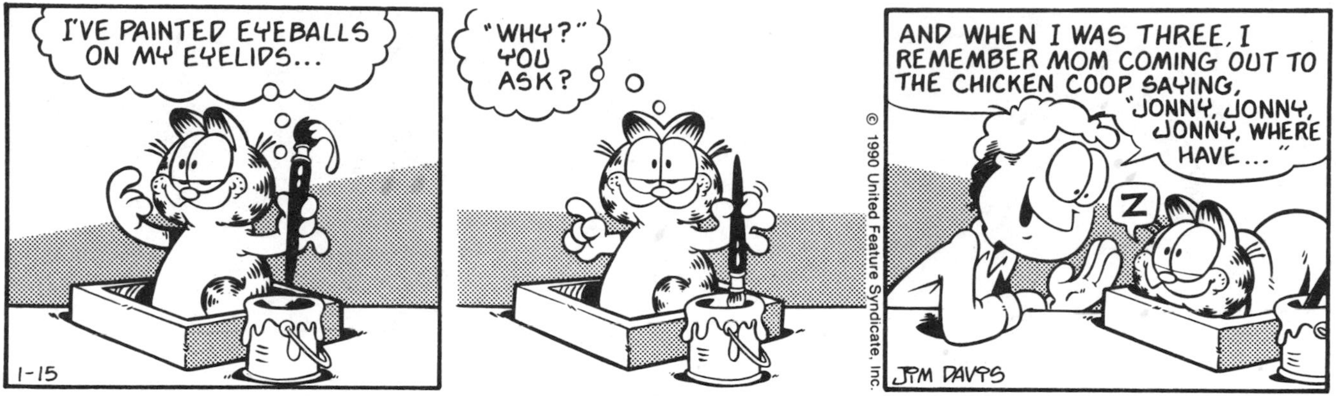
I'VE PAINTED EYEBALLS ON MY EYELIDS...
"WHY?" YOU ASK?
AND WHEN I WAS THREE, I REMEMBER MOM COMING OUT TO THE CHICKEN COOP SAYING, "JONNY, JONNY, JONNY, WHERE HAVE..."
Z
1-15
© 1990 United Feature Syndicate, Inc.
JIM DAVIS

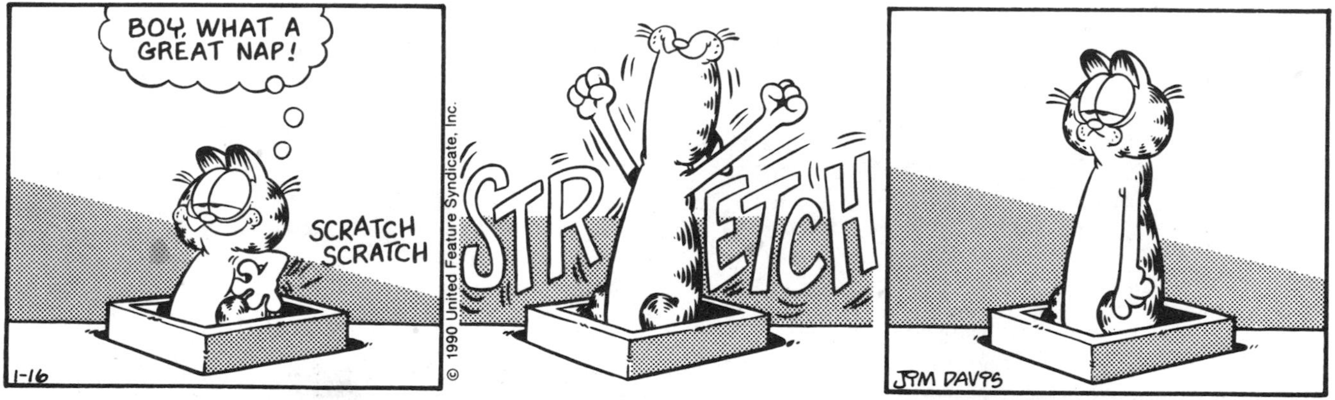
BOY, WHAT A GREAT NAP!
SCRATCH SCRATCH
STRETCH
1-16
© 1990 United Feature Syndicate, Inc.
JIM DAVIS

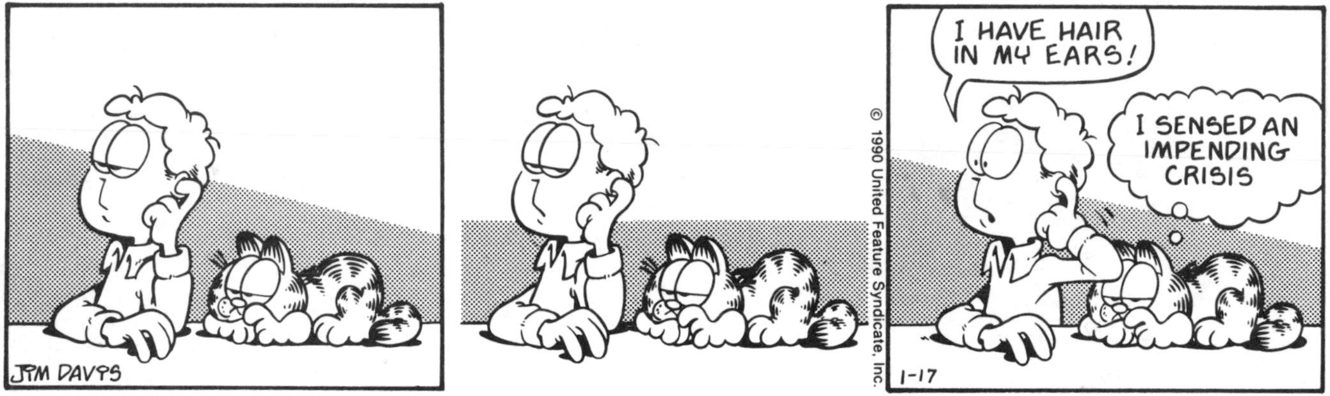
JIM DAVIS
© 1990 United Feature Syndicate, Inc.
I HAVE HAIR IN MY EARS!
I SENSED AN IMPENDING CRISIS
1-17

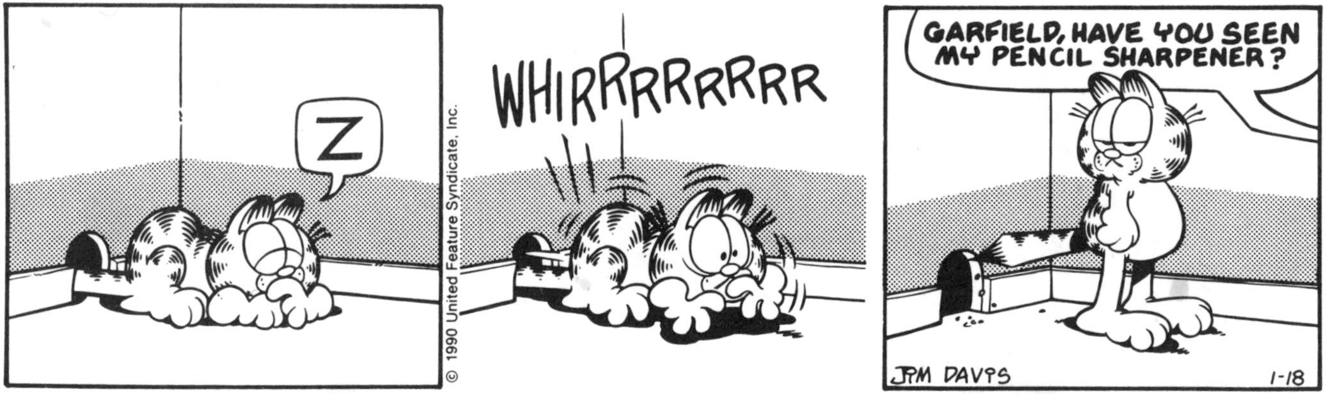
Z
© 1990 United Feature Syndicate, Inc.
WHIRRRRRRRR
GARFIELD, HAVE YOU SEEN MY PENCIL SHARPENER?
JIM DAVIS
1-18

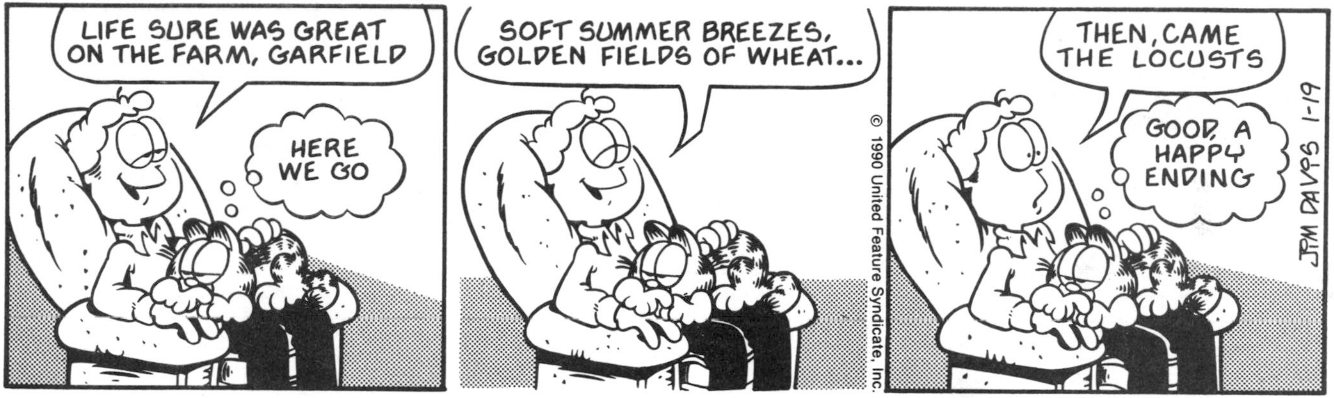
LIFE SURE WAS GREAT ON THE FARM, GARFIELD
HERE WE GO
SOFT SUMMER BREEZES, GOLDEN FIELDS OF WHEAT...
© 1990 United Feature Syndicate, Inc.
THEN, CAME THE LOCUSTS
GOOD, A HAPPY ENDING
JIM DAVIS 1-19

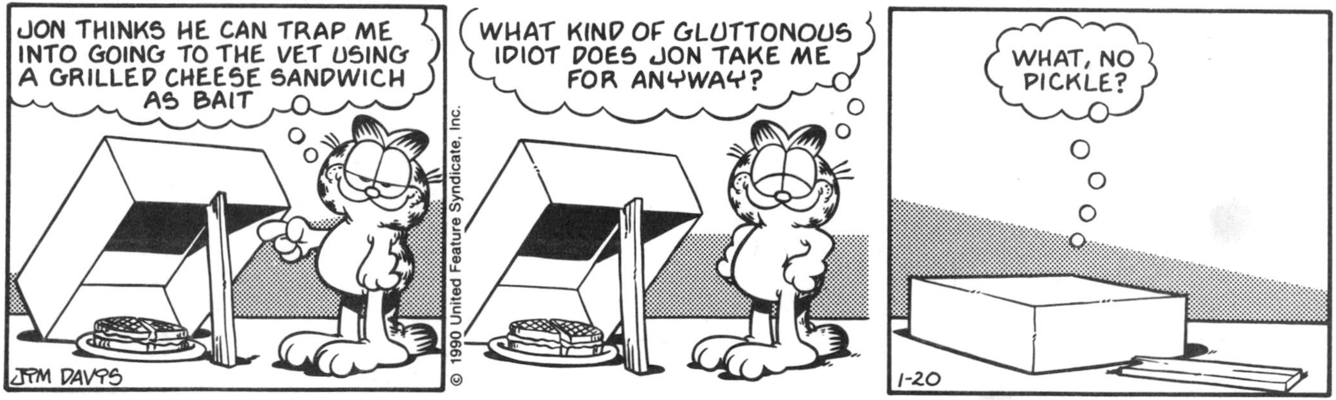
JON THINKS HE CAN TRAP ME INTO GOING TO THE VET USING A GRILLED CHEESE SANDWICH AS BAIT
JIM DAVIS
© 1990 United Feature Syndicate, Inc.
WHAT KIND OF GLUTTONOUS IDIOT DOES JON TAKE ME FOR ANYWAY?
WHAT, NO PICKLE?
1-20

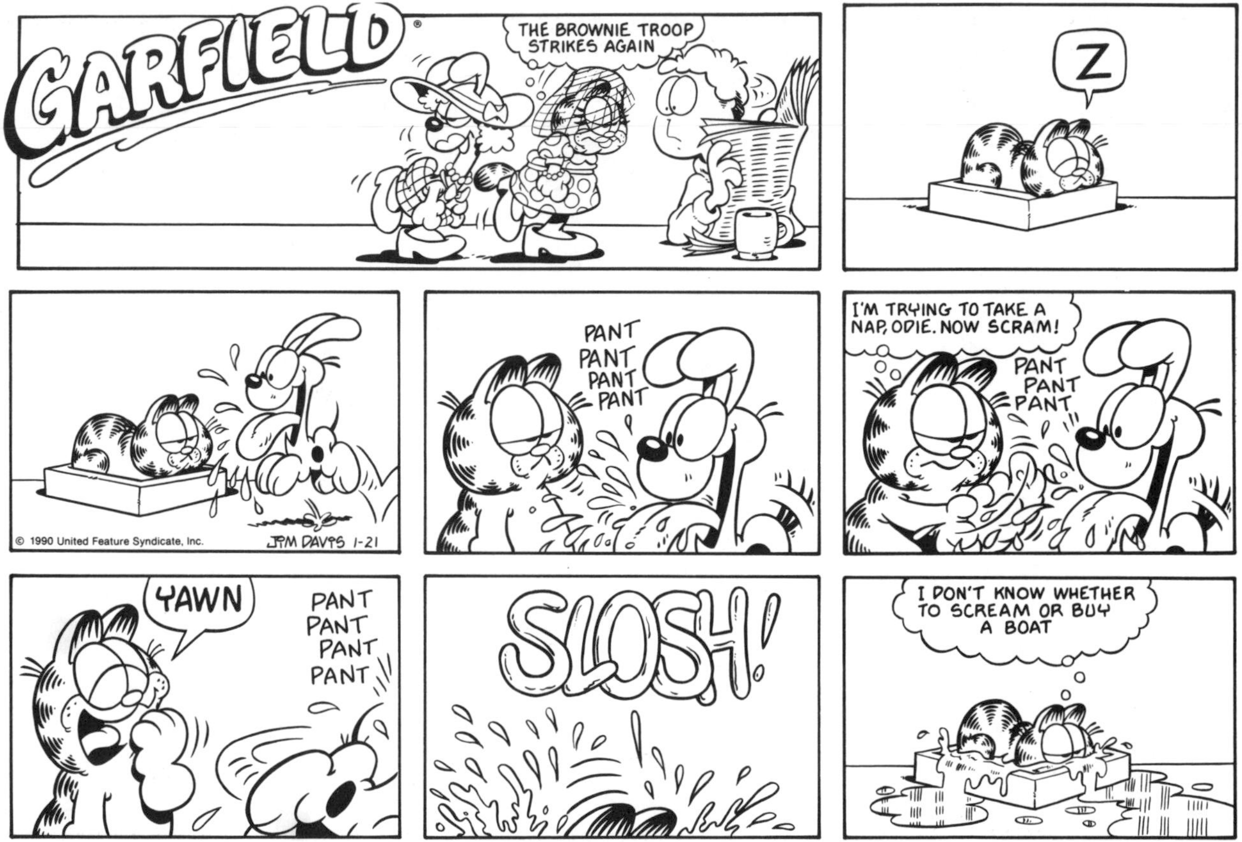
GARFIELD®
THE BROWNIE TROOP STRIKES AGAIN
Z
PANT PANT PANT PANT
I'M TRYING TO TAKE A NAP, ODIE. NOW SCRAM!
PANT PANT PANT
YAWN
PANT PANT PANT PANT
SLOSH!
I DON'T KNOW WHETHER TO SCREAM OR BUY A BOAT
JIM DAVIS 1-21

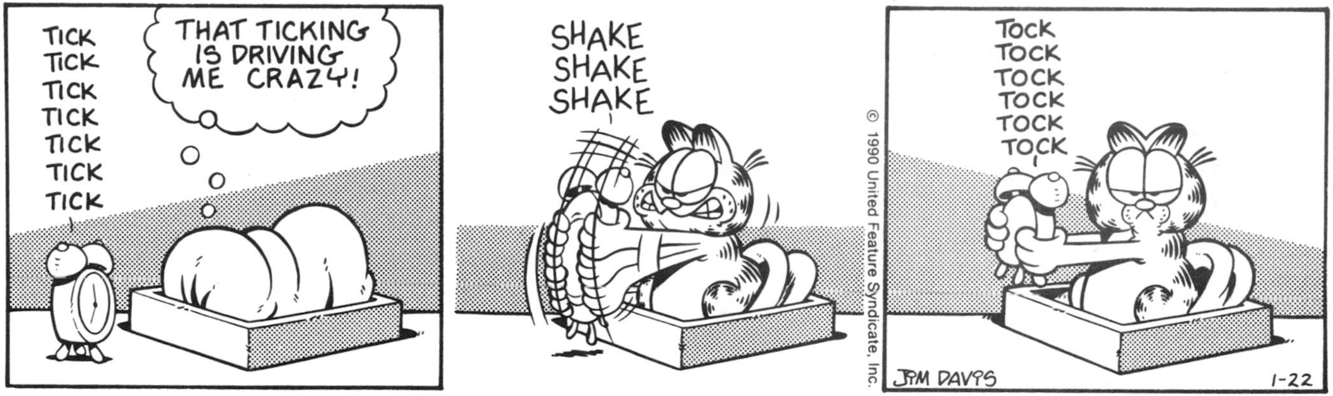
TICK
TICK
TICK
TICK
TICK
TICK
TICK
THAT TICKING IS DRIVING ME CRAZY!
SHAKE
SHAKE
SHAKE
© 1990 United Feature Syndicate, Inc.
TOCK
TOCK
TOCK
TOCK
TOCK
TOCK
JIM DAVIS
1-22

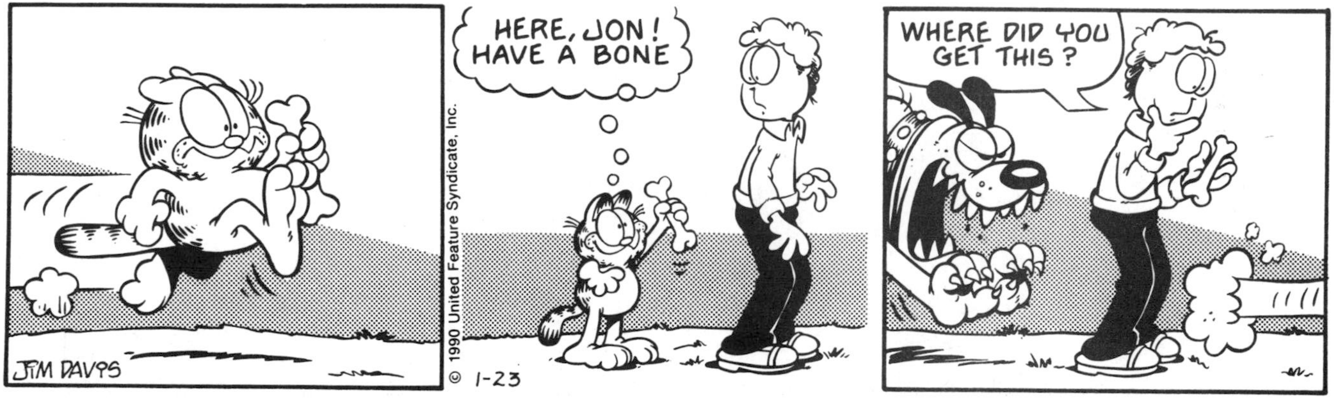
JIM DAVIS
© 1990 United Feature Syndicate, Inc.
HERE, JON! HAVE A BONE
1-23
WHERE DID YOU GET THIS?

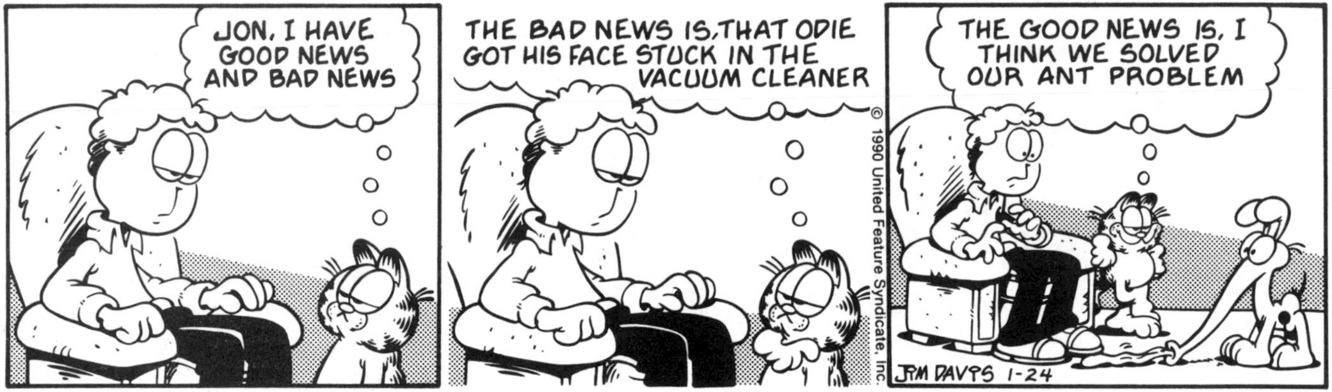
JON, I HAVE GOOD NEWS AND BAD NEWS
THE BAD NEWS IS, THAT ODIE GOT HIS FACE STUCK IN THE VACUUM CLEANER
© 1990 United Feature Syndicate, Inc.
THE GOOD NEWS IS, I THINK WE SOLVED OUR ANT PROBLEM
JIM DAVIS 1-24

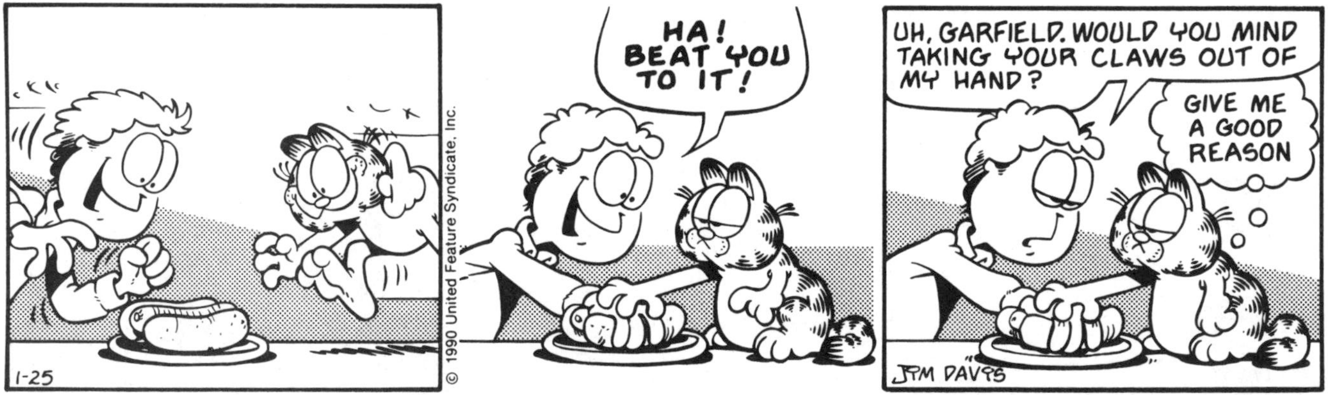
1-25
© 1990 United Feature Syndicate, Inc.
HA! BEAT YOU TO IT!
UH, GARFIELD. WOULD YOU MIND TAKING YOUR CLAWS OUT OF MY HAND?
GIVE ME A GOOD REASON
JIM DAVIS

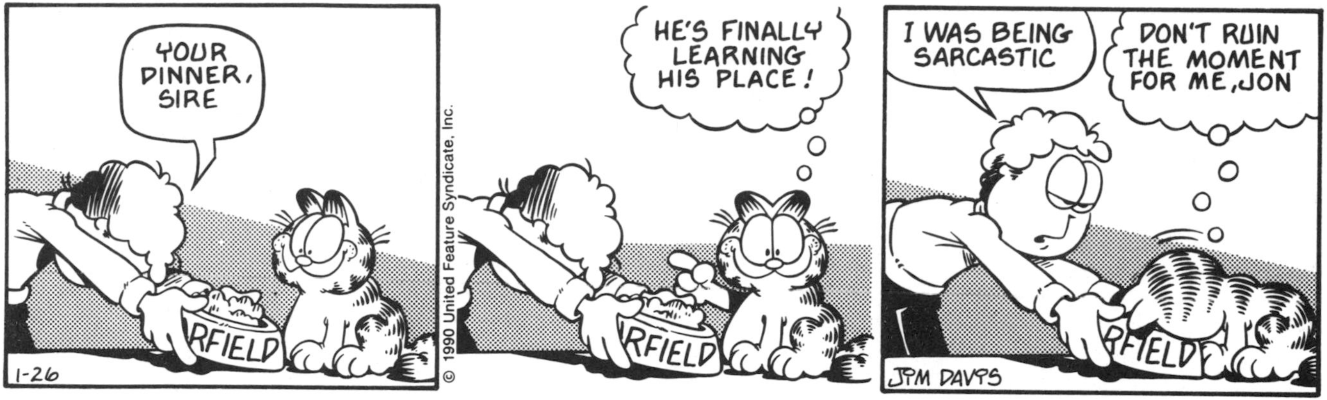
YOUR DINNER, SIRE
1-26
© 1990 United Feature Syndicate, Inc.
HE'S FINALLY LEARNING HIS PLACE!
I WAS BEING SARCASTIC
DON'T RUIN THE MOMENT FOR ME, JON
JIM DAVIS

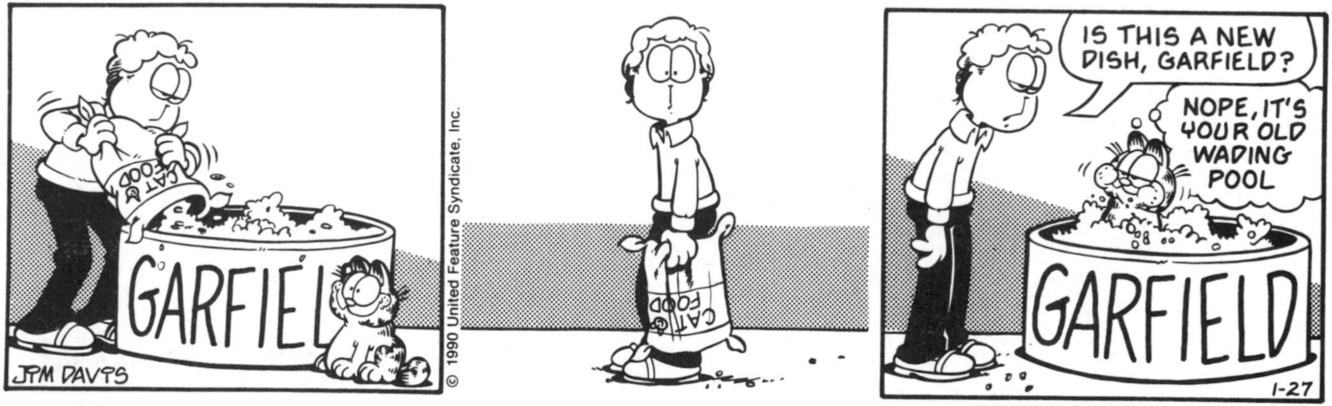
CAT FOOD
GARFIEL
JIM DAVIS
© 1990 United Feature Syndicate, Inc.
CAT FOOD
IS THIS A NEW DISH, GARFIELD?
NOPE, IT'S YOUR OLD WADING POOL
GARFIELD
1-27

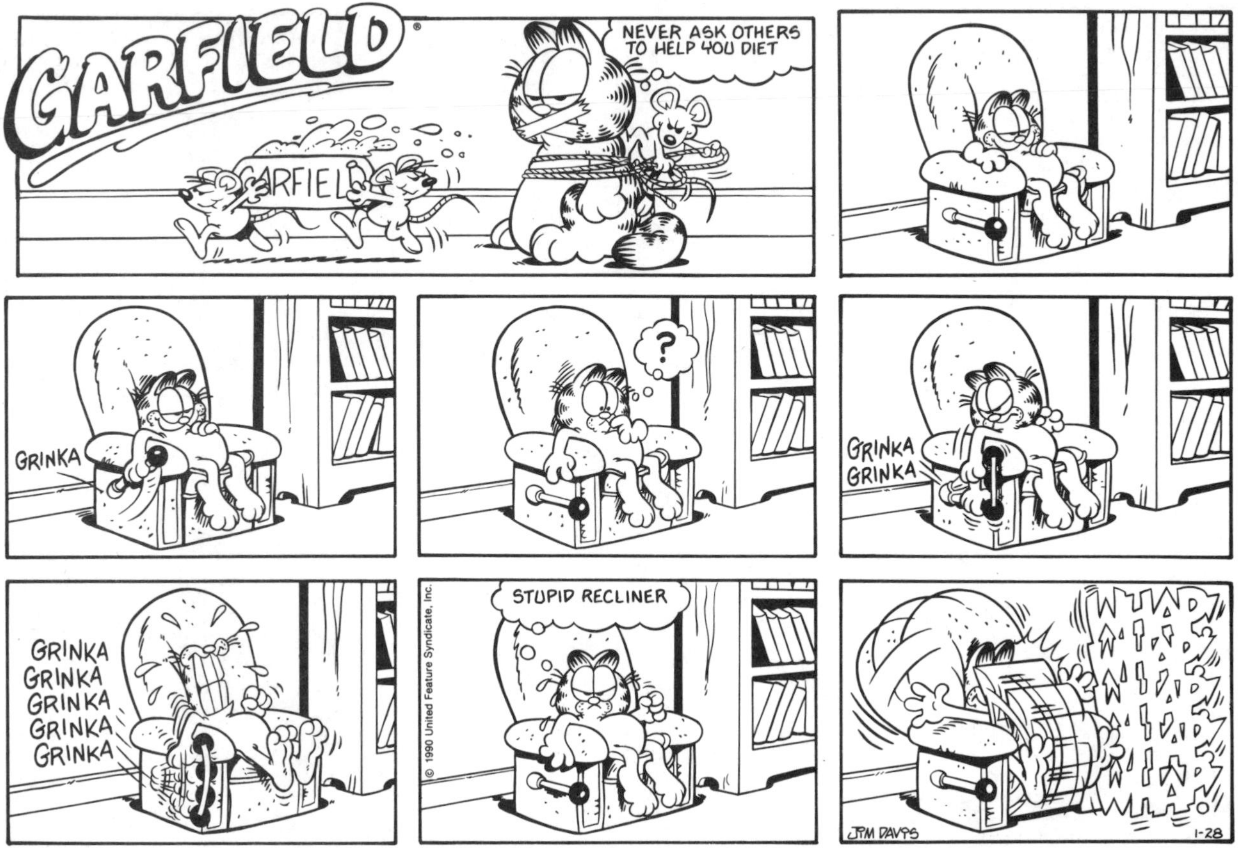
GARFIELD
GARFIELD
NEVER ASK OTHERS TO HELP YOU DIET
GRINKA
?
GRINKA GRINKA
GRINKA GRINKA GRINKA GRINKA GRINKA
© 1990 United Feature Syndicate, Inc.
STUPID RECLINER
JIM DAVIS
1-28

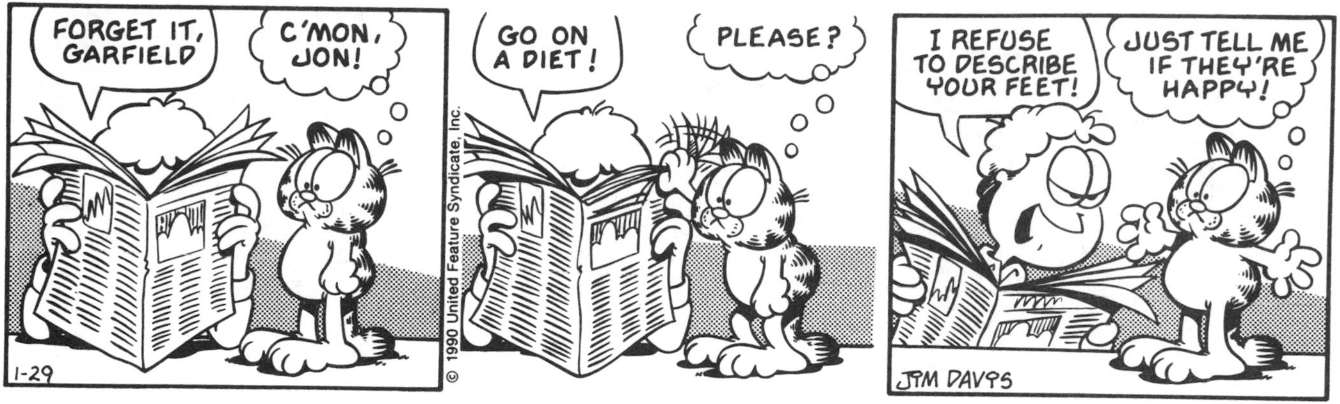
FORGET IT, GARFIELD
C'MON, JON!
GO ON A DIET!
PLEASE?
I REFUSE TO DESCRIBE YOUR FEET!
JUST TELL ME IF THEY'RE HAPPY!
1-29
© 1990 United Feature Syndicate, Inc.
JIM DAVIS

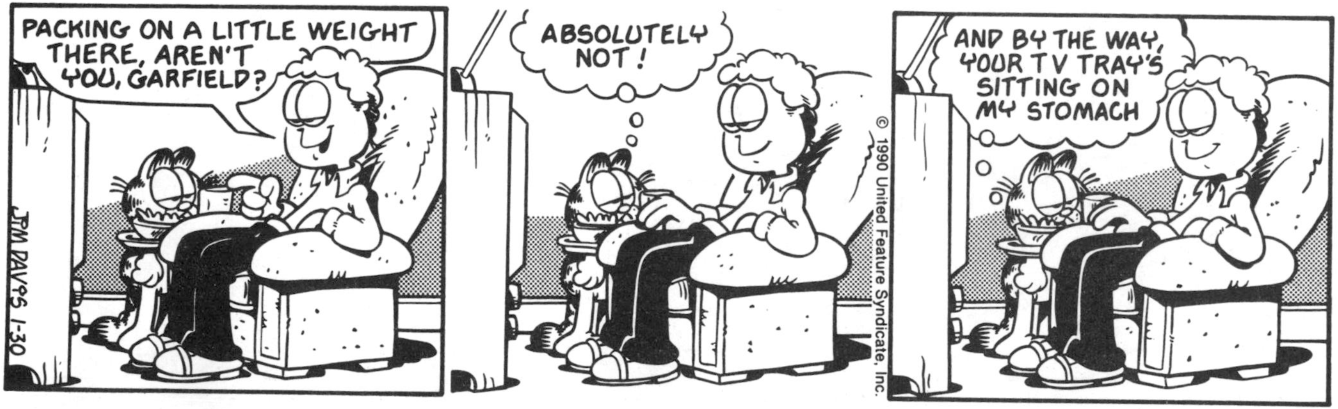
PACKING ON A LITTLE WEIGHT THERE, AREN'T YOU, GARFIELD?
ABSOLUTELY NOT!
AND BY THE WAY, YOUR TV TRAY'S SITTING ON MY STOMACH
JIM DAVIS 1-30
© 1990 United Feature Syndicate, Inc.

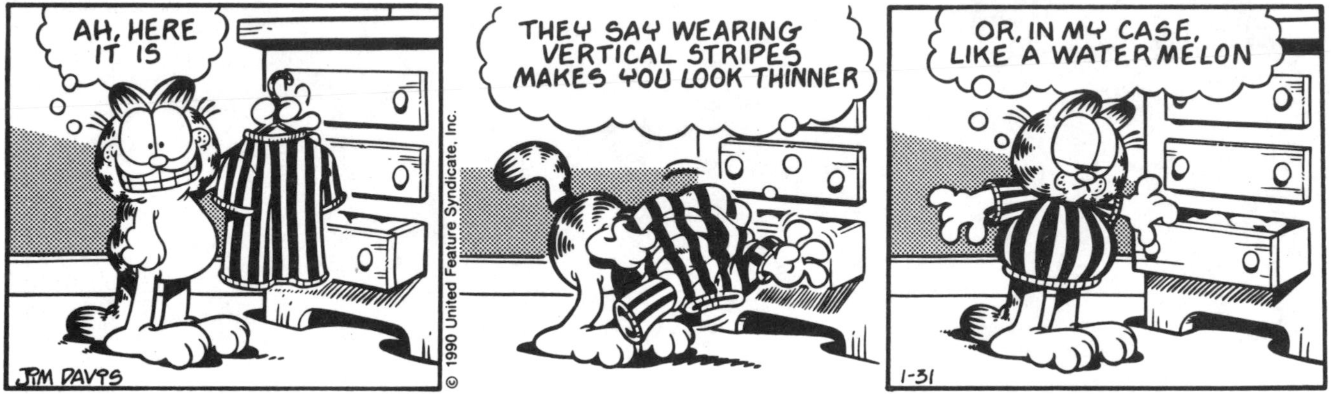
AH, HERE IT IS
THEY SAY WEARING VERTICAL STRIPES MAKES YOU LOOK THINNER
OR, IN MY CASE, LIKE A WATERMELON
JIM DAVIS
1-31
© 1990 United Feature Syndicate, Inc.

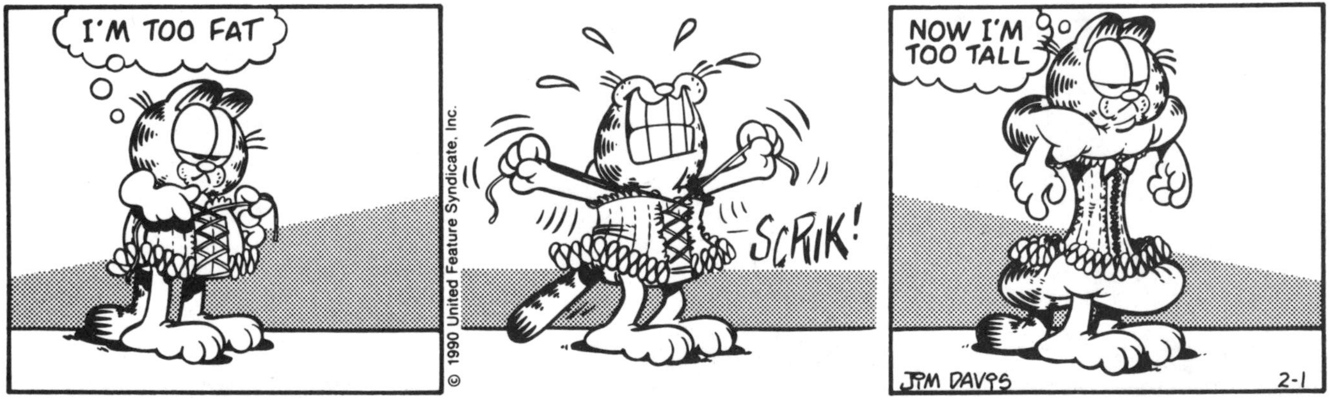
I'M TOO FAT
SCRIK!
NOW I'M TOO TALL
JIM DAVIS
2-1
© 1990 United Feature Syndicate, Inc.

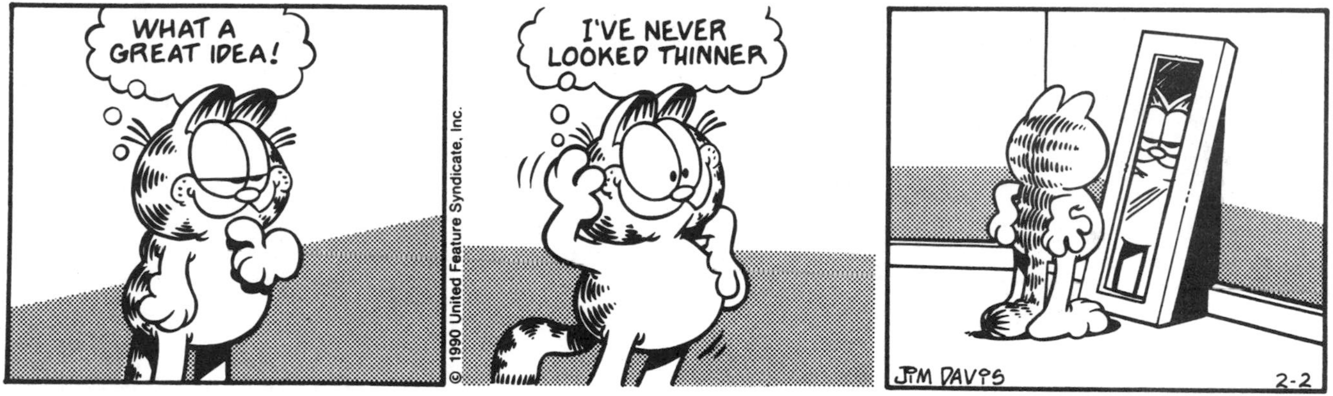
WHAT A GREAT IDEA!
I'VE NEVER LOOKED THINNER
© 1990 United Feature Syndicate, Inc.
JIM DAVIS
2-2

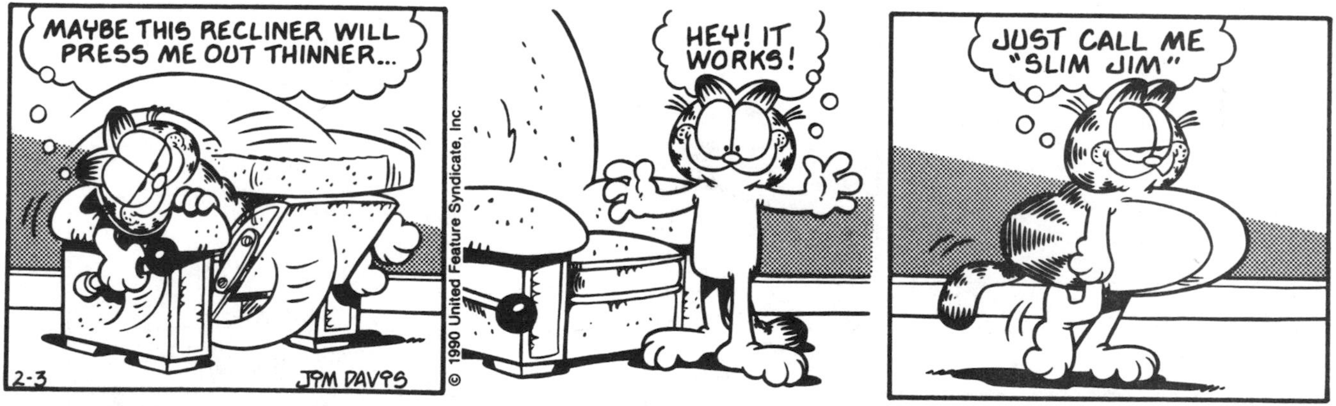
MAYBE THIS RECLINER WILL PRESS ME OUT THINNER...
2-3
JIM DAVIS
© 1990 United Feature Syndicate, Inc.
HEY! IT WORKS!
JUST CALL ME "SLIM JIM"

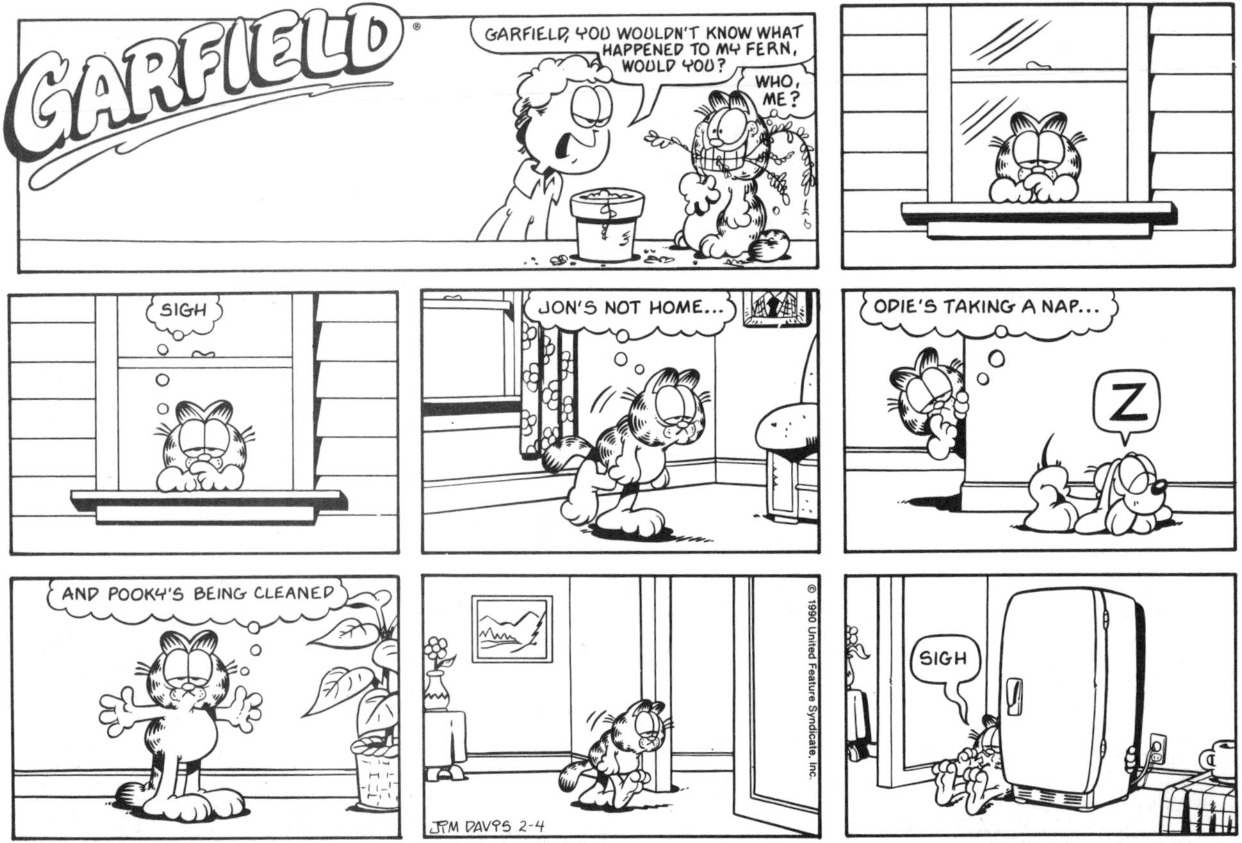
GARFIELD®
GARFIELD, YOU WOULDN'T KNOW WHAT HAPPENED TO MY FERN, WOULD YOU?
WHO, ME?
SIGH
JON'S NOT HOME...
ODIE'S TAKING A NAP...
Z
AND POOKY'S BEING CLEANED
JIM DAVIS 2-4
© 1990 United Feature Syndicate, Inc.
SIGH

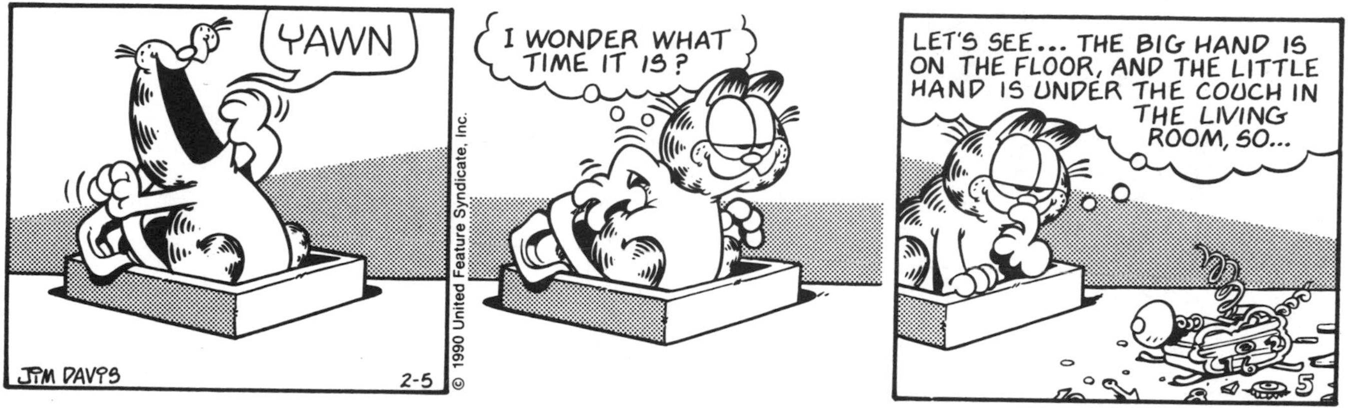

YAWN
JIM DAVIS
2-5
© 1990 United Feature Syndicate, Inc.
I WONDER WHAT TIME IT IS?
LET'S SEE... THE BIG HAND IS ON THE FLOOR, AND THE LITTLE HAND IS UNDER THE COUCH IN THE LIVING ROOM, SO...

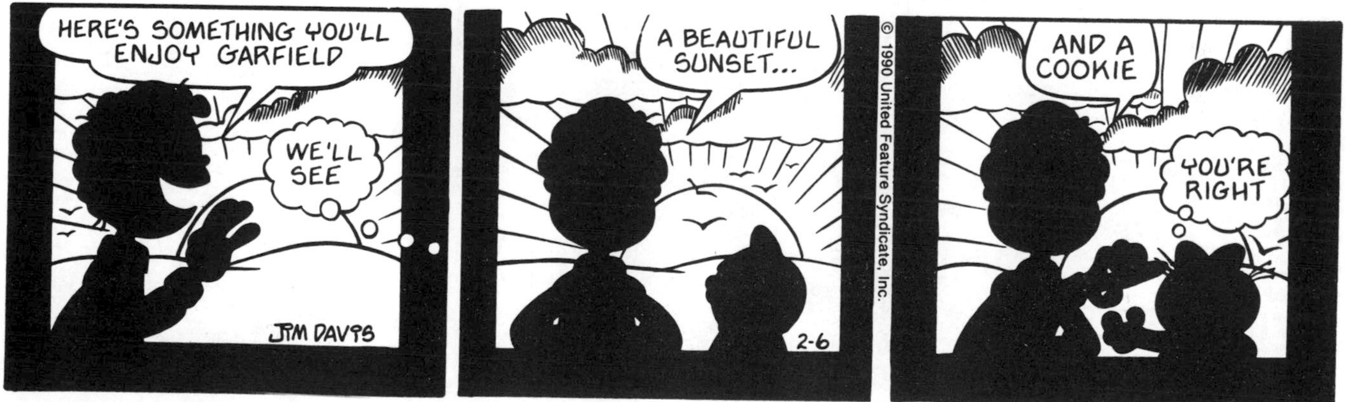

HERE'S SOMETHING YOU'LL ENJOY GARFIELD
WE'LL SEE
JIM DAVIS
A BEAUTIFUL SUNSET...
2-6
© 1990 United Feature Syndicate, Inc.
AND A COOKIE
YOU'RE RIGHT

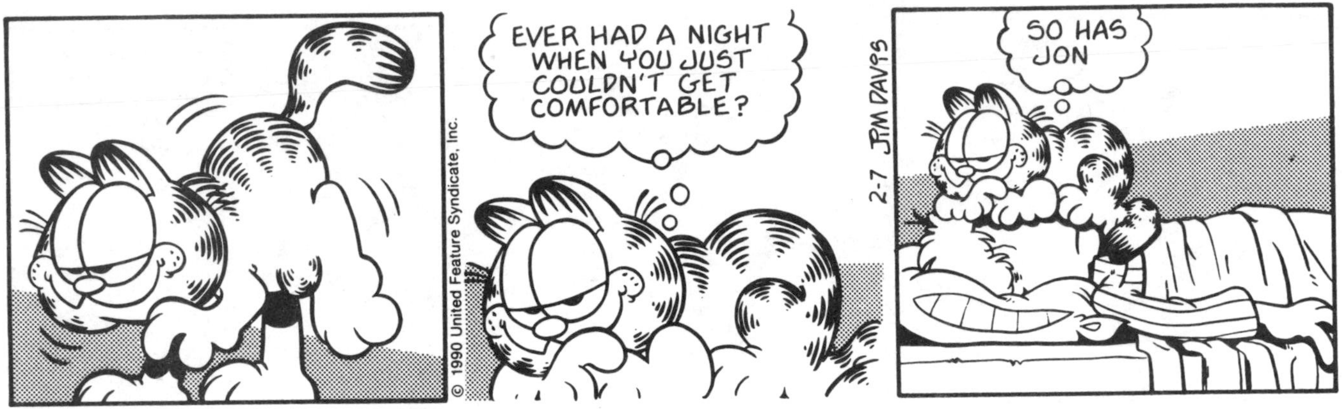

EVER HAD A NIGHT WHEN YOU JUST COULDN'T GET COMFORTABLE?
SO HAS JON
JIM DAVIS 2-7
© 1990 United Feature Syndicate, Inc.

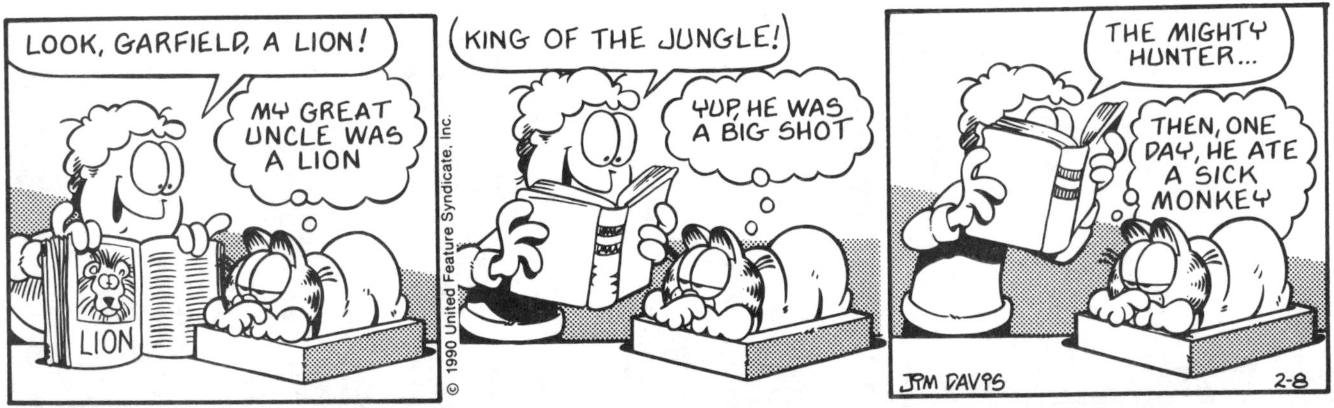

LOOK, GARFIELD, A LION!
MY GREAT UNCLE WAS A LION
LION
KING OF THE JUNGLE!
YUP, HE WAS A BIG SHOT
THE MIGHTY HUNTER...
THEN, ONE DAY, HE ATE A SICK MONKEY
JIM DAVIS 2-8
© 1990 United Feature Syndicate, Inc.

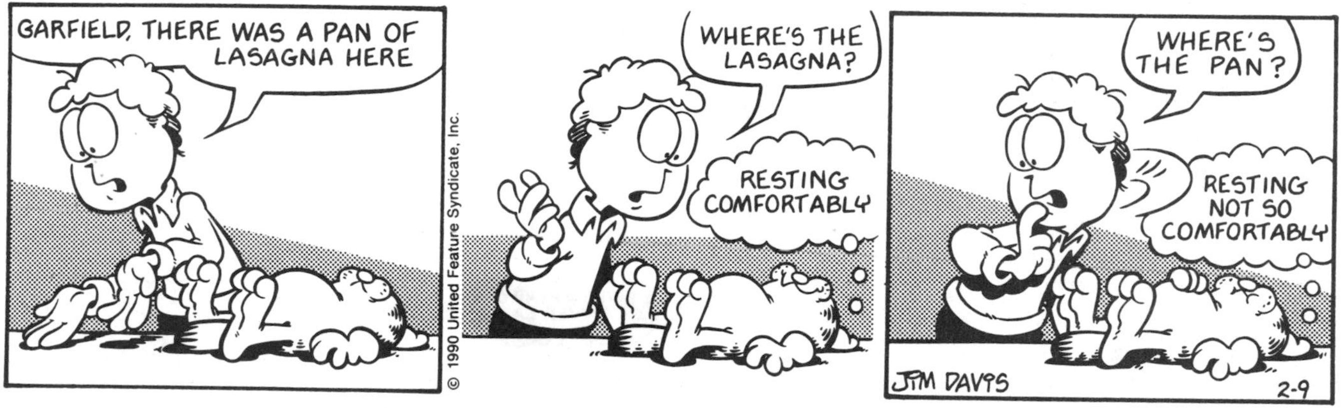
GARFIELD, THERE WAS A PAN OF LASAGNA HERE
WHERE'S THE LASAGNA?
RESTING COMFORTABLY
WHERE'S THE PAN?
RESTING NOT SO COMFORTABLY
JIM DAVIS
2-9
© 1990 United Feature Syndicate, Inc.

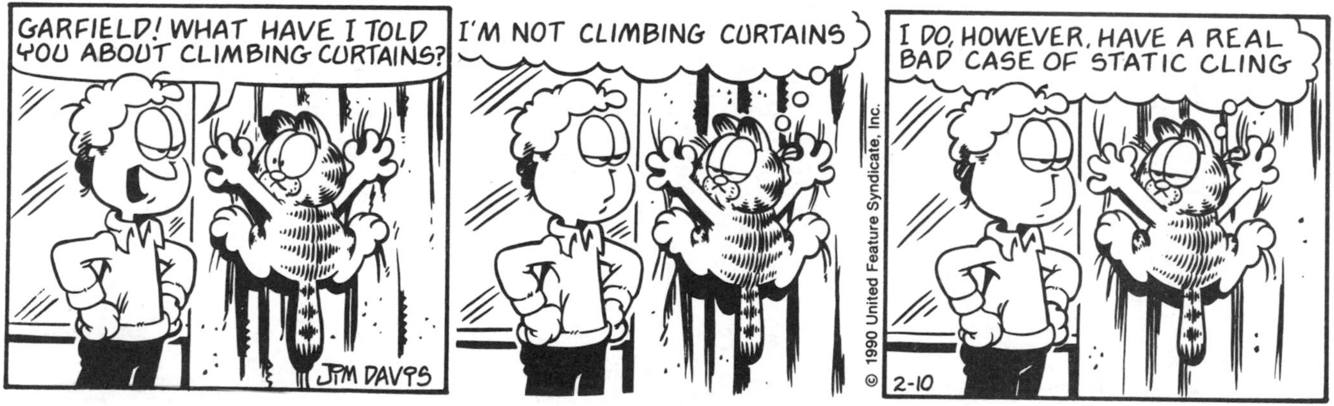
GARFIELD! WHAT HAVE I TOLD YOU ABOUT CLIMBING CURTAINS?
JIM DAVIS
I'M NOT CLIMBING CURTAINS
I DO, HOWEVER, HAVE A REAL BAD CASE OF STATIC CLING
2-10
© 1990 United Feature Syndicate, Inc.

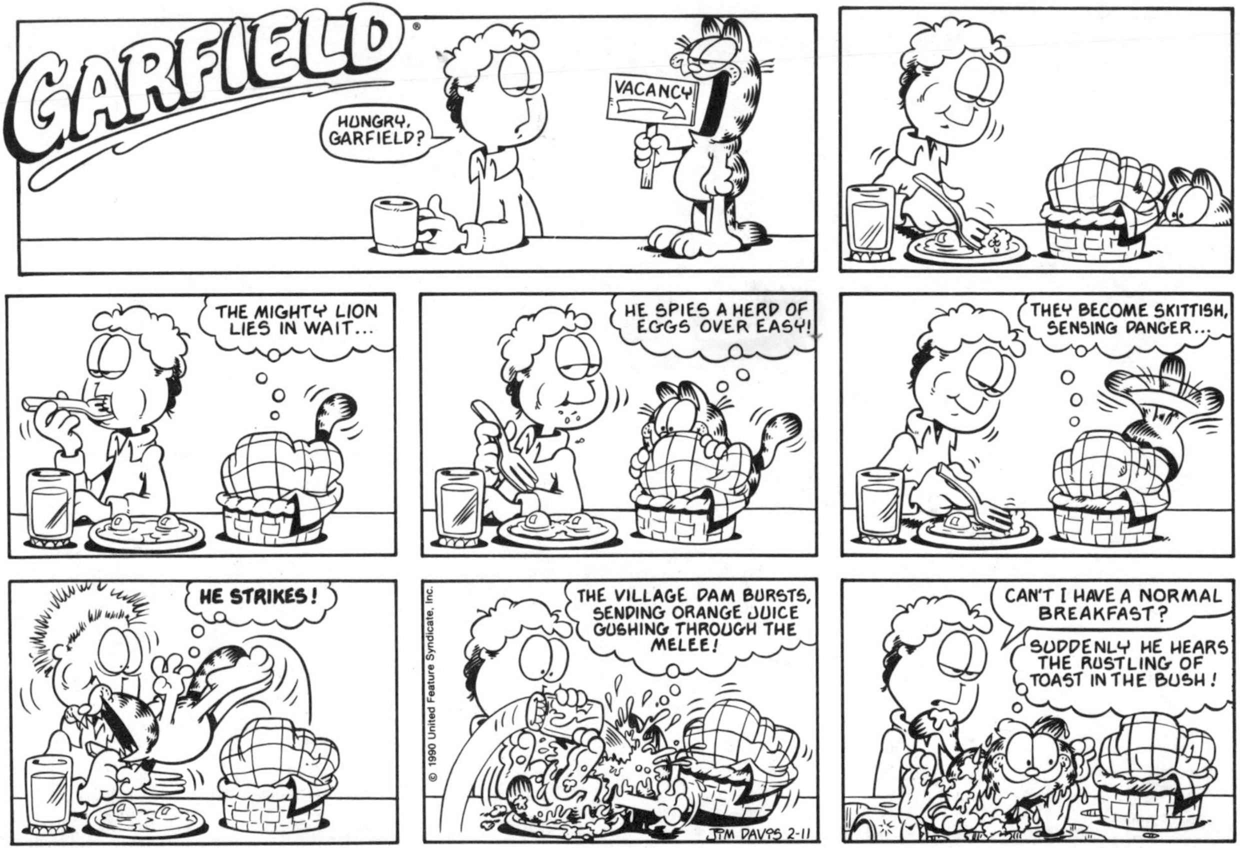
GARFIELD®
HUNGRY, GARFIELD?
VACANCY
THE MIGHTY LION LIES IN WAIT...
HE SPIES A HERD OF EGGS OVER EASY!
THEY BECOME SKITTISH, SENSING DANGER...
HE STRIKES!
© 1990 United Feature Syndicate, Inc.
THE VILLAGE DAM BURSTS, SENDING ORANGE JUICE GUSHING THROUGH THE MELEE!
JIM DAVIS 2-11
CAN'T I HAVE A NORMAL BREAKFAST?
SUDDENLY HE HEARS THE RUSTLING OF TOAST IN THE BUSH!

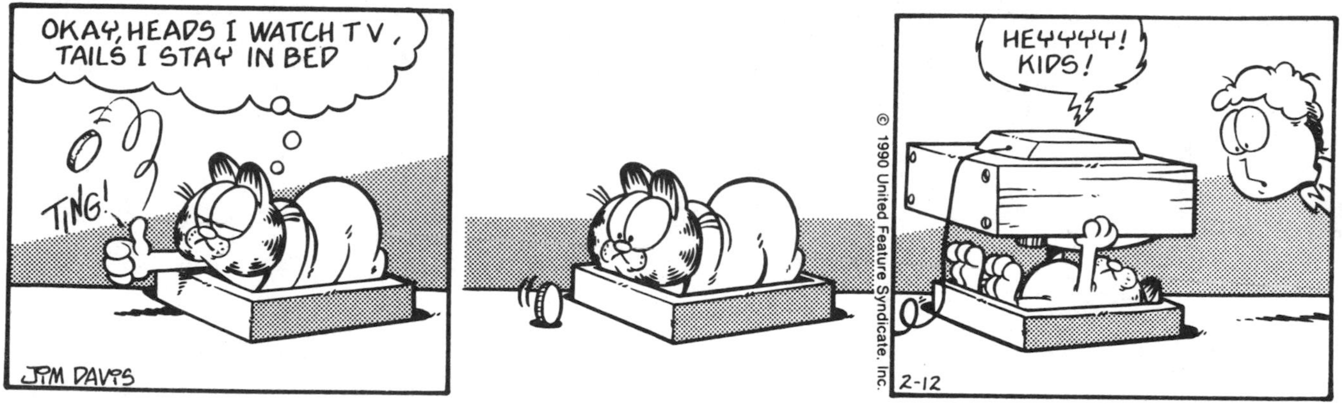
OKAY, HEADS I WATCH TV, TAILS I STAY IN BED
TING!
JIM DAVIS
© 1990 United Feature Syndicate, Inc.
HEYYYY! KIDS!
2-12

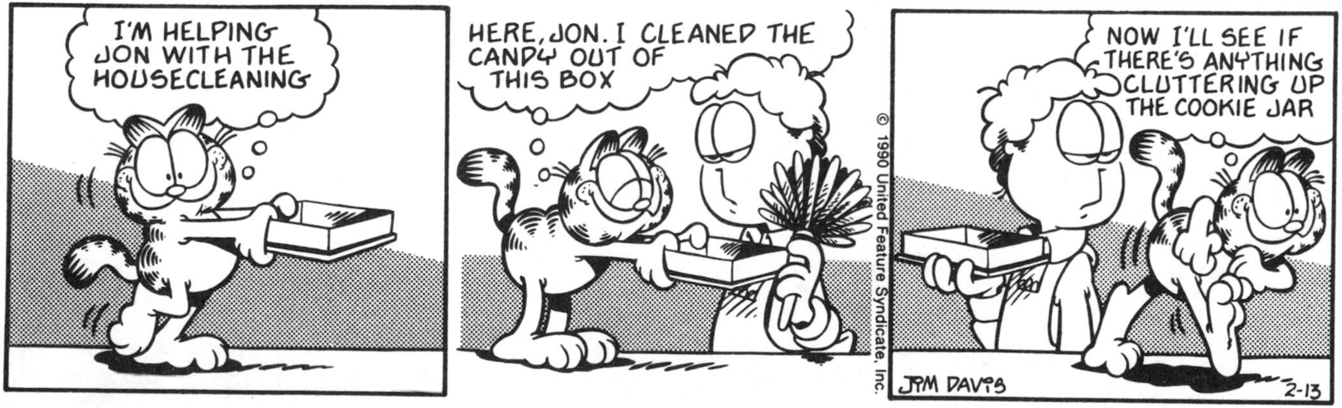
I'M HELPING JON WITH THE HOUSECLEANING
HERE, JON. I CLEANED THE CANDY OUT OF THIS BOX
© 1990 United Feature Syndicate, Inc.
NOW I'LL SEE IF THERE'S ANYTHING CLUTTERING UP THE COOKIE JAR
JIM DAVIS
2-13

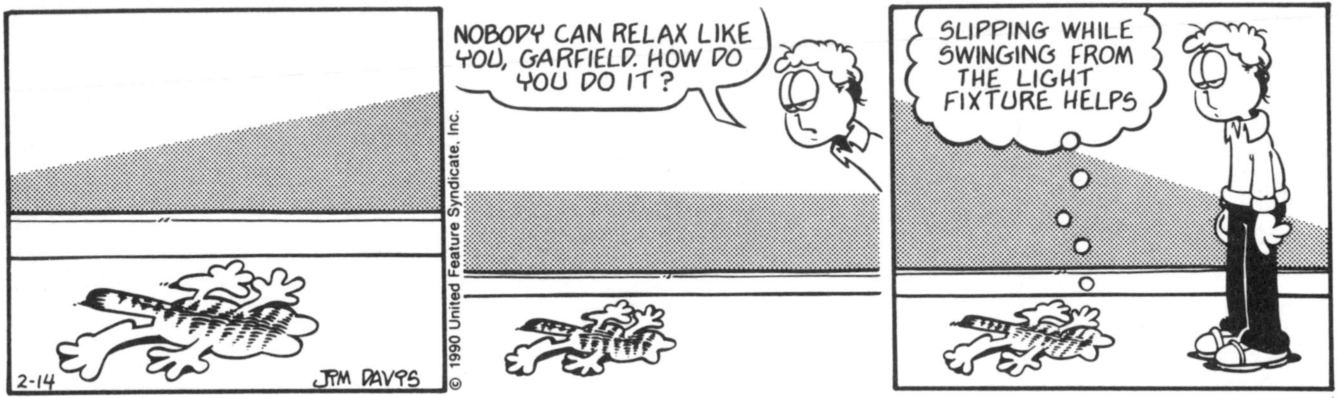

2-14
JIM DAVIS
© 1990 United Feature Syndicate, Inc.
NOBODY CAN RELAX LIKE YOU, GARFIELD. HOW DO YOU DO IT?
SLIPPING WHILE SWINGING FROM THE LIGHT FIXTURE HELPS

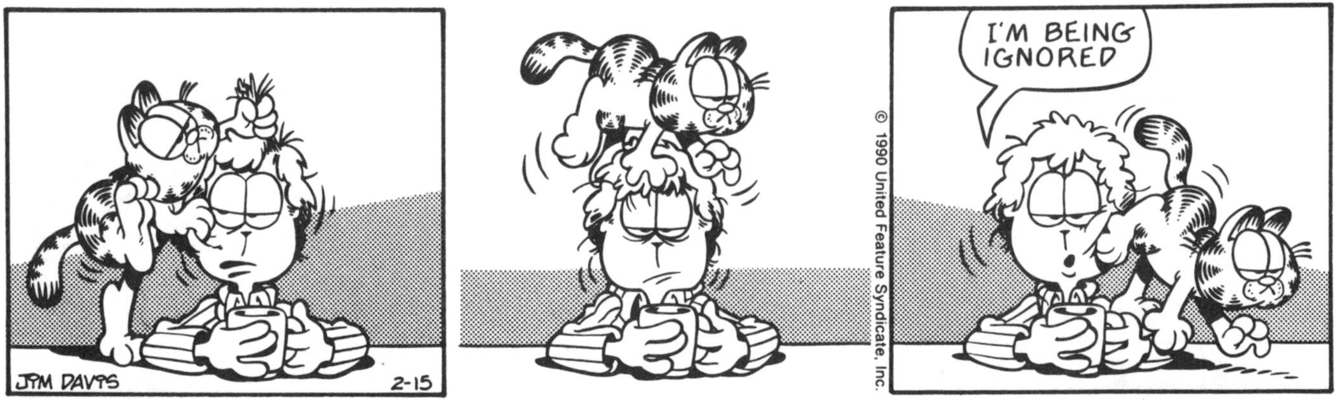

JIM DAVIS
2-15
© 1990 United Feature Syndicate, Inc.
I'M BEING IGNORED

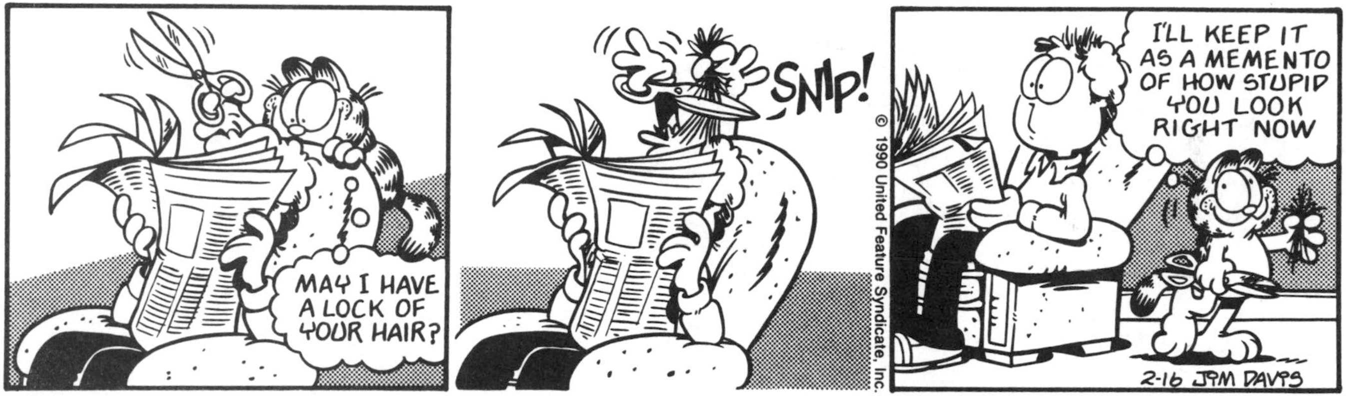
MAY I HAVE A LOCK OF YOUR HAIR?
SNIP!
I'LL KEEP IT AS A MEMENTO OF HOW STUPID YOU LOOK RIGHT NOW
© 1990 United Feature Syndicate, Inc.
2-16 JIM DAVIS

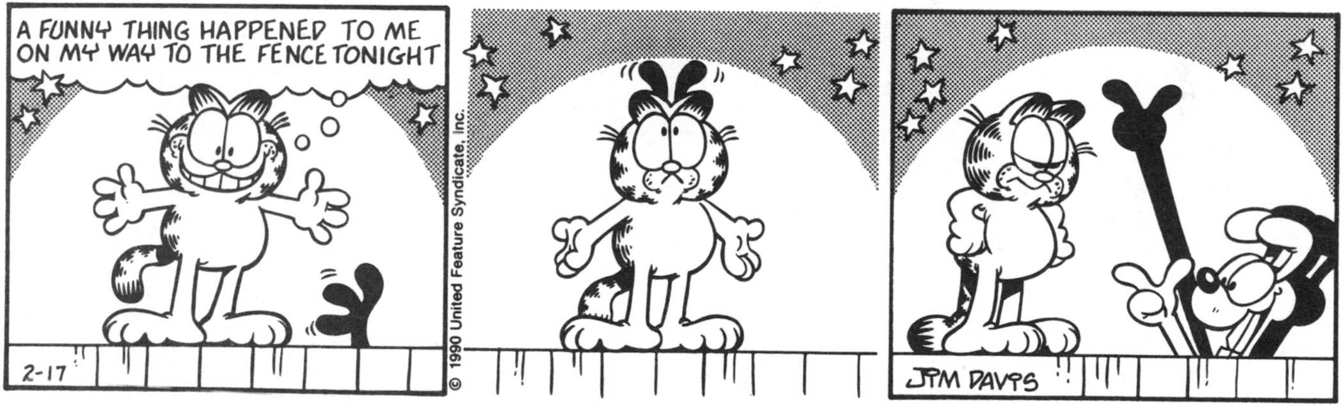
A FUNNY THING HAPPENED TO ME ON MY WAY TO THE FENCE TONIGHT
2-17
© 1990 United Feature Syndicate, Inc.
JIM DAVIS

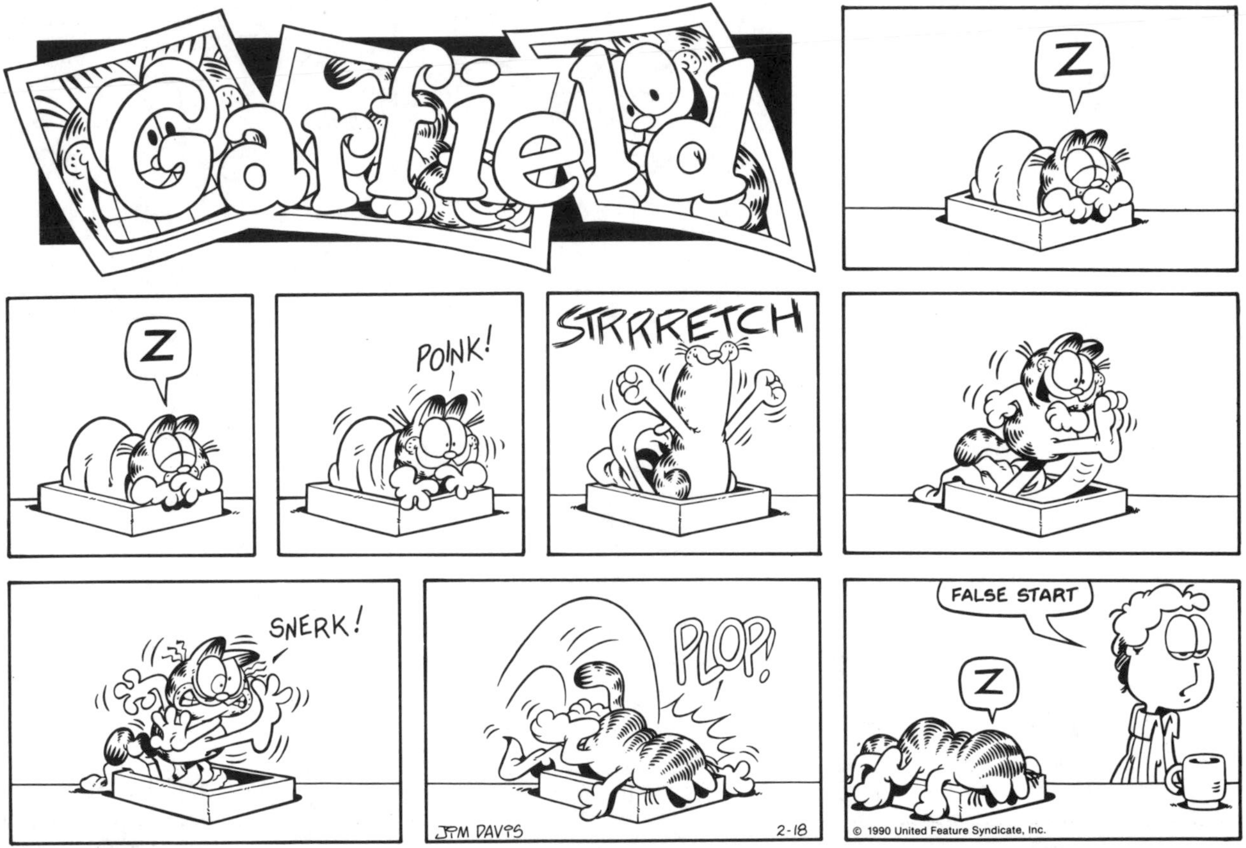
Garfield
Z
Z
POINK!
STRRRETCH
SNERK!
PLOP!
JIM DAVIS
2-18
FALSE START
Z
© 1990 United Feature Syndicate, Inc.

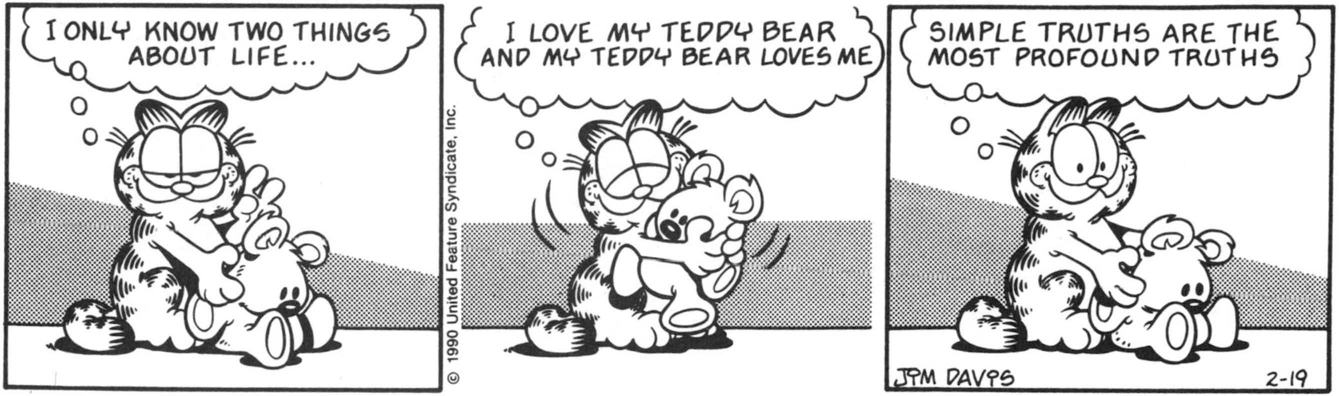
I ONLY KNOW TWO THINGS ABOUT LIFE...
© 1990 United Feature Syndicate, Inc.
I LOVE MY TEDDY BEAR AND MY TEDDY BEAR LOVES ME
SIMPLE TRUTHS ARE THE MOST PROFOUND TRUTHS
JIM DAVIS
2-19

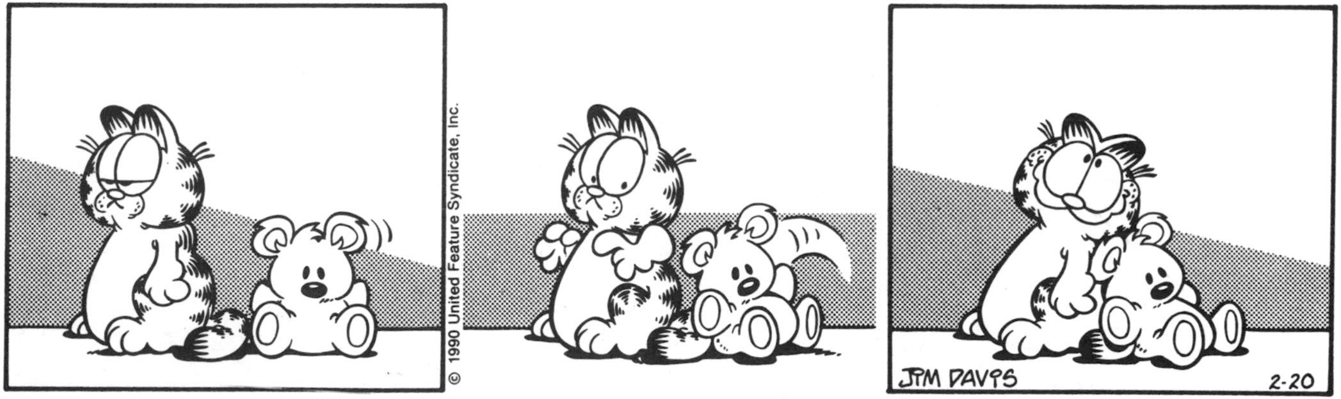
© 1990 United Feature Syndicate, Inc.
JIM DAVIS
2-20

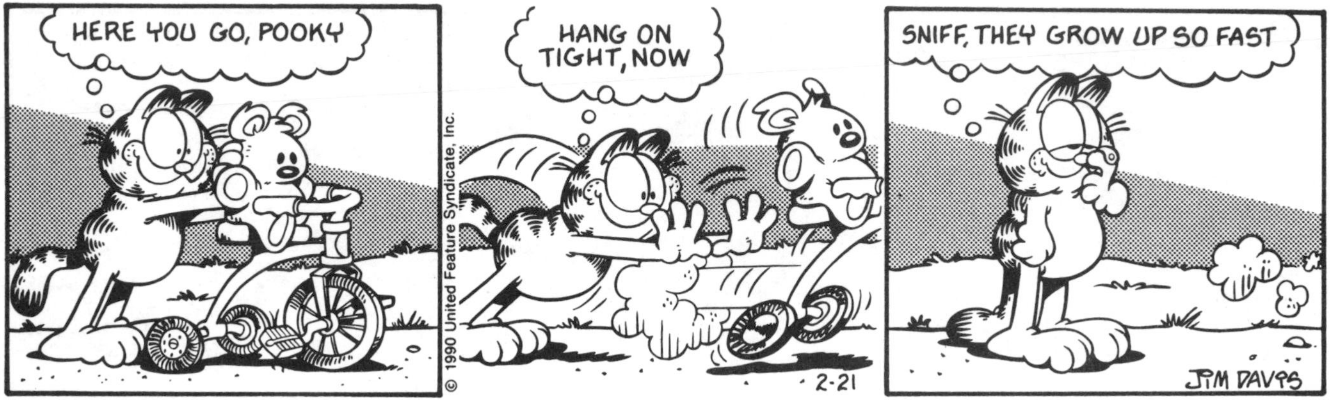
HERE YOU GO, POOKY
HANG ON TIGHT, NOW
SNIFF, THEY GROW UP SO FAST
© 1990 United Feature Syndicate, Inc.
2-21
JIM DAVIS

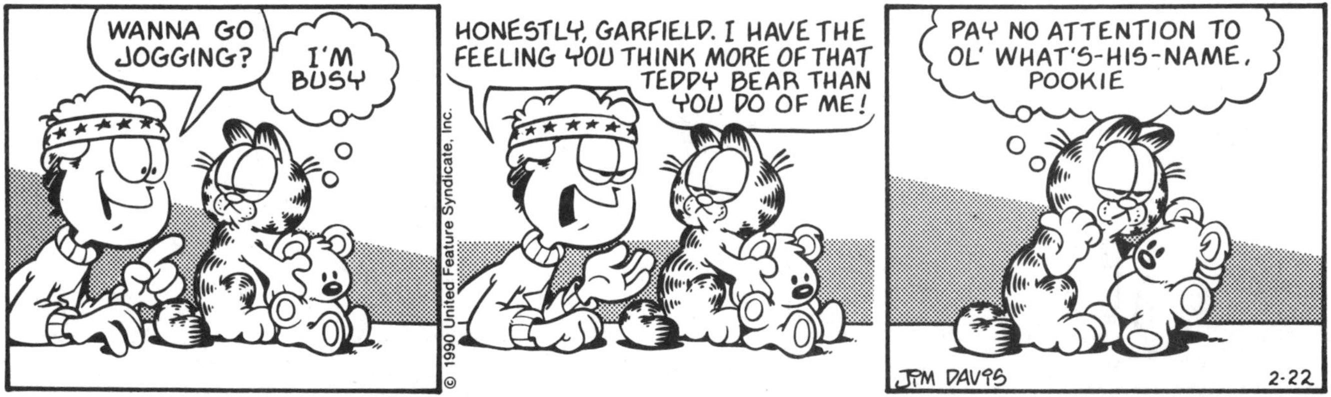
WANNA GO JOGGING?
I'M BUSY
HONESTLY, GARFIELD. I HAVE THE FEELING YOU THINK MORE OF THAT TEDDY BEAR THAN YOU DO OF ME!
PAY NO ATTENTION TO OL' WHAT'S-HIS-NAME, POOKIE
© 1990 United Feature Syndicate, Inc.
JIM DAVIS
2-22

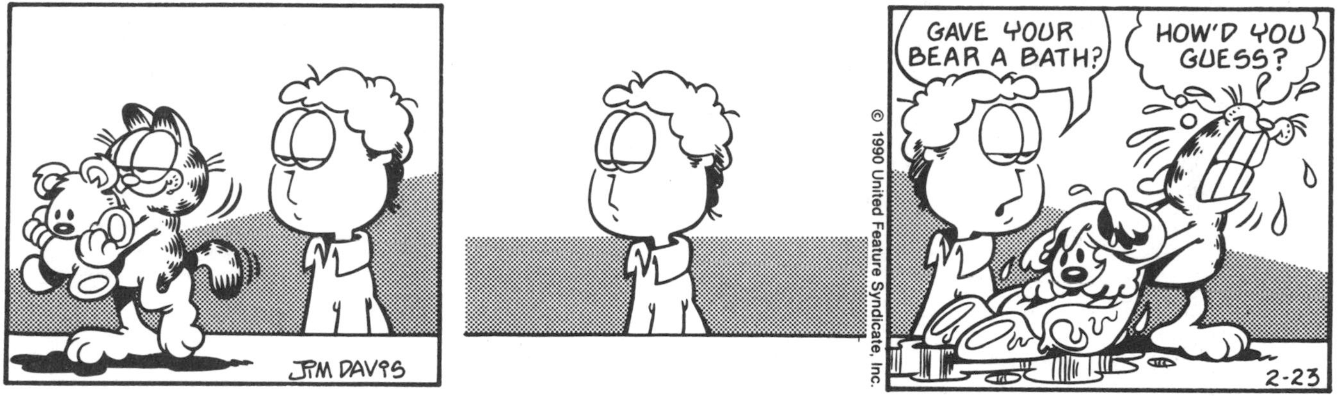
JIM DAVIS
GAVE YOUR BEAR A BATH?
HOW'D YOU GUESS?
© 1990 United Feature Syndicate, Inc.
2-23

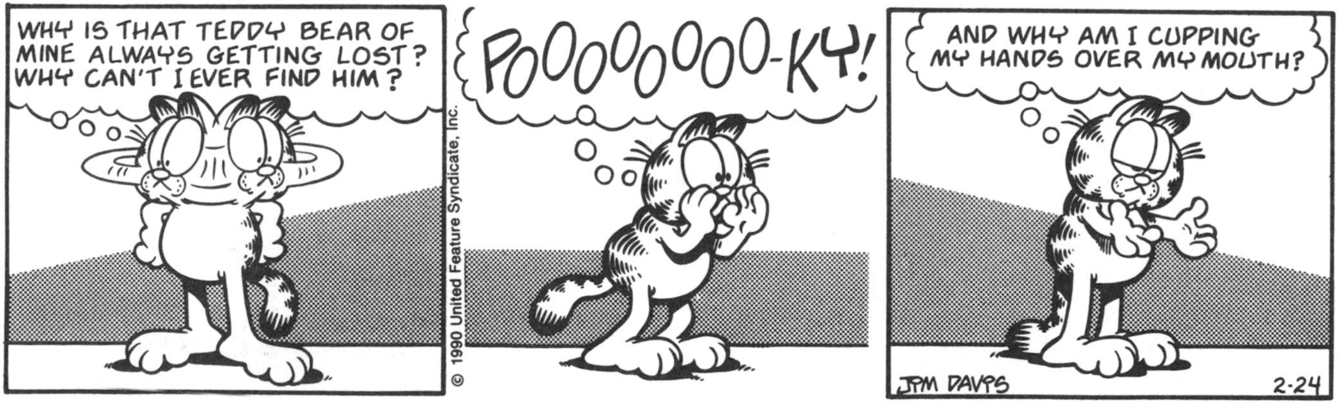
WHY IS THAT TEDDY BEAR OF MINE ALWAYS GETTING LOST? WHY CAN'T I EVER FIND HIM?
© 1990 United Feature Syndicate, Inc.
POOOOOOOOO-KY!
AND WHY AM I CUPPING MY HANDS OVER MY MOUTH?
JIM DAVIS
2-24

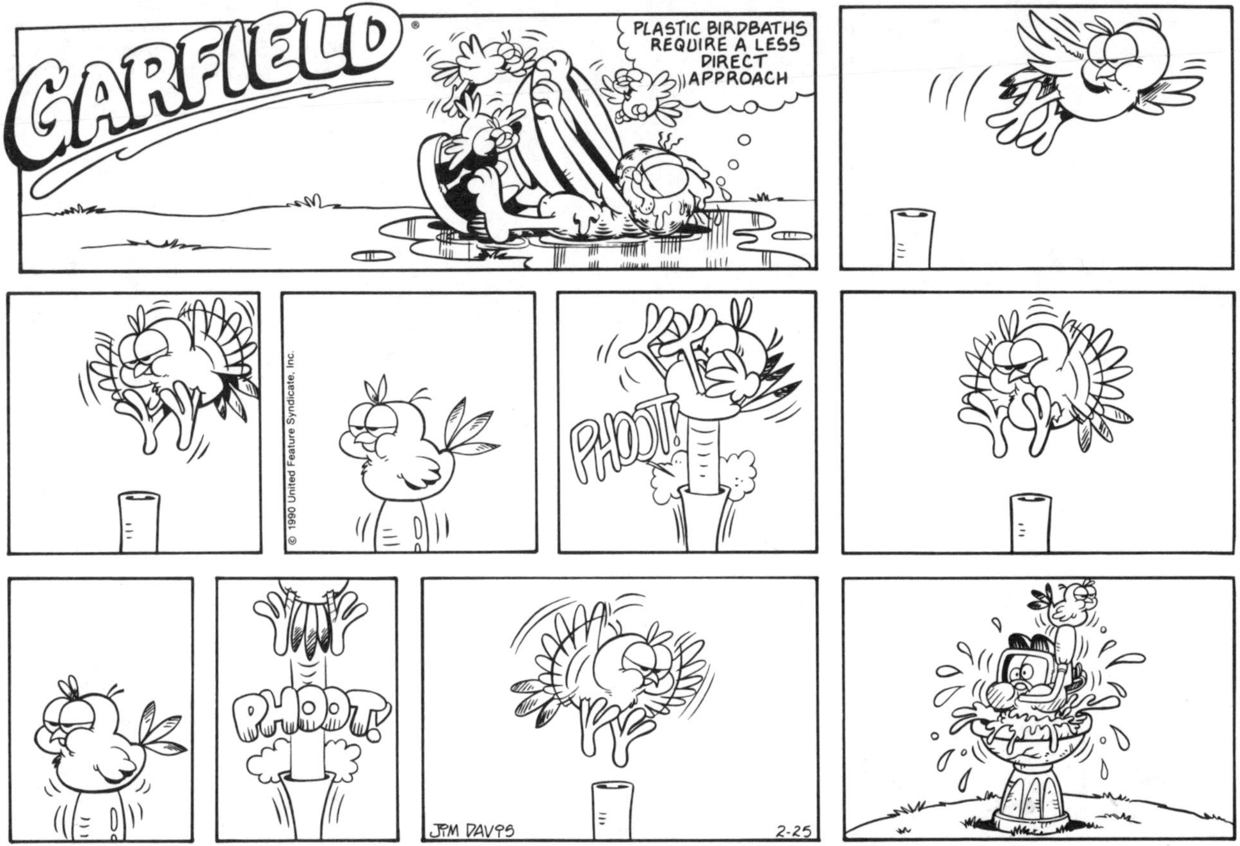
GARFIELD
PLASTIC BIRDBATHS REQUIRE A LESS DIRECT APPROACH
© 1990 United Feature Syndicate, Inc.
PHOOT!
PHOOT!
JIM DAVIS
2-25

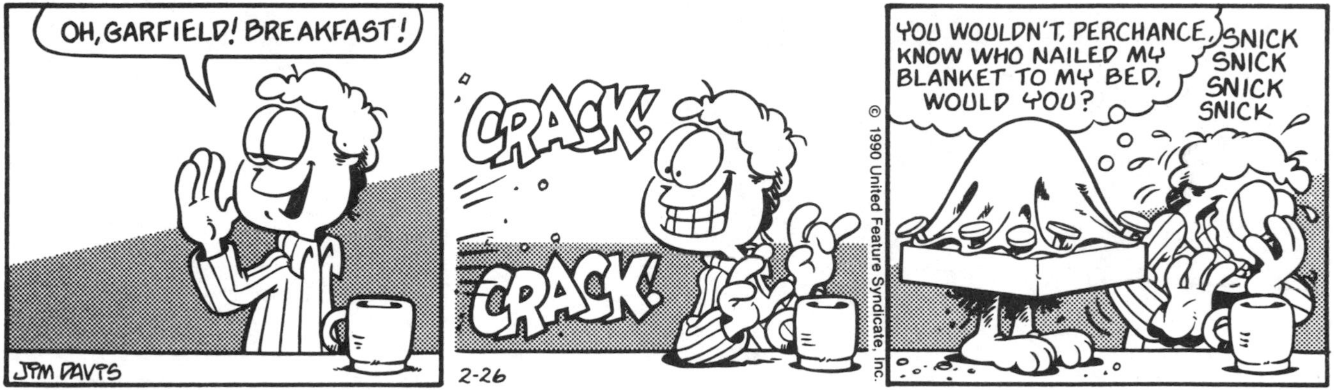
OH, GARFIELD! BREAKFAST!
CRACK!
CRACK!
YOU WOULDN'T, PERCHANCE, KNOW WHO NAILED MY BLANKET TO MY BED, WOULD YOU?
SNICK SNICK SNICK SNICK
JIM DAVIS
2-26
© 1990 United Feature Syndicate, Inc.

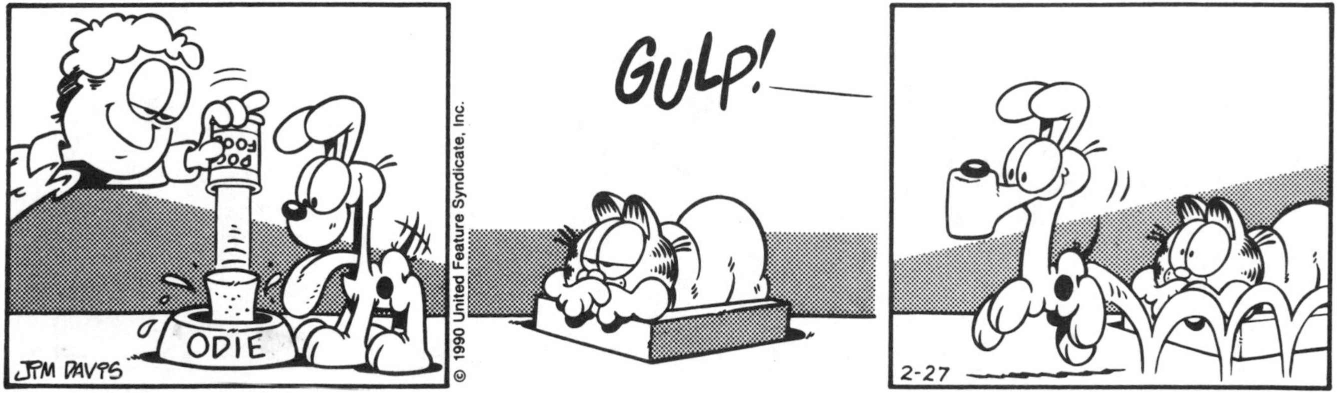
DOG FOOD
ODIE
GULP!
JIM DAVIS
2-27
© 1990 United Feature Syndicate, Inc.

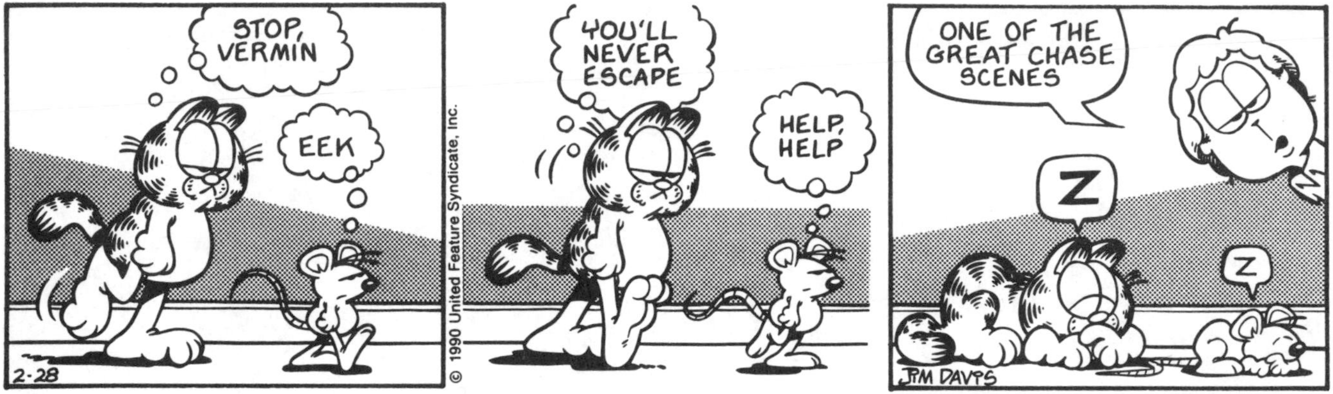
STOP, VERMIN
EEK
2-28
© 1990 United Feature Syndicate, Inc.
YOU'LL NEVER ESCAPE
HELP, HELP
ONE OF THE GREAT CHASE SCENES
Z
Z
JIM DAVIS

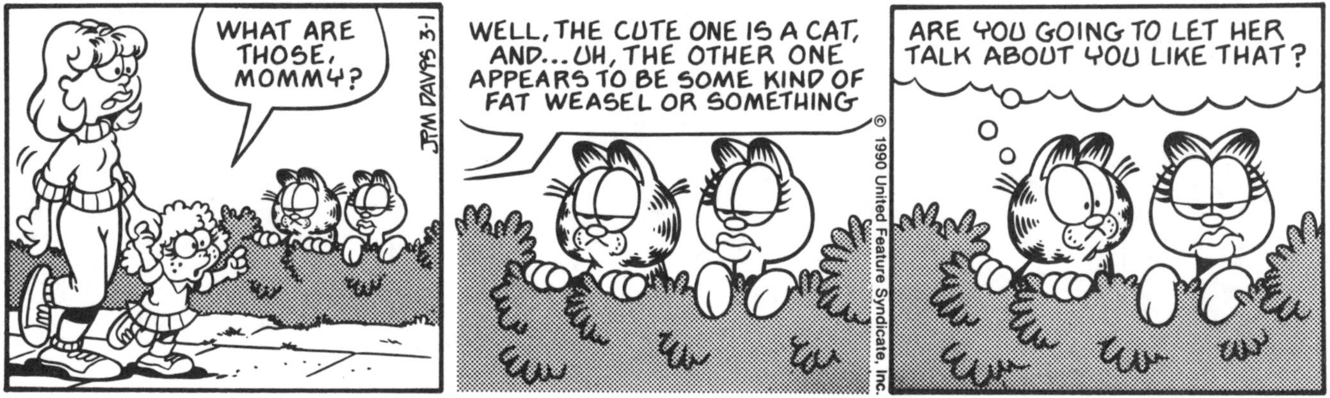
WHAT ARE THOSE, MOMMY?
JIM DAVIS 3-1
WELL, THE CUTE ONE IS A CAT, AND...UH, THE OTHER ONE APPEARS TO BE SOME KIND OF FAT WEASEL OR SOMETHING
© 1990 United Feature Syndicate, Inc.
ARE YOU GOING TO LET HER TALK ABOUT YOU LIKE THAT?

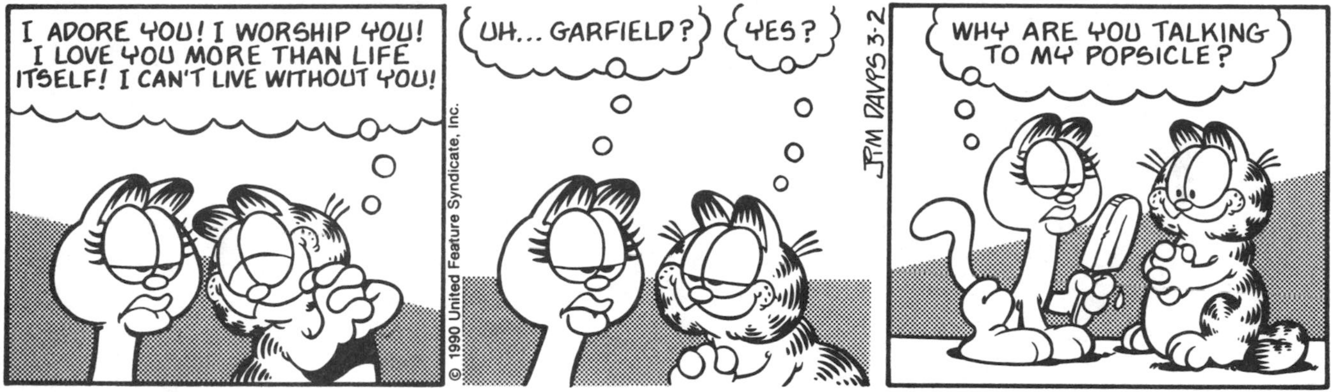
I ADORE YOU! I WORSHIP YOU! I LOVE YOU MORE THAN LIFE ITSELF! I CAN'T LIVE WITHOUT YOU!
UH... GARFIELD?
YES?
WHY ARE YOU TALKING TO MY POPSICLE?
© 1990 United Feature Syndicate, Inc.
JIM DAVIS 3-2

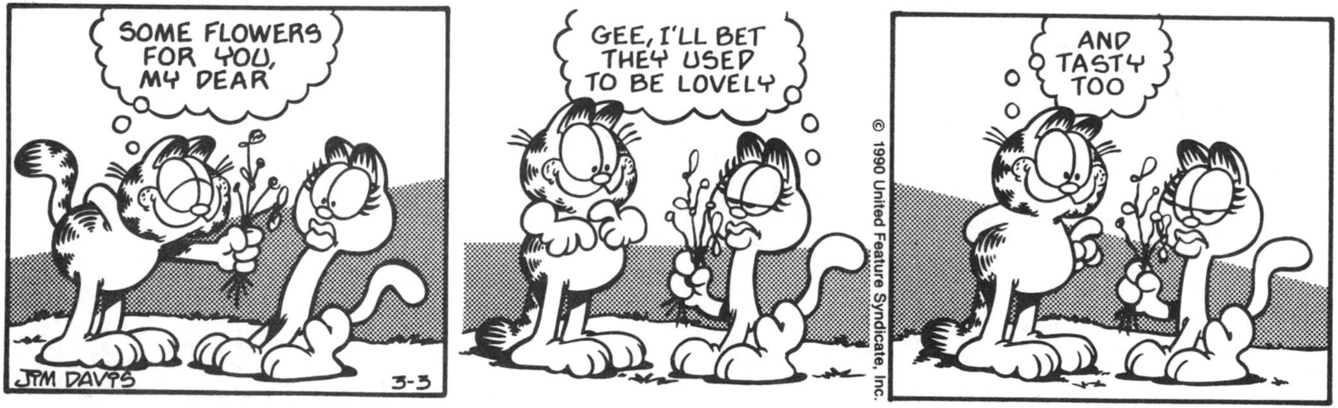
SOME FLOWERS FOR YOU, MY DEAR
GEE, I'LL BET THEY USED TO BE LOVELY
AND TASTY TOO
JIM DAVIS 3-3
© 1990 United Feature Syndicate, Inc.

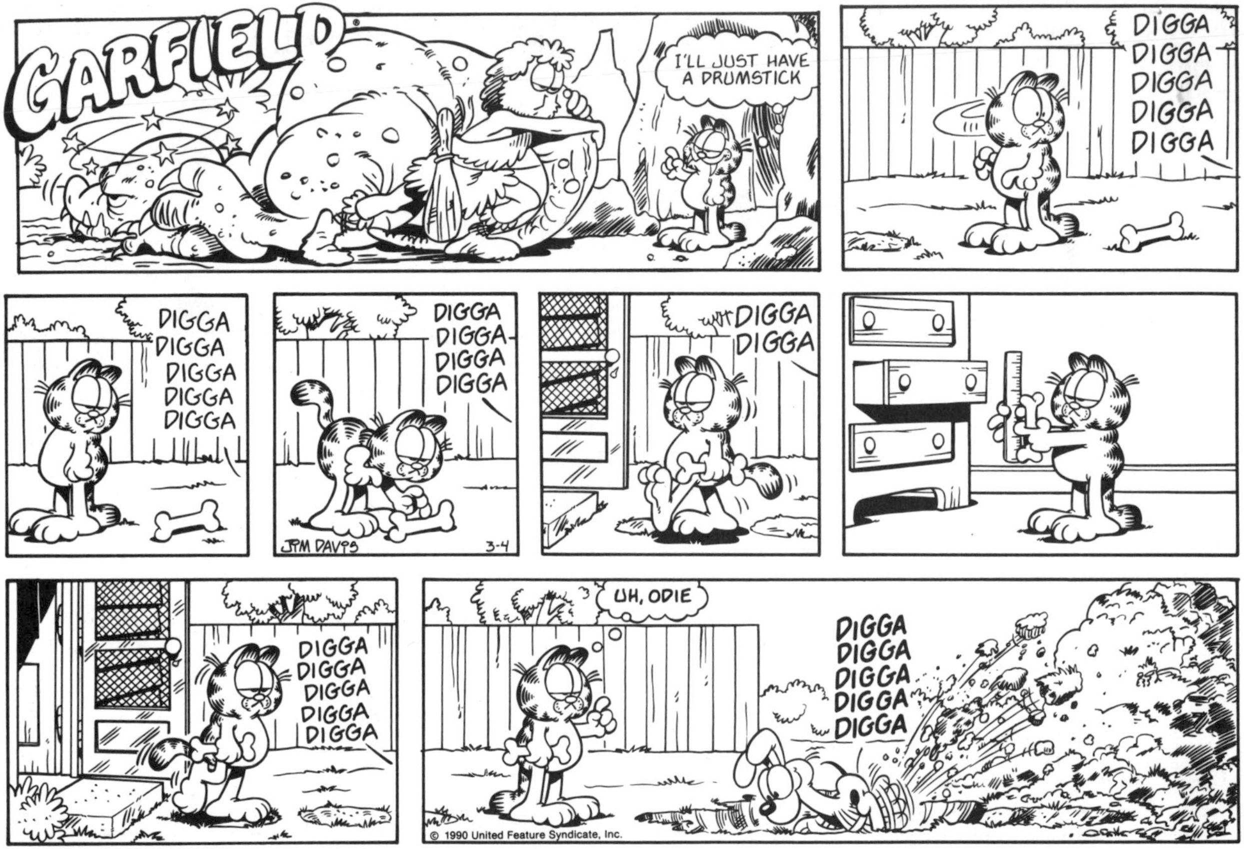
GARFIELD
I'LL JUST HAVE A DRUMSTICK
DIGGA DIGGA DIGGA DIGGA DIGGA
DIGGA DIGGA DIGGA DIGGA DIGGA
DIGGA DIGGA DIGGA DIGGA
JIM DAVIS
3-4
DIGGA DIGGA
DIGGA DIGGA DIGGA DIGGA DIGGA
UH, ODIE
DIGGA DIGGA DIGGA DIGGA DIGGA
© 1990 United Feature Syndicate, Inc.

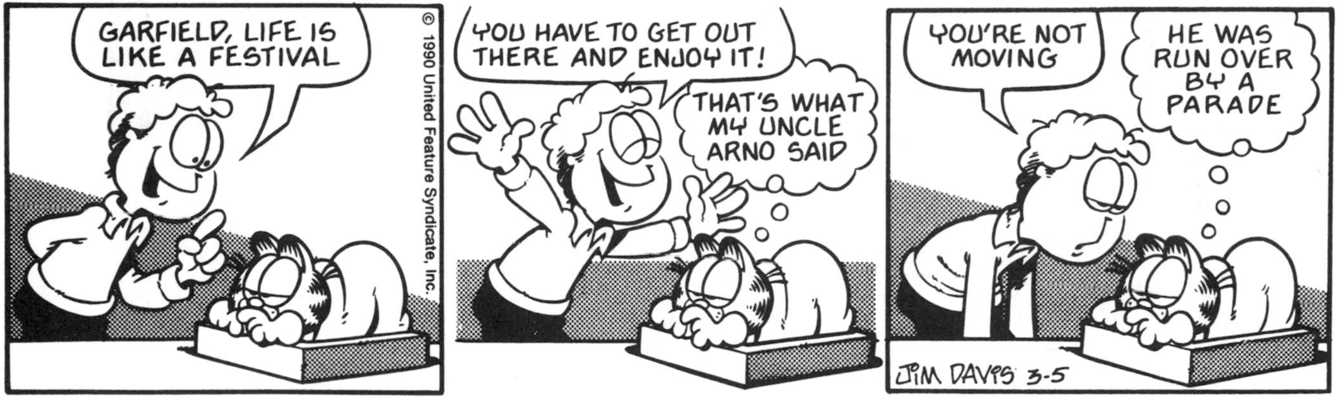
GARFIELD, LIFE IS LIKE A FESTIVAL
© 1990 United Feature Syndicate, Inc.
YOU HAVE TO GET OUT THERE AND ENJOY IT!
THAT'S WHAT MY UNCLE ARNO SAID
YOU'RE NOT MOVING
HE WAS RUN OVER BY A PARADE
JIM DAVIS 3-5

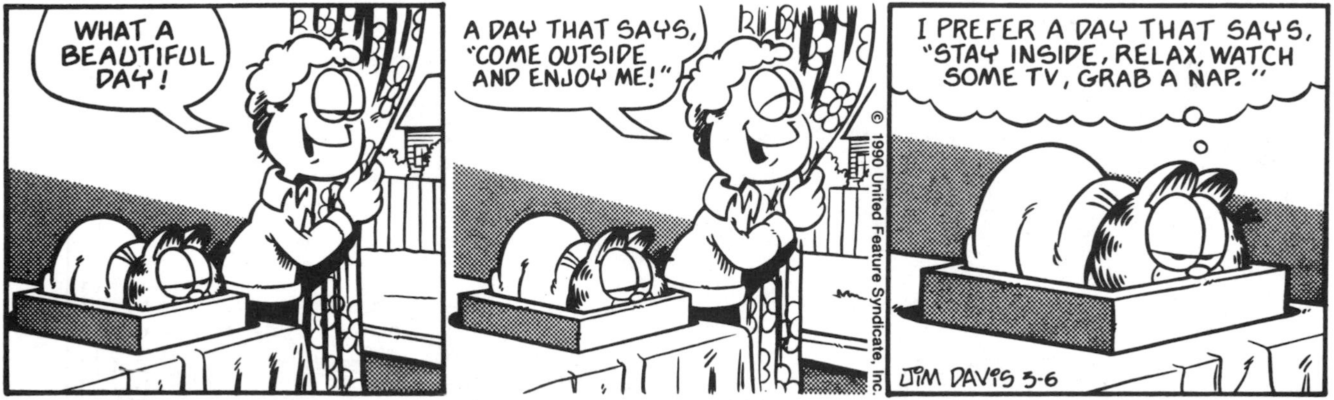
WHAT A BEAUTIFUL DAY!
A DAY THAT SAYS, "COME OUTSIDE AND ENJOY ME!"
© 1990 United Feature Syndicate, Inc.
I PREFER A DAY THAT SAYS, "STAY INSIDE, RELAX, WATCH SOME TV, GRAB A NAP."
JIM DAVIS 3-6

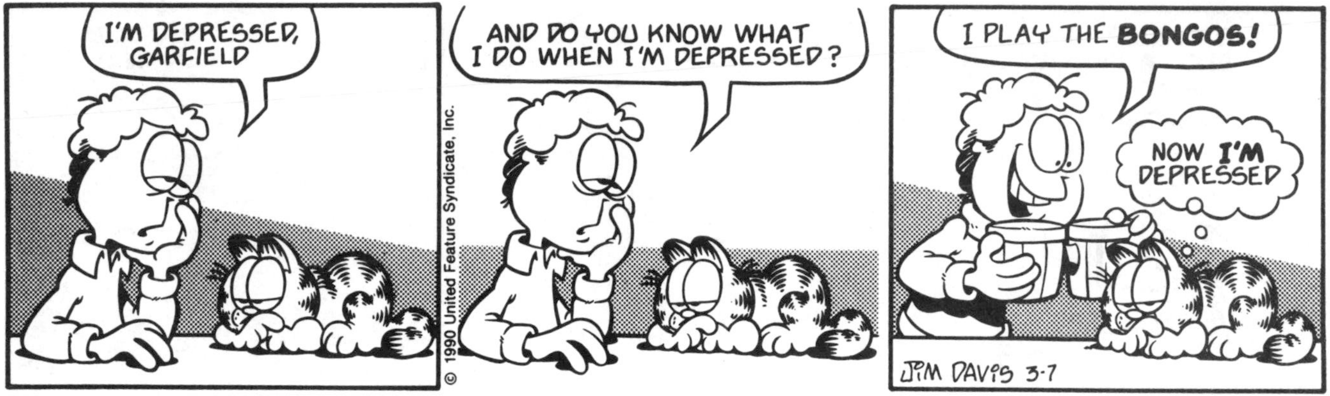
I'M DEPRESSED, GARFIELD
AND DO YOU KNOW WHAT I DO WHEN I'M DEPRESSED?
I PLAY THE BONGOS!
NOW I'M DEPRESSED
JIM DAVIS 3-7
© 1990 United Feature Syndicate, Inc.

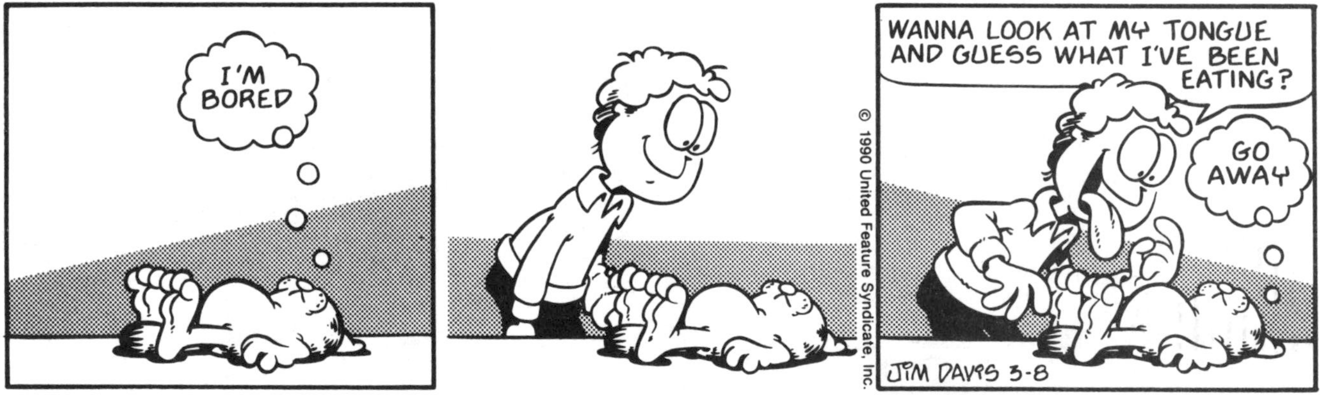
I'M BORED
WANNA LOOK AT MY TONGUE AND GUESS WHAT I'VE BEEN EATING?
GO AWAY
JIM DAVIS 3-8
© 1990 United Feature Syndicate, Inc.

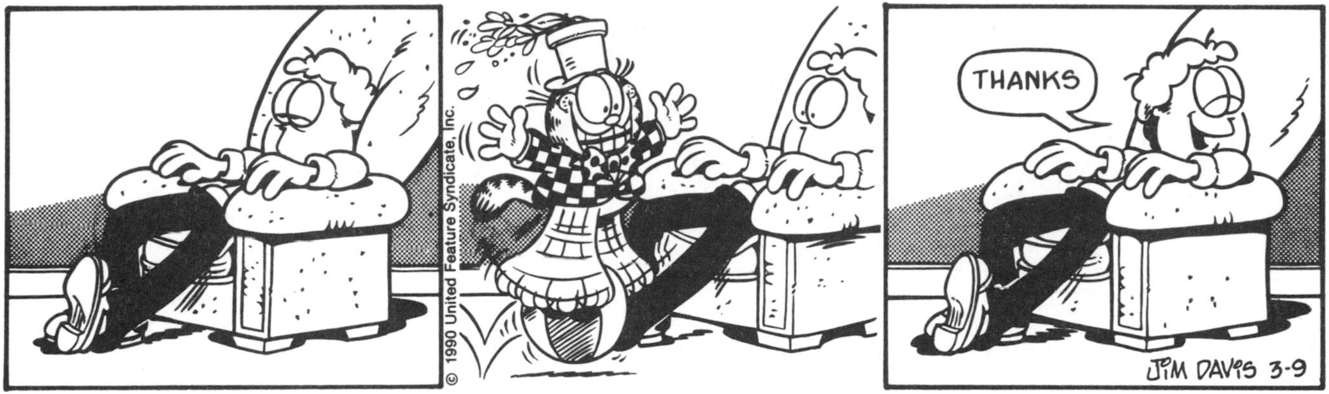
THANKS
© 1990 United Feature Syndicate, Inc.
JIM DAVIS 3-9

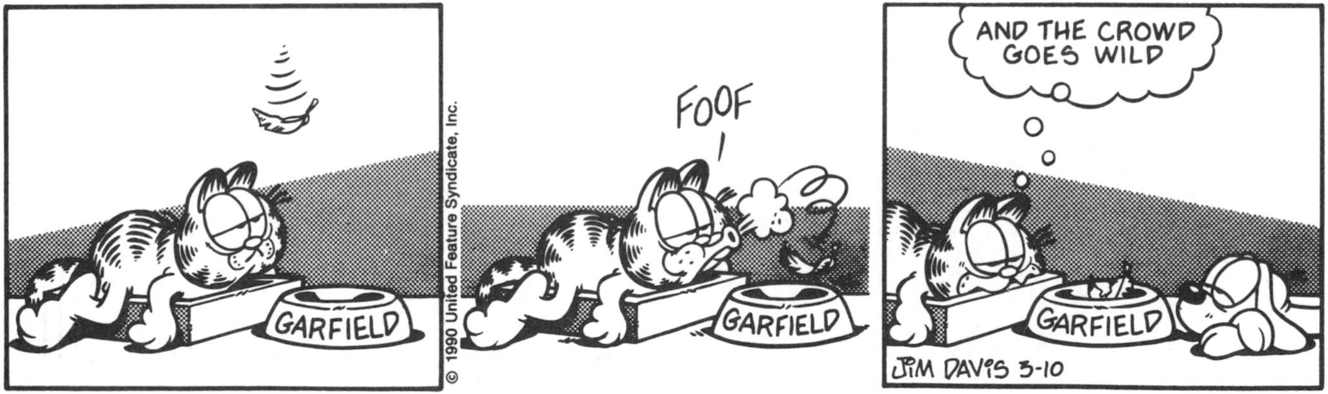
FOOF
AND THE CROWD GOES WILD
© 1990 United Feature Syndicate, Inc.
JIM DAVIS 3-10

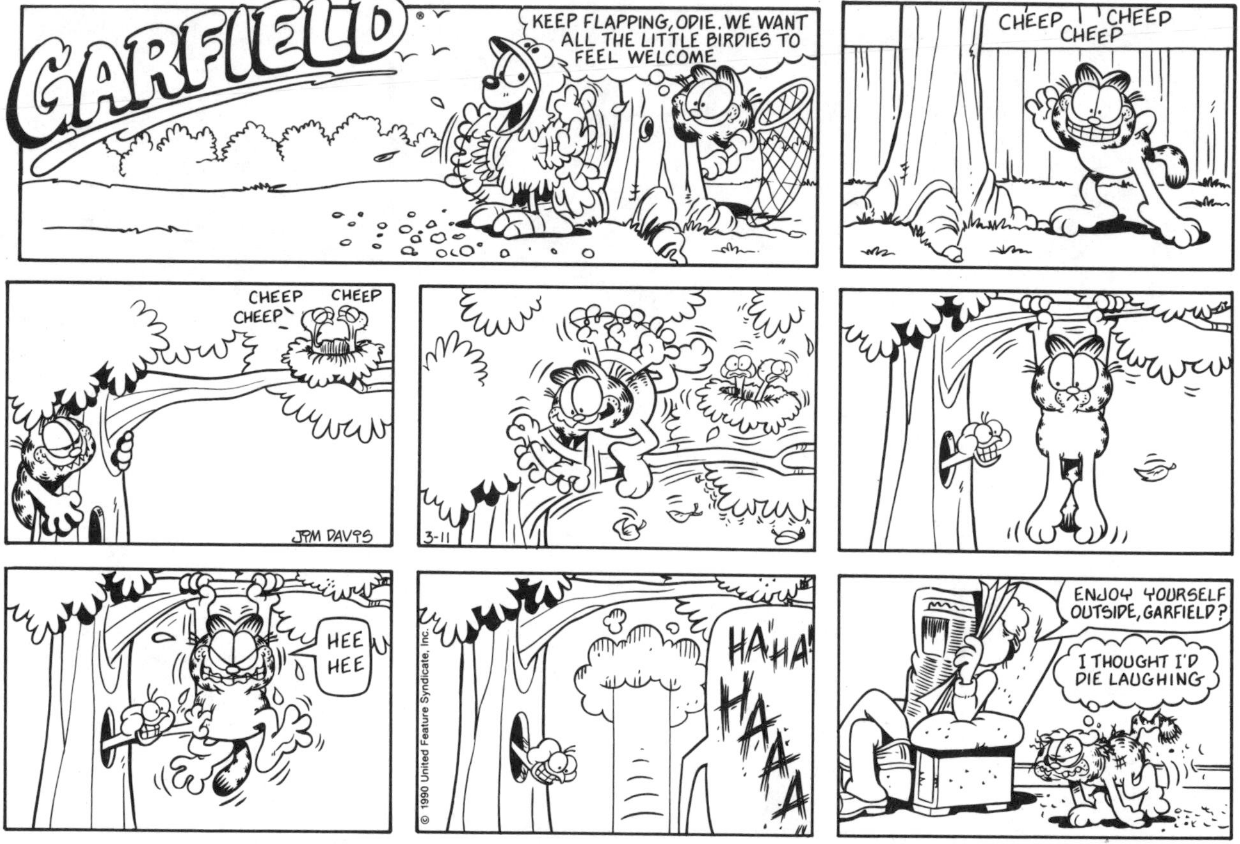
GARFIELD
KEEP FLAPPING, ODIE. WE WANT ALL THE LITTLE BIRDIES TO FEEL WELCOME
CHEEP CHEEP CHEEP
CHEEP CHEEP CHEEP
JIM DAVIS
3-11
HEE HEE
© 1990 United Feature Syndicate, Inc.
HA HA! HA A A A
ENJOY YOURSELF OUTSIDE, GARFIELD?
I THOUGHT I'D DIE LAUGHING

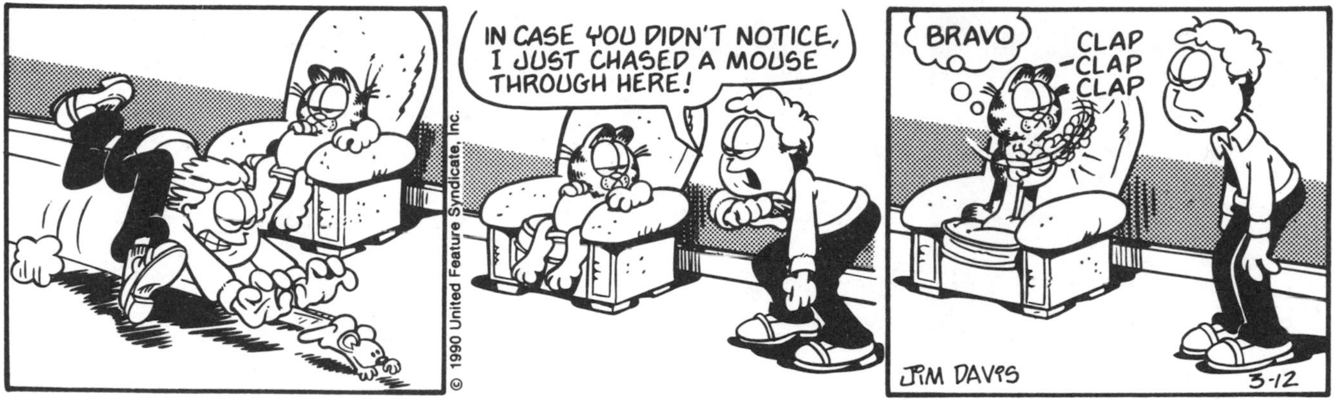
© 1990 United Feature Syndicate, Inc.
IN CASE YOU DIDN'T NOTICE, I JUST CHASED A MOUSE THROUGH HERE!
BRAVO
CLAP
CLAP
CLAP
JIM DAVIS
3-12

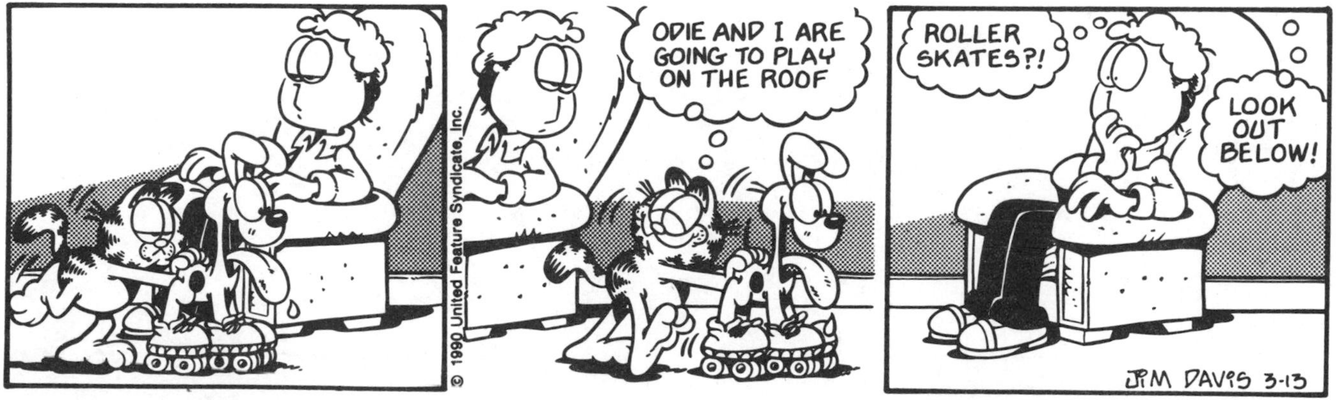
© 1990 United Feature Syndicate, Inc.
ODIE AND I ARE GOING TO PLAY ON THE ROOF
ROLLER SKATES?!
LOOK OUT BELOW!
JIM DAVIS 3-13

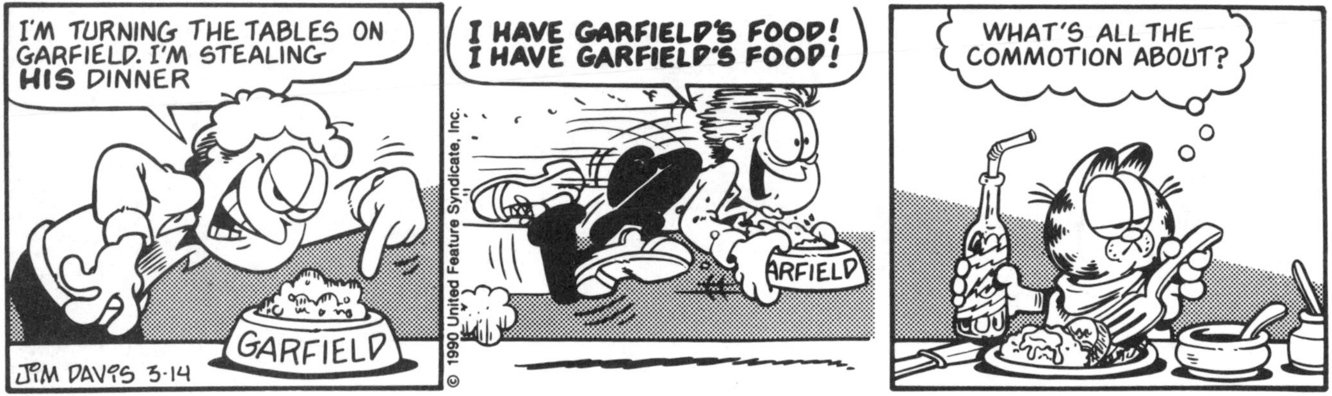
I'M TURNING THE TABLES ON GARFIELD. I'M STEALING **HIS** DINNER
GARFIELD
JIM DAVIS 3-14
© 1990 United Feature Syndicate, Inc.
I HAVE GARFIELD'S FOOD! I HAVE GARFIELD'S FOOD!
ARFIELD
WHAT'S ALL THE COMMOTION ABOUT?

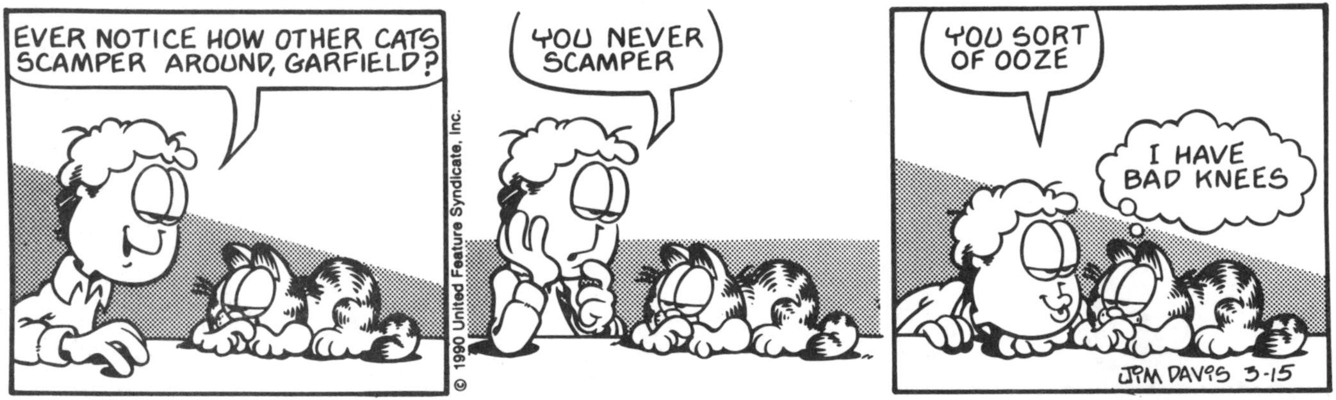
EVER NOTICE HOW OTHER CATS SCAMPER AROUND, GARFIELD?
© 1990 United Feature Syndicate, Inc.
YOU NEVER SCAMPER
YOU SORT OF OOZE
I HAVE BAD KNEES
JIM DAVIS 3-15

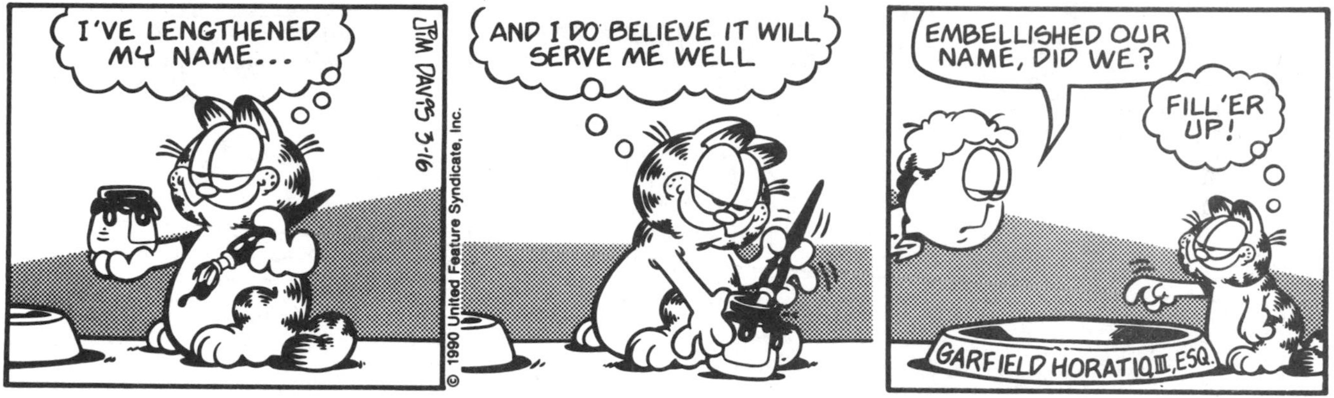
I'VE LENGTHENED MY NAME...
JIM DAVIS 3-16
© 1990 United Feature Syndicate, Inc.
AND I DO BELIEVE IT WILL SERVE ME WELL
EMBELLISHED OUR NAME, DID WE?
FILL'ER UP!
GARFIELD HORATIO III, ESQ.

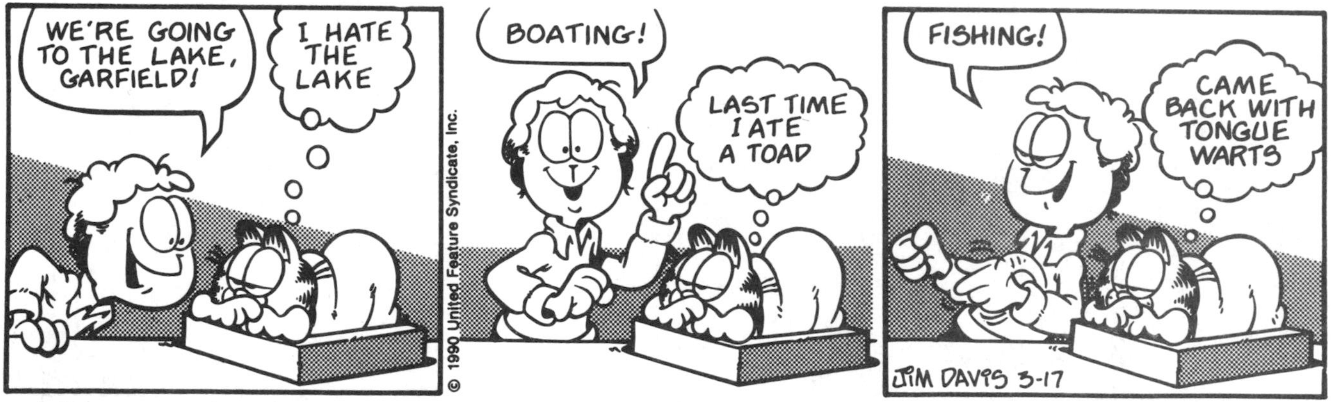
WE'RE GOING TO THE LAKE, GARFIELD!
I HATE THE LAKE
© 1990 United Feature Syndicate, Inc.
BOATING!
LAST TIME I ATE A TOAD
FISHING!
CAME BACK WITH TONGUE WARTS
JIM DAVIS 3-17

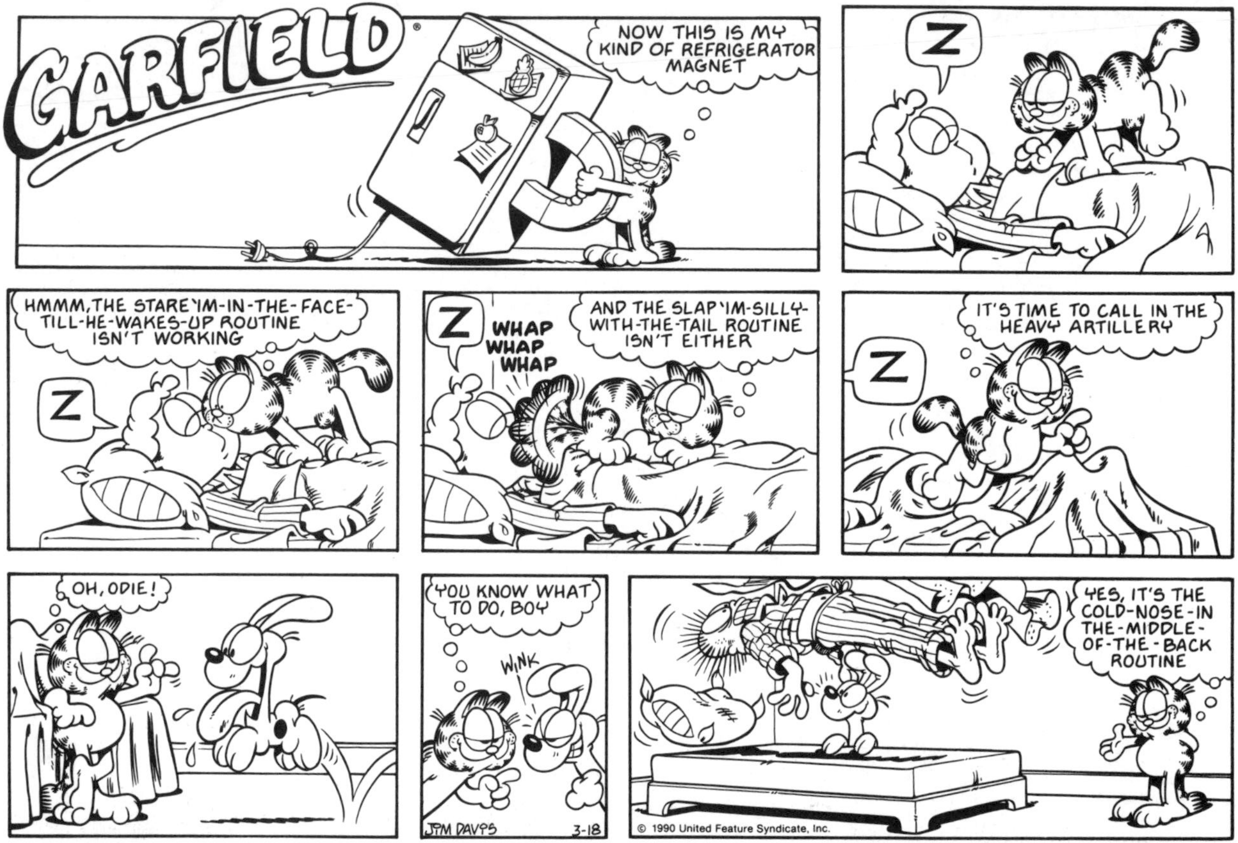
GARFIELD®
NOW THIS IS MY KIND OF REFRIGERATOR MAGNET
Z
HMMM, THE STARE 'IM-IN-THE-FACE-TILL-HE-WAKES-UP ROUTINE ISN'T WORKING
Z
Z
WHAP WHAP WHAP
AND THE SLAP 'IM-SILLY-WITH-THE-TAIL ROUTINE ISN'T EITHER
IT'S TIME TO CALL IN THE HEAVY ARTILLERY
Z
OH, ODIE!
YOU KNOW WHAT TO DO, BOY
WINK
YES, IT'S THE COLD-NOSE-IN-THE-MIDDLE-OF-THE-BACK ROUTINE
JIM DAVIS
3-18
© 1990 United Feature Syndicate, Inc.

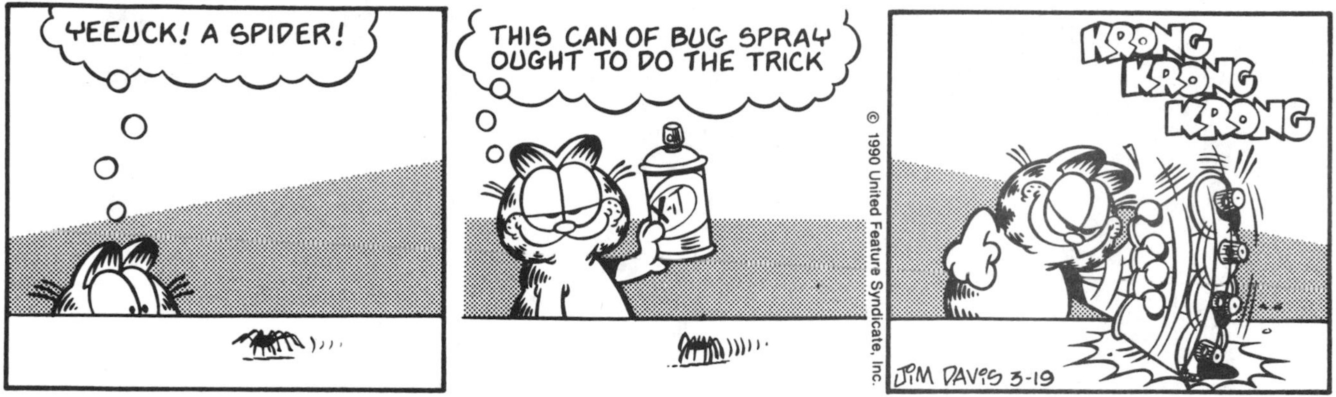

YEEUCK! A SPIDER!
THIS CAN OF BUG SPRAY OUGHT TO DO THE TRICK
KRONG KRONG KRONG
© 1990 United Feature Syndicate, Inc.
JIM DAVIS 3-19

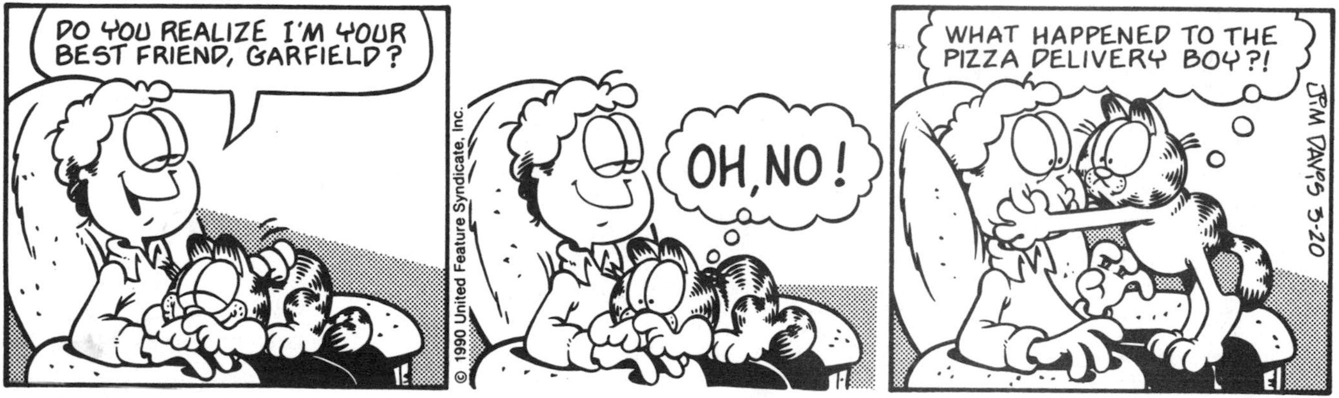

DO YOU REALIZE I'M YOUR BEST FRIEND, GARFIELD?
OH, NO!
WHAT HAPPENED TO THE PIZZA DELIVERY BOY?!
© 1990 United Feature Syndicate, Inc.
JIM DAVIS 3-20

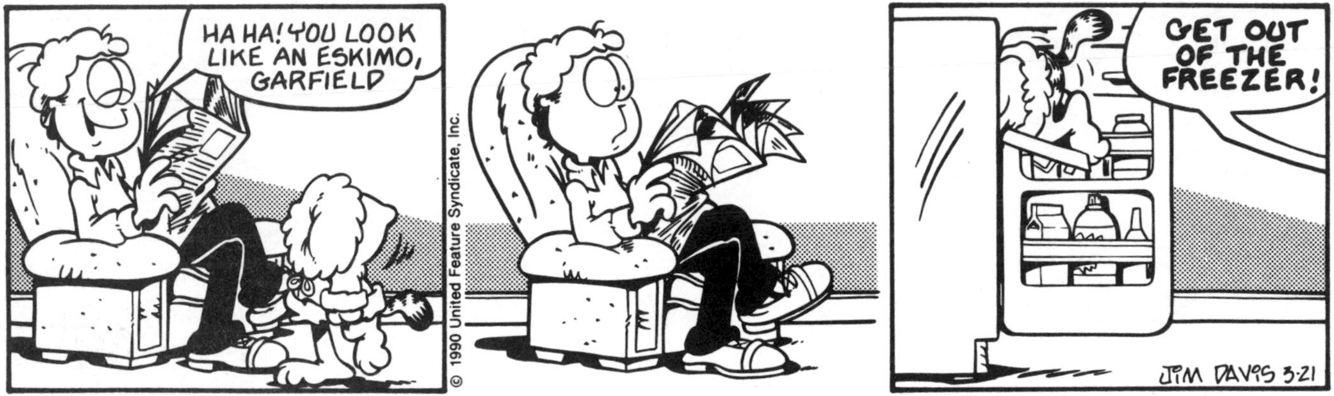
HA HA! YOU LOOK LIKE AN ESKIMO, GARFIELD
GET OUT OF THE FREEZER!
© 1990 United Feature Syndicate, Inc.
JIM DAVIS 3-21

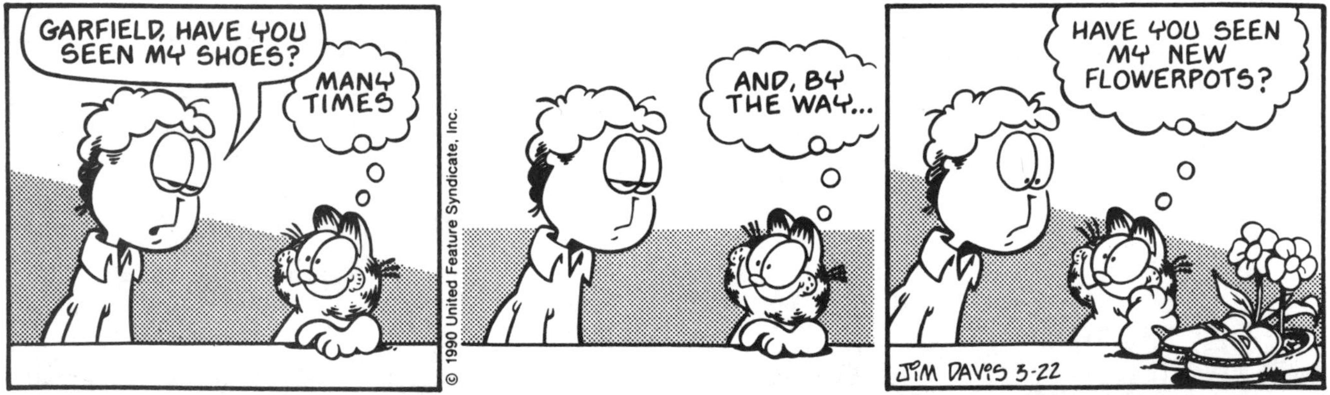
GARFIELD, HAVE YOU SEEN MY SHOES?
MANY TIMES
AND, BY THE WAY...
HAVE YOU SEEN MY NEW FLOWERPOTS?
© 1990 United Feature Syndicate, Inc.
JIM DAVIS 3-22

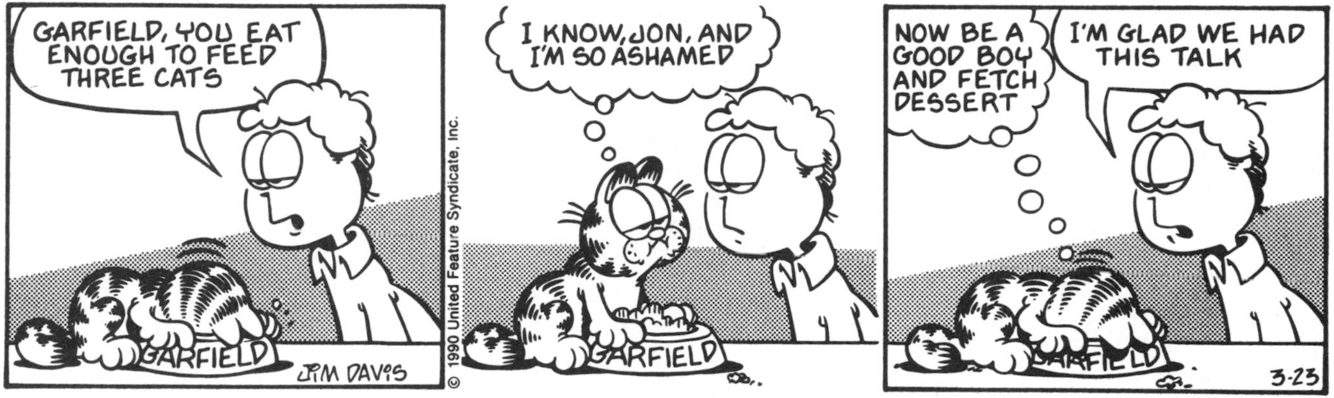
GARFIELD, YOU EAT ENOUGH TO FEED THREE CATS
GARFIELD
JIM DAVIS
© 1990 United Feature Syndicate, Inc.
I KNOW, JON, AND I'M SO ASHAMED
GARFIELD
NOW BE A GOOD BOY AND FETCH DESSERT
I'M GLAD WE HAD THIS TALK
GARFIELD
3-23

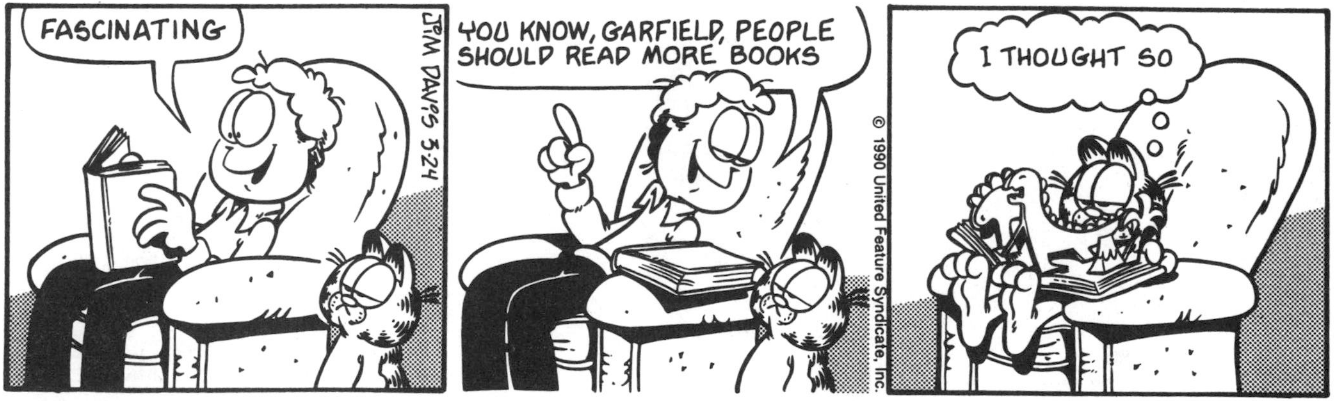
FASCINATING
JIM DAVIS 3-24
YOU KNOW, GARFIELD, PEOPLE SHOULD READ MORE BOOKS
© 1990 United Feature Syndicate, Inc.
I THOUGHT SO

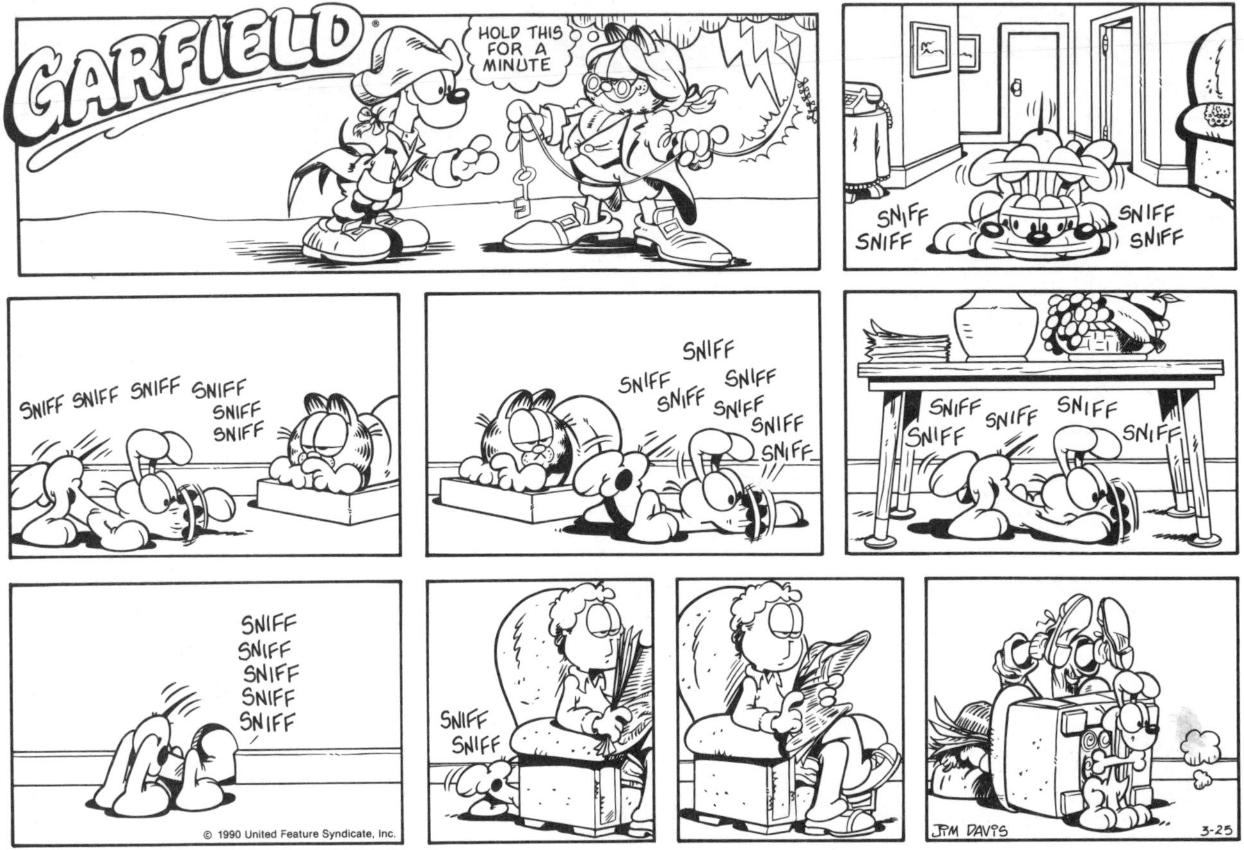
GARFIELD
HOLD THIS FOR A MINUTE
SNIFF SNIFF
SNIFF SNIFF
SNIFF SNIFF SNIFF SNIFF SNIFF SNIFF
SNIFF SNIFF SNIFF SNIFF SNIFF SNIFF SNIFF
SNIFF SNIFF SNIFF SNIFF SNIFF
SNIFF SNIFF SNIFF SNIFF SNIFF
SNIFF SNIFF
JPM DAVIS
3-25

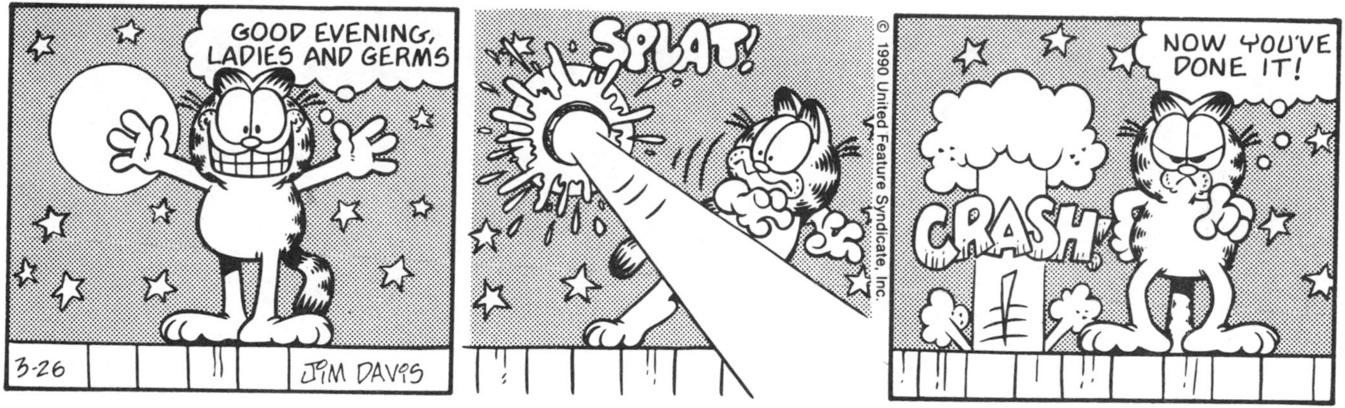
GOOD EVENING, LADIES AND GERMS
3-26
JIM DAVIS
SPLAT!
© 1990 United Feature Syndicate, Inc.
CRASH!
NOW YOU'VE DONE IT!

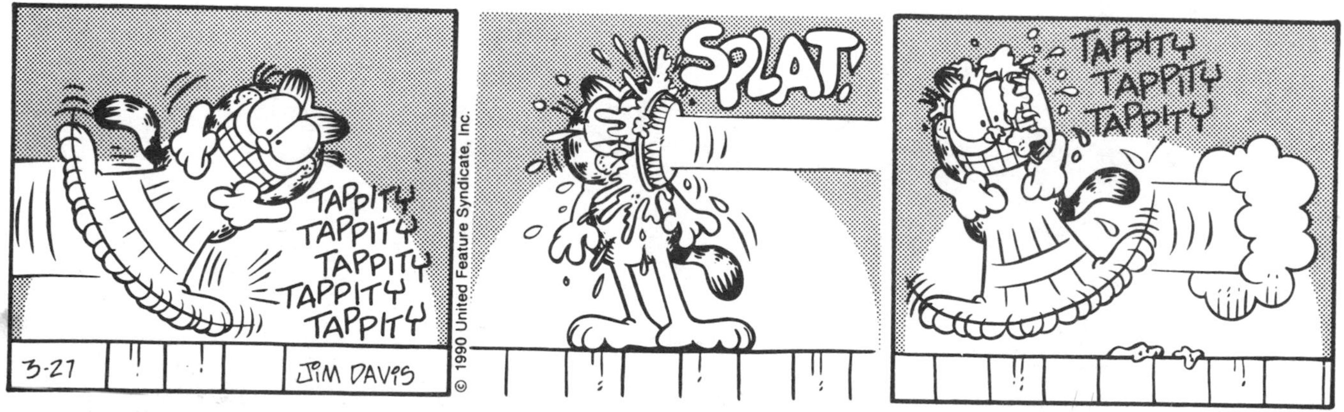
TAPPITY TAPPITY TAPPITY TAPPITY TAPPITY
3-27
JIM DAVIS
© 1990 United Feature Syndicate, Inc.
SPLAT!
TAPPITY TAPPITY TAPPITY

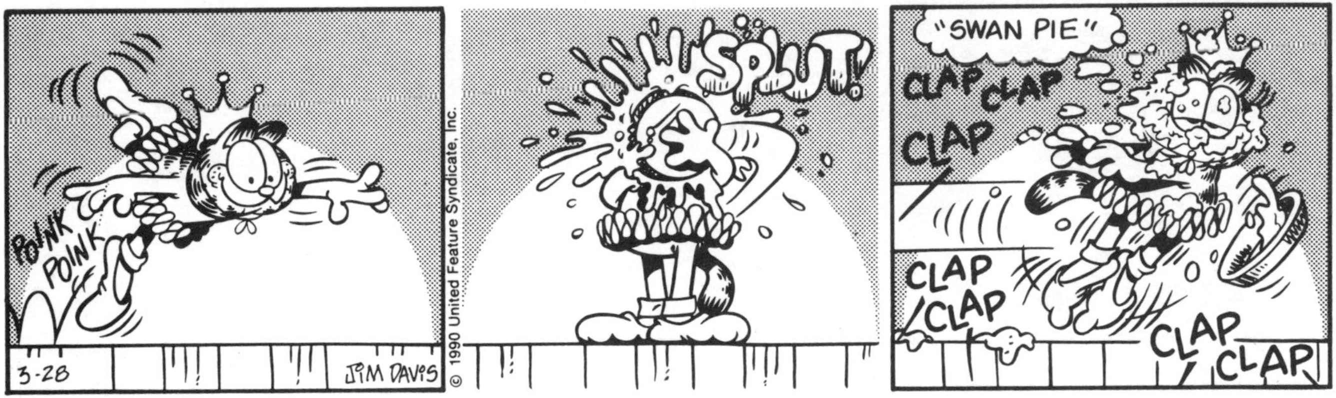
POINK
POINK
3-28
JIM DAVIS
© 1990 United Feature Syndicate, Inc.
SPLUT!
"SWAN PIE"
CLAP CLAP
CLAP
CLAP
CLAP
CLAP
CLAP

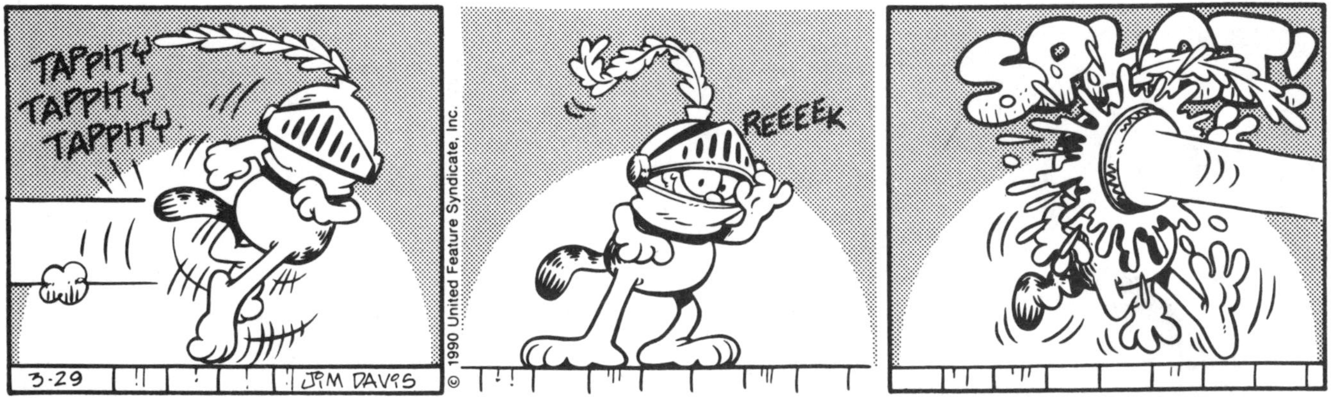
TAPPITY
TAPPITY
TAPPITY
3-29
JIM DAVIS
© 1990 United Feature Syndicate, Inc.
REEEEK
SPLAT!

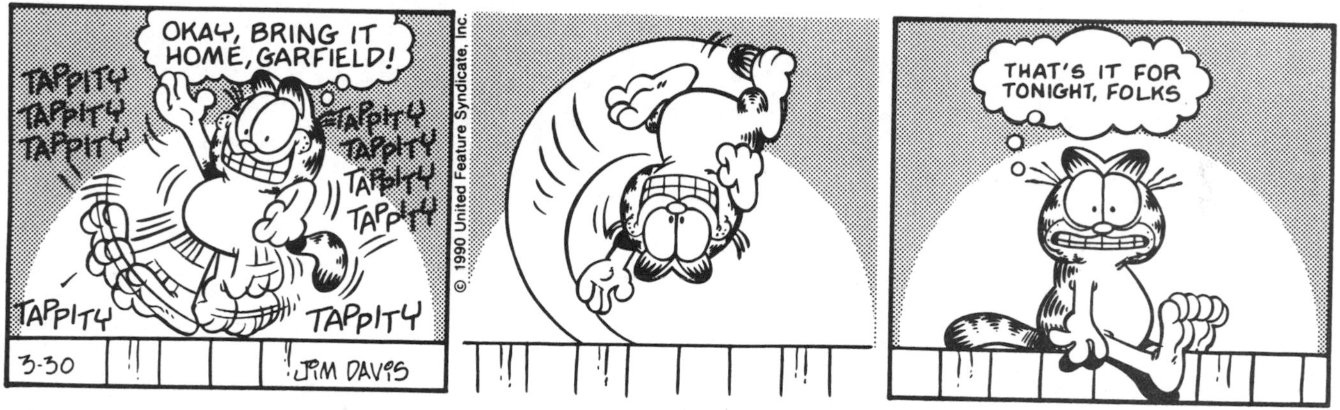
TAPPITY TAPPITY TAPPITY
OKAY, BRING IT HOME, GARFIELD!
TAPPITY TAPPITY TAPPITY TAPPITY
TAPPITY
TAPPITY
3-30
JIM DAVIS
© 1990 United Feature Syndicate, Inc.
THAT'S IT FOR TONIGHT, FOLKS

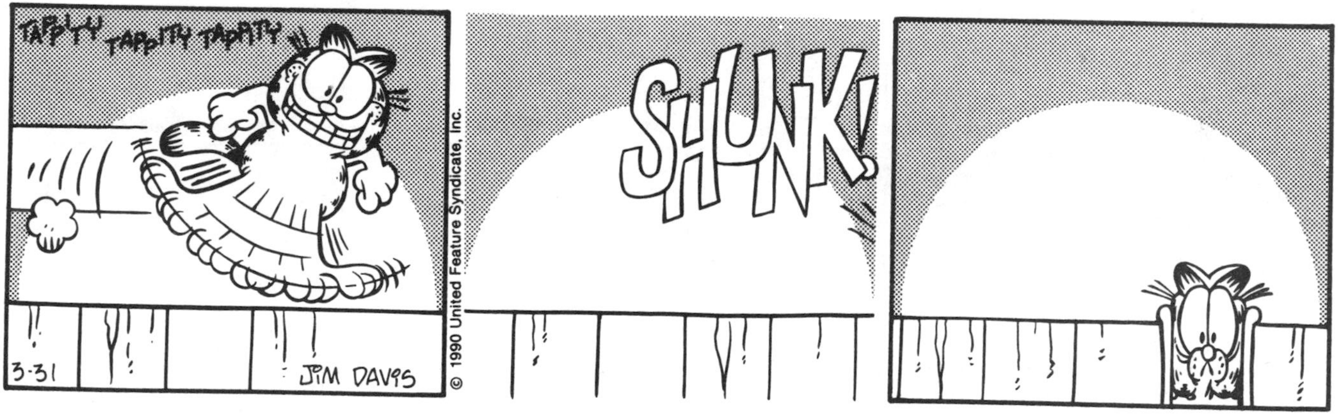
TAPPITY TAPPITY TAPPITY
3-31
JIM DAVIS
© 1990 United Feature Syndicate, Inc.
SHUNK!

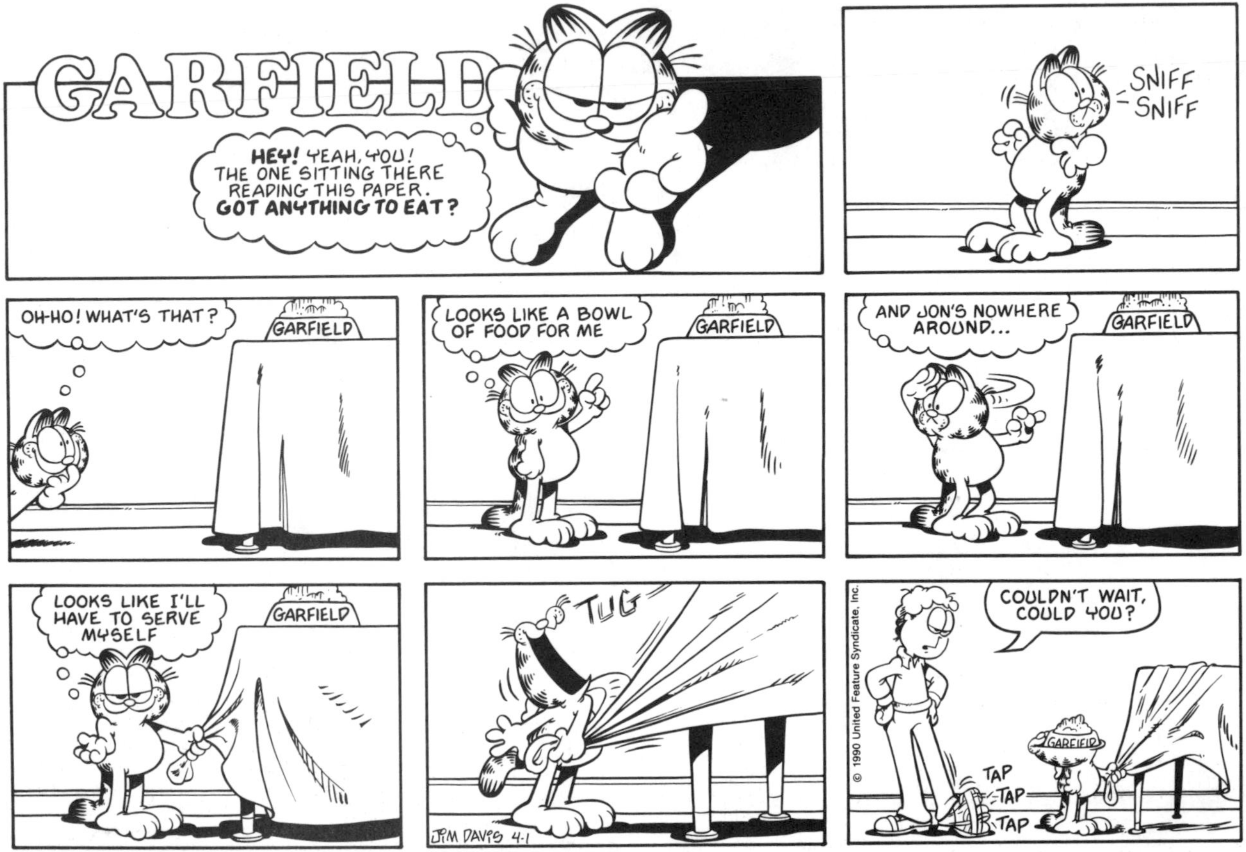
GARFIELD
HEY! YEAH, YOU! THE ONE SITTING THERE READING THIS PAPER. GOT ANYTHING TO EAT?
SNIFF SNIFF
OH-HO! WHAT'S THAT?
GARFIELD
LOOKS LIKE A BOWL OF FOOD FOR ME
GARFIELD
AND JON'S NOWHERE AROUND...
GARFIELD
LOOKS LIKE I'LL HAVE TO SERVE MYSELF
GARFIELD
TUG
JIM DAVIS 4-1
© 1990 United Feature Syndicate, Inc.
COULDN'T WAIT, COULD YOU?
TAP TAP TAP
GARFIELD

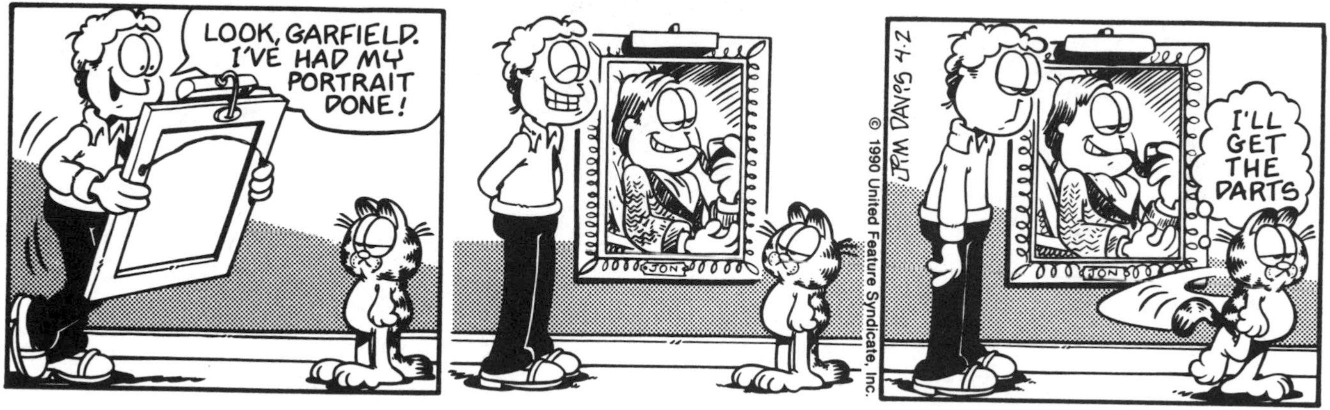
LOOK, GARFIELD. I'VE HAD MY PORTRAIT DONE!
JON
JON
I'LL GET THE DARTS
JPM DAVIS 4-2
© 1990 United Feature Syndicate, Inc.

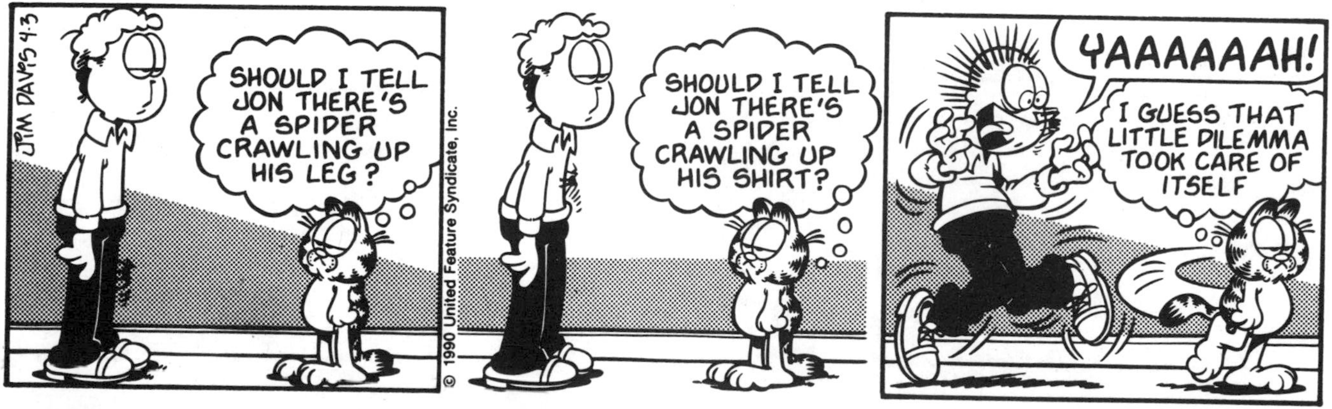
JPM DAVIS 4-3
SHOULD I TELL JON THERE'S A SPIDER CRAWLING UP HIS LEG?
© 1990 United Feature Syndicate, Inc.
SHOULD I TELL JON THERE'S A SPIDER CRAWLING UP HIS SHIRT?
YAAAAAAH!
I GUESS THAT LITTLE DILEMMA TOOK CARE OF ITSELF

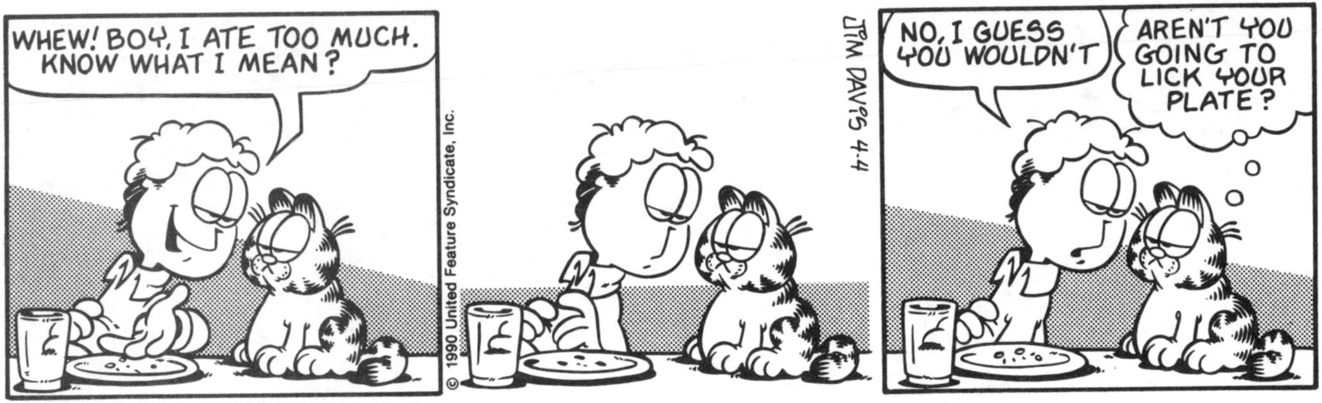

WHEW! BOY, I ATE TOO MUCH. KNOW WHAT I MEAN?
© 1990 United Feature Syndicate, Inc.
JIM DAVIS 4-4
NO, I GUESS YOU WOULDN'T
AREN'T YOU GOING TO LICK YOUR PLATE?

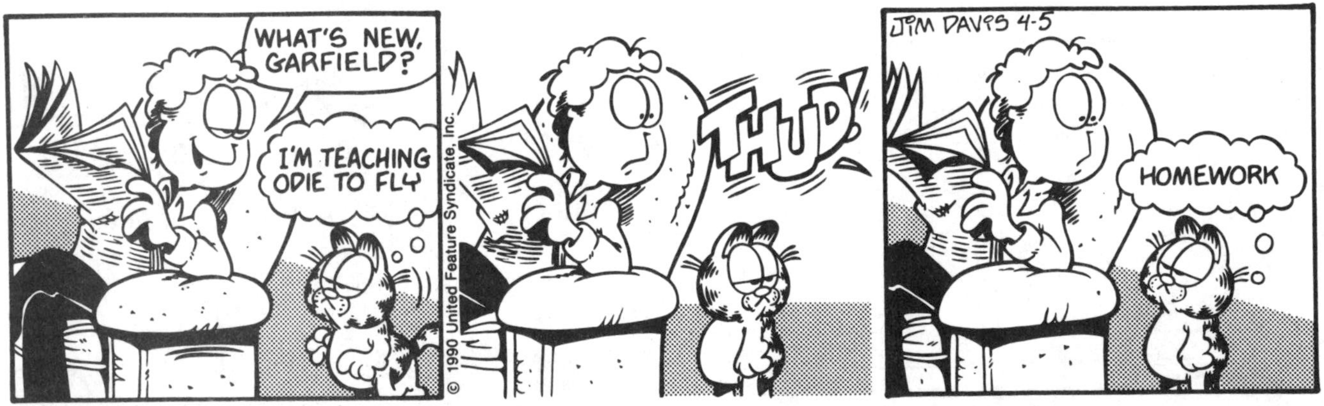

WHAT'S NEW, GARFIELD?
I'M TEACHING ODIE TO FLY
© 1990 United Feature Syndicate, Inc.
THUD!
JIM DAVIS 4-5
HOMEWORK

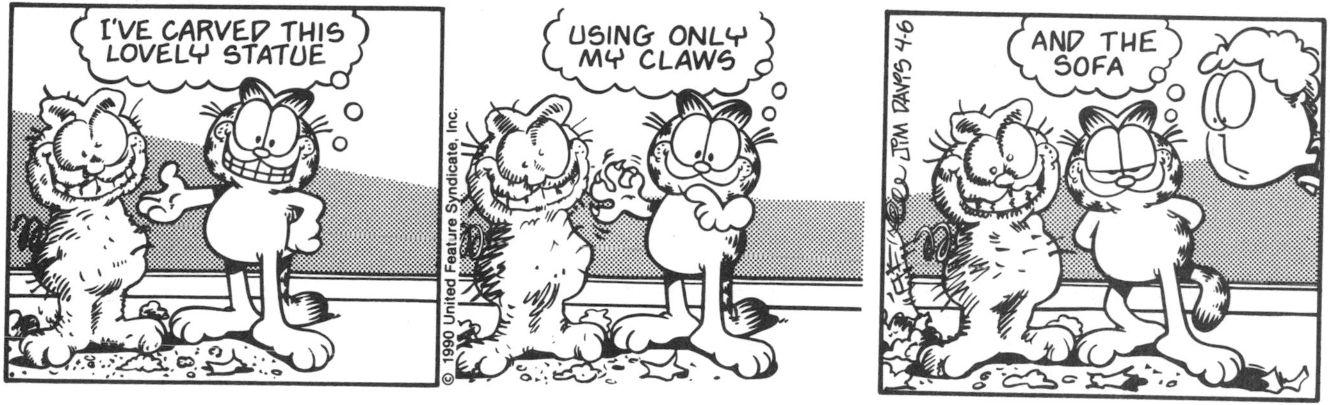
I'VE CARVED THIS LOVELY STATUE
USING ONLY MY CLAWS
© 1990 United Feature Syndicate, Inc.
AND THE SOFA
JIM DAVIS 4-6

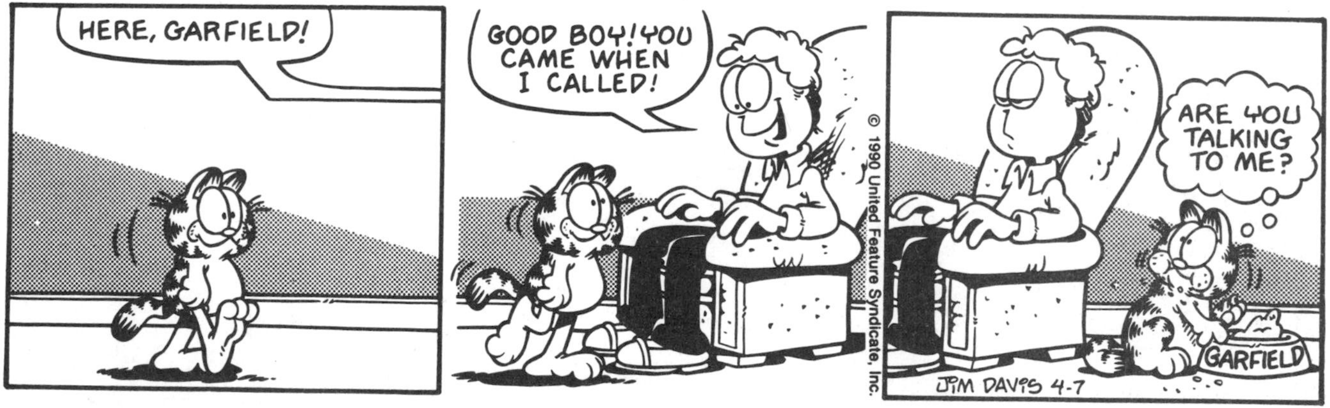
HERE, GARFIELD!
GOOD BOY! YOU CAME WHEN I CALLED!
© 1990 United Feature Syndicate, Inc.
ARE YOU TALKING TO ME?
GARFIELD
JIM DAVIS 4-7

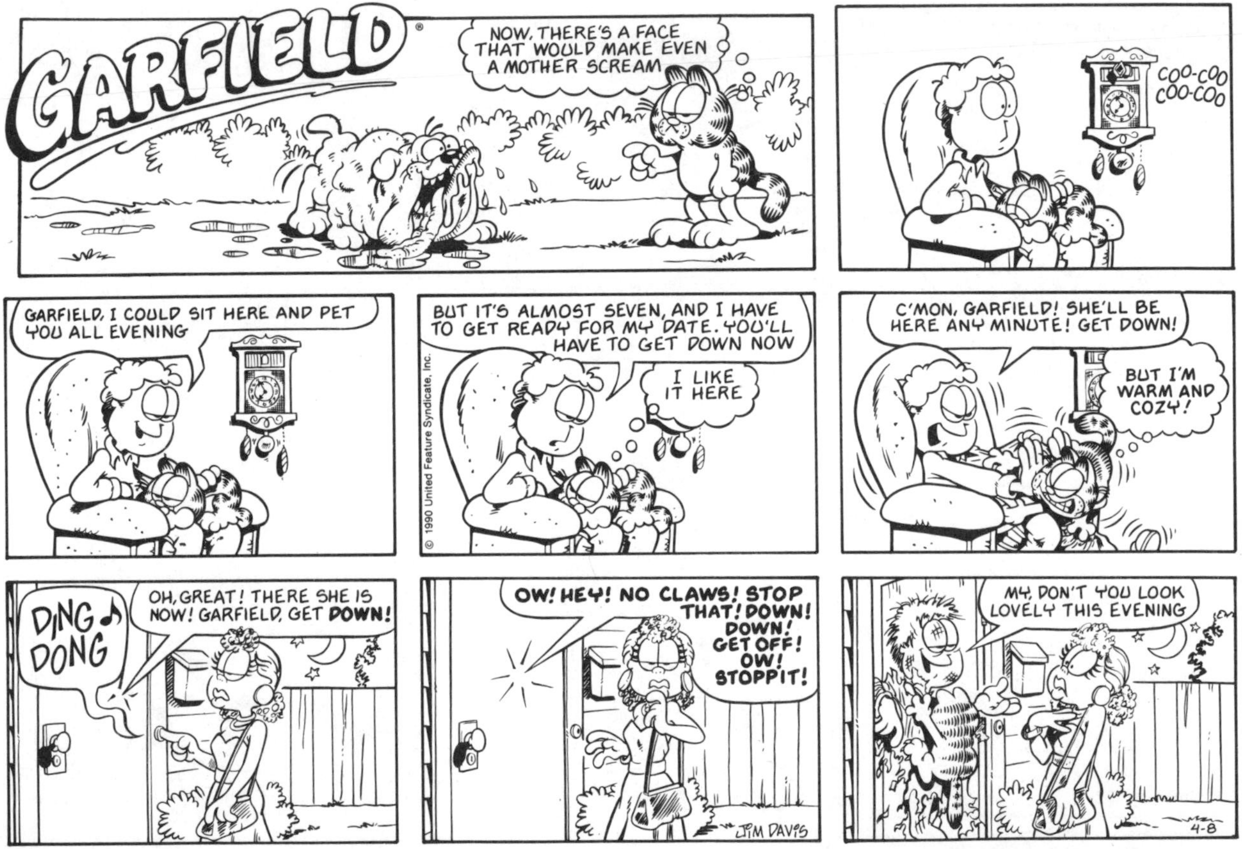

GARFIELD®
NOW, THERE'S A FACE THAT WOULD MAKE EVEN A MOTHER SCREAM
COO-COO COO-COO
GARFIELD, I COULD SIT HERE AND PET YOU ALL EVENING
BUT IT'S ALMOST SEVEN, AND I HAVE TO GET READY FOR MY DATE. YOU'LL HAVE TO GET DOWN NOW
I LIKE IT HERE
© 1990 United Feature Syndicate, Inc.
C'MON, GARFIELD! SHE'LL BE HERE ANY MINUTE! GET DOWN!
BUT I'M WARM AND COZY!
DING DONG ♪
OH, GREAT! THERE SHE IS NOW! GARFIELD, GET DOWN!
OW! HEY! NO CLAWS! STOP THAT! DOWN! DOWN! GET OFF! OW! STOPPIT!
JIM DAVIS
MY, DON'T YOU LOOK LOVELY THIS EVENING
4-8

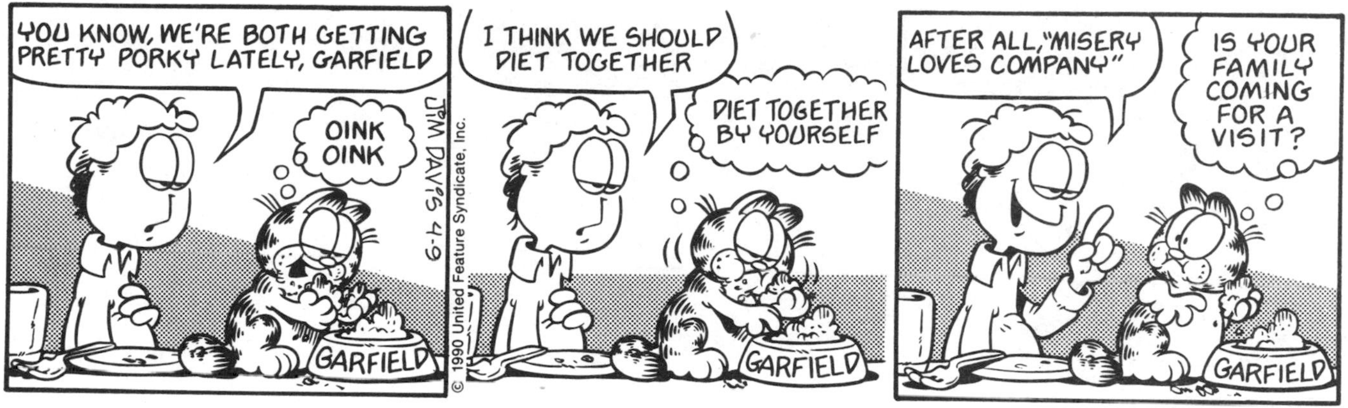
YOU KNOW, WE'RE BOTH GETTING PRETTY PORKY LATELY, GARFIELD
OINK OINK
GARFIELD
JIM DAVIS 4-9
© 1990 United Feature Syndicate, Inc.
I THINK WE SHOULD DIET TOGETHER
DIET TOGETHER BY YOURSELF
GARFIELD
AFTER ALL, "MISERY LOVES COMPANY"
IS YOUR FAMILY COMING FOR A VISIT?
GARFIELD

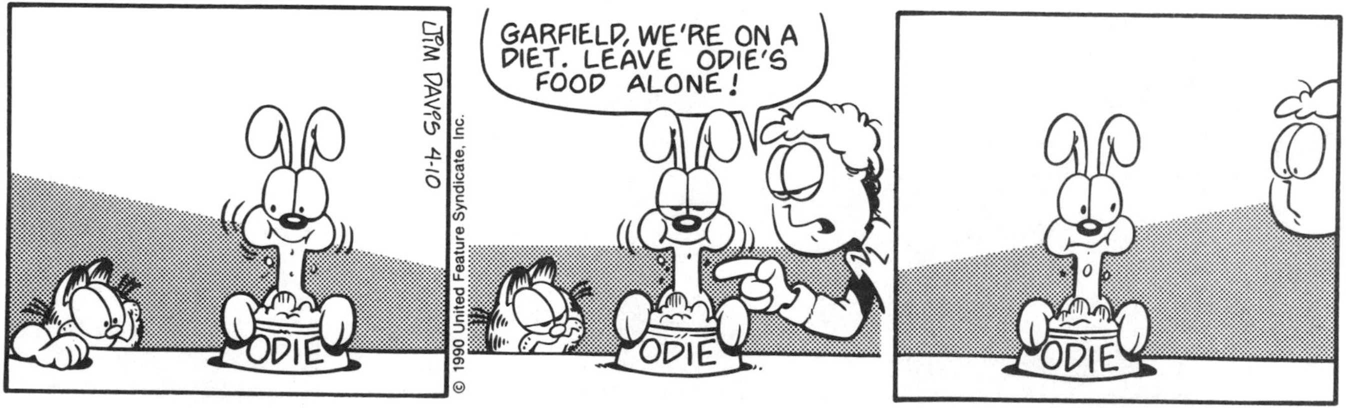
JIM DAVIS 4-10
ODIE
© 1990 United Feature Syndicate, Inc.
GARFIELD, WE'RE ON A DIET. LEAVE ODIE'S FOOD ALONE!
ODIE
ODIE

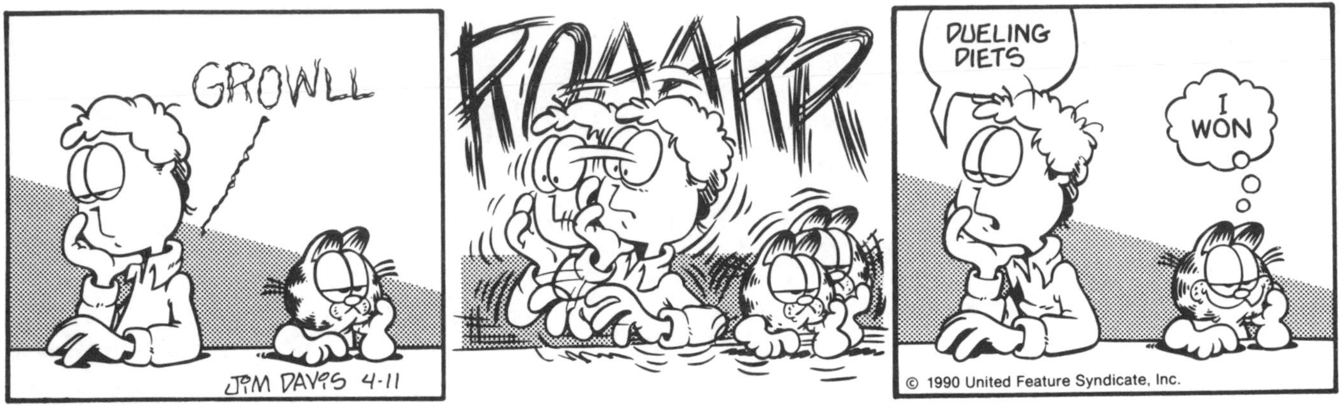
GROWLL
JIM DAVIS 4-11
ROAARR
DUELING DIETS
I WON
© 1990 United Feature Syndicate, Inc.

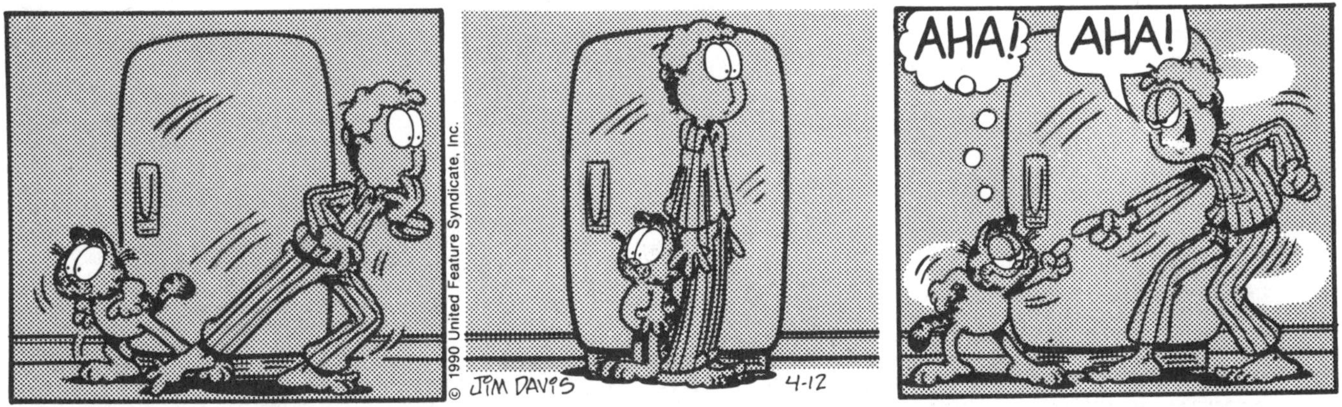
© 1990 United Feature Syndicate, Inc.
JIM DAVIS
4-12
AHA!
AHA!

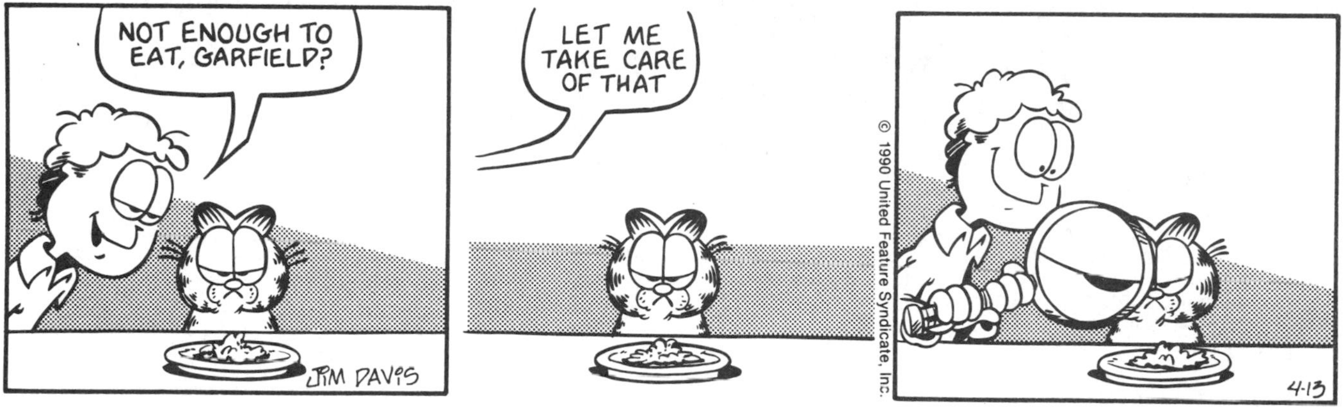
NOT ENOUGH TO EAT, GARFIELD?
JIM DAVIS
LET ME TAKE CARE OF THAT
4-13

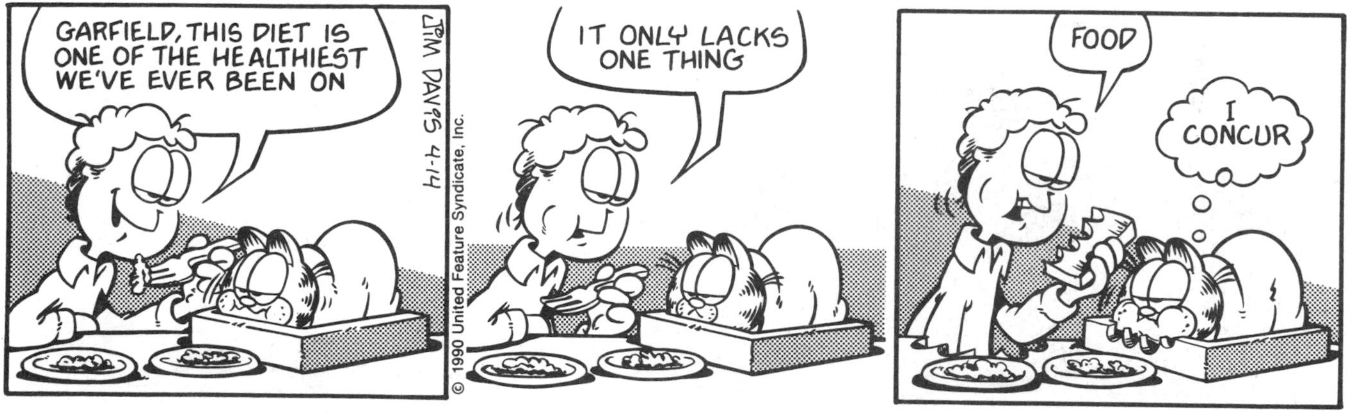
GARFIELD, THIS DIET IS ONE OF THE HEALTHIEST WE'VE EVER BEEN ON
JIM DAVIS 4-14
IT ONLY LACKS ONE THING
FOOD
I CONCUR

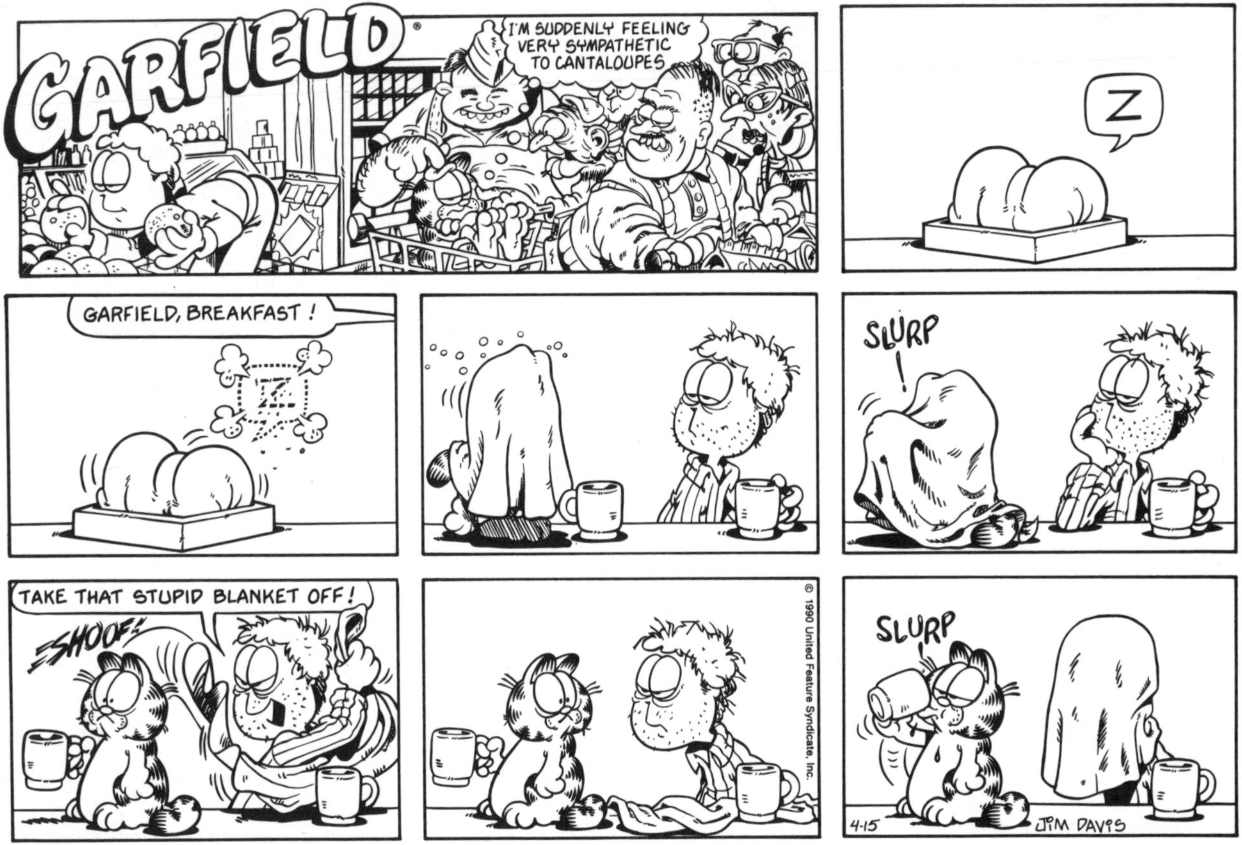
GARFIELD®
I'M SUDDENLY FEELING VERY SYMPATHETIC TO CANTALOUPES
Z
GARFIELD, BREAKFAST!
SLURP
TAKE THAT STUPID BLANKET OFF!
SHOOF!
© 1990 United Feature Syndicate, Inc.
SLURP
4-15
JIM DAVIS

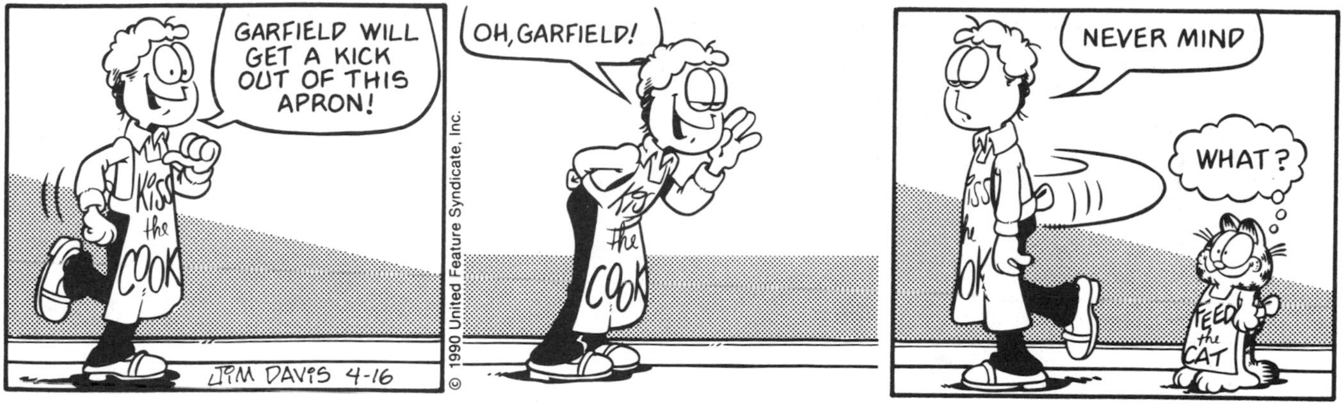
GARFIELD WILL GET A KICK OUT OF THIS APRON!
KISS the COOK
JIM DAVIS 4-16
© 1990 United Feature Syndicate, Inc.
OH, GARFIELD!
KISS the COOK
NEVER MIND
WHAT?
FEED the CAT

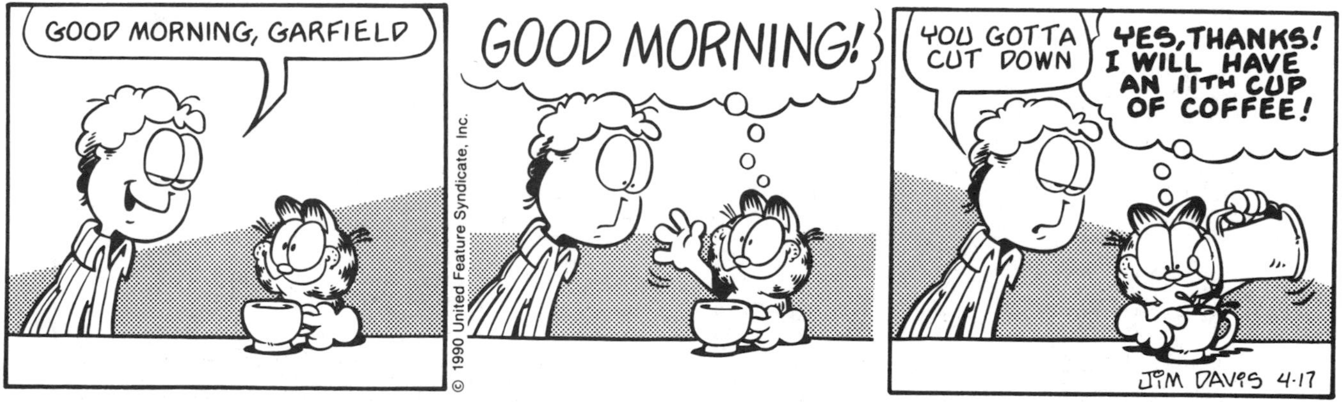
GOOD MORNING, GARFIELD
© 1990 United Feature Syndicate, Inc.
GOOD MORNING!
YOU GOTTA CUT DOWN
YES, THANKS! I WILL HAVE AN 11TH CUP OF COFFEE!
JIM DAVIS 4-17

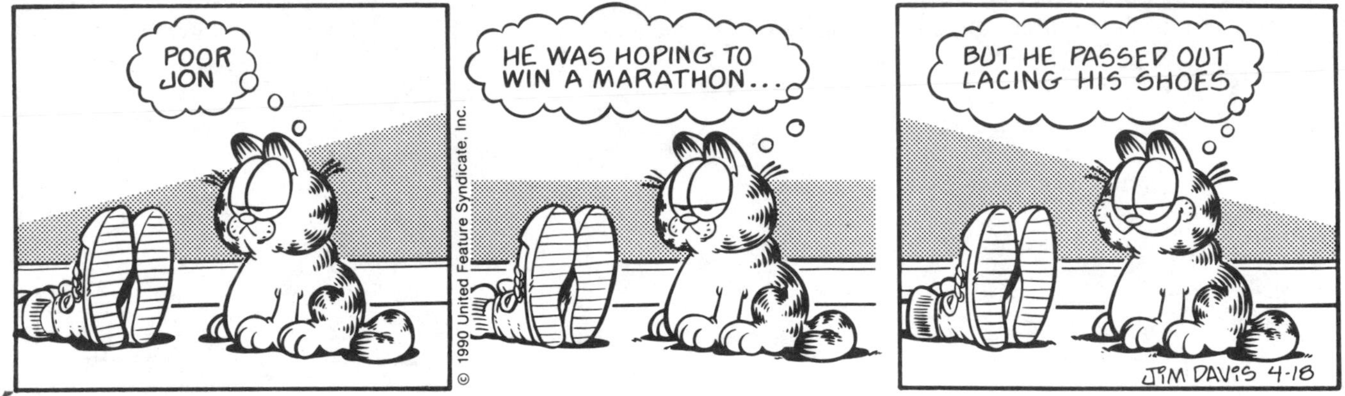
POOR JON
HE WAS HOPING TO WIN A MARATHON...
BUT HE PASSED OUT LACING HIS SHOES
© 1990 United Feature Syndicate, Inc.
JIM DAVIS 4-18

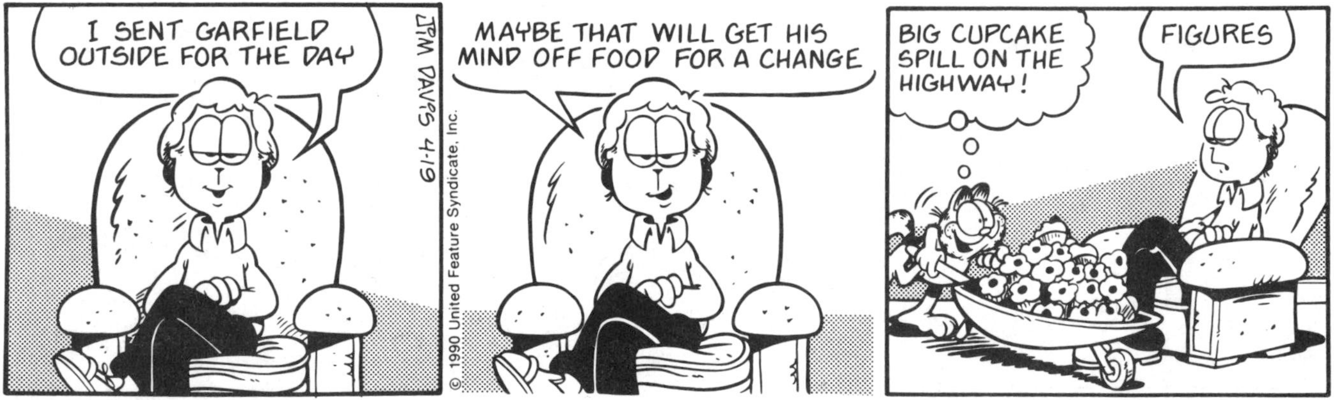
I SENT GARFIELD OUTSIDE FOR THE DAY
JIM DAVIS 4-19
© 1990 United Feature Syndicate, Inc.
MAYBE THAT WILL GET HIS MIND OFF FOOD FOR A CHANGE
BIG CUPCAKE SPILL ON THE HIGHWAY!
FIGURES

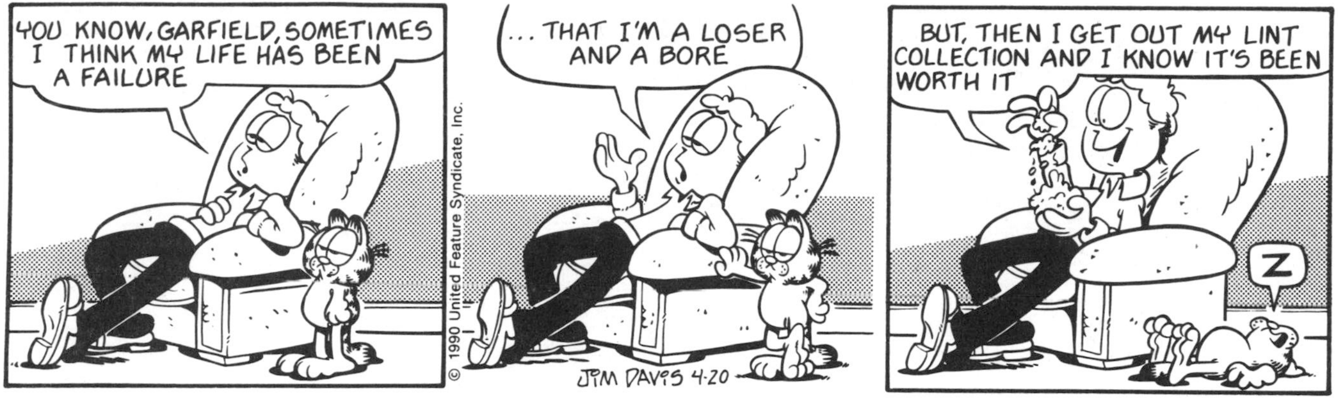
YOU KNOW, GARFIELD, SOMETIMES I THINK MY LIFE HAS BEEN A FAILURE
... THAT I'M A LOSER AND A BORE
BUT, THEN I GET OUT MY LINT COLLECTION AND I KNOW IT'S BEEN WORTH IT
Z
© 1990 United Feature Syndicate, Inc.
JIM DAVIS 4-20

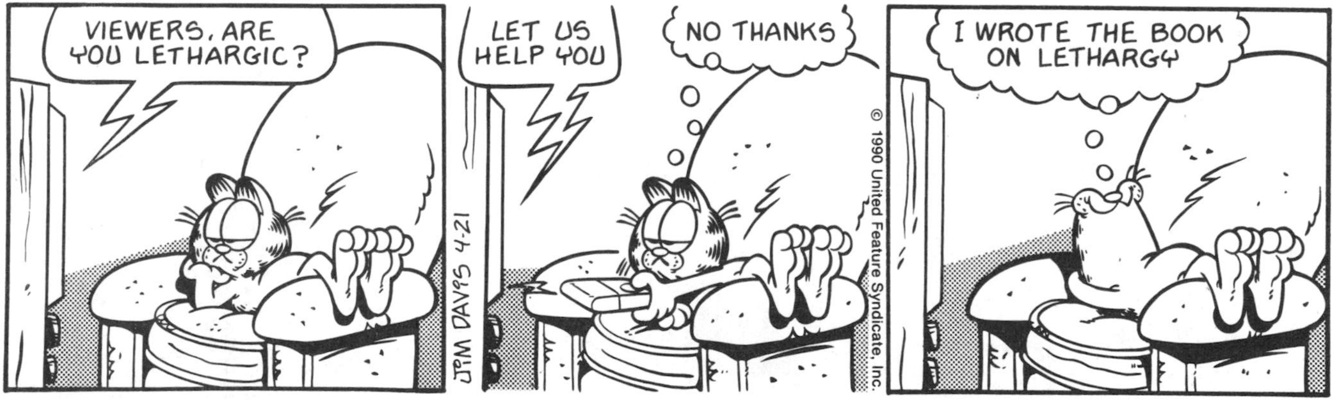
VIEWERS, ARE YOU LETHARGIC?
LET US HELP YOU
NO THANKS
I WROTE THE BOOK ON LETHARGY
JIM DAVIS 4-21
© 1990 United Feature Syndicate, Inc.

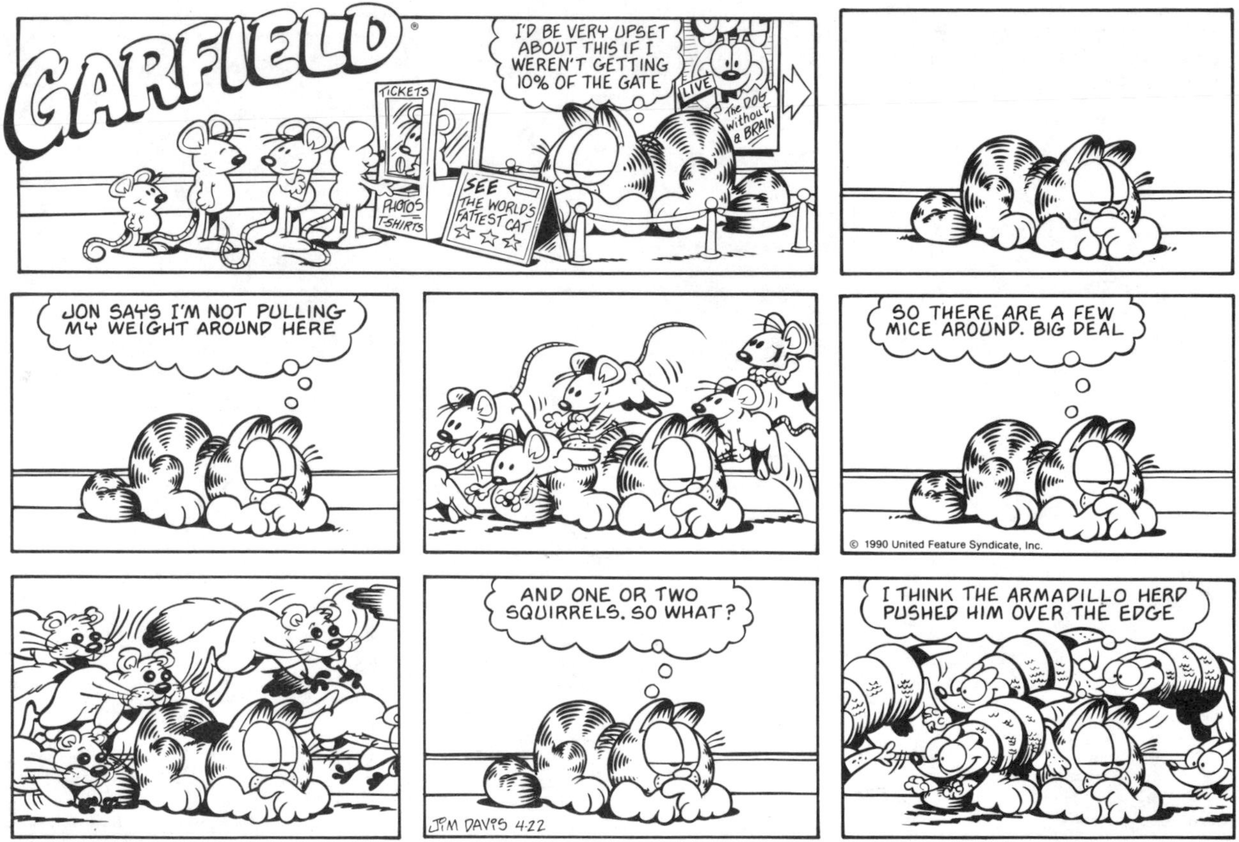
GARFIELD®
TICKETS
PHOTOS
T-SHIRTS
SEE THE WORLD'S FATTEST CAT
I'D BE VERY UPSET ABOUT THIS IF I WEREN'T GETTING 10% OF THE GATE
LIVE
The DOG without a BRAIN
JON SAYS I'M NOT PULLING MY WEIGHT AROUND HERE
SO THERE ARE A FEW MICE AROUND. BIG DEAL
© 1990 United Feature Syndicate, Inc.
AND ONE OR TWO SQUIRRELS. SO WHAT?
JIM DAVIS 4-22
I THINK THE ARMADILLO HERD PUSHED HIM OVER THE EDGE

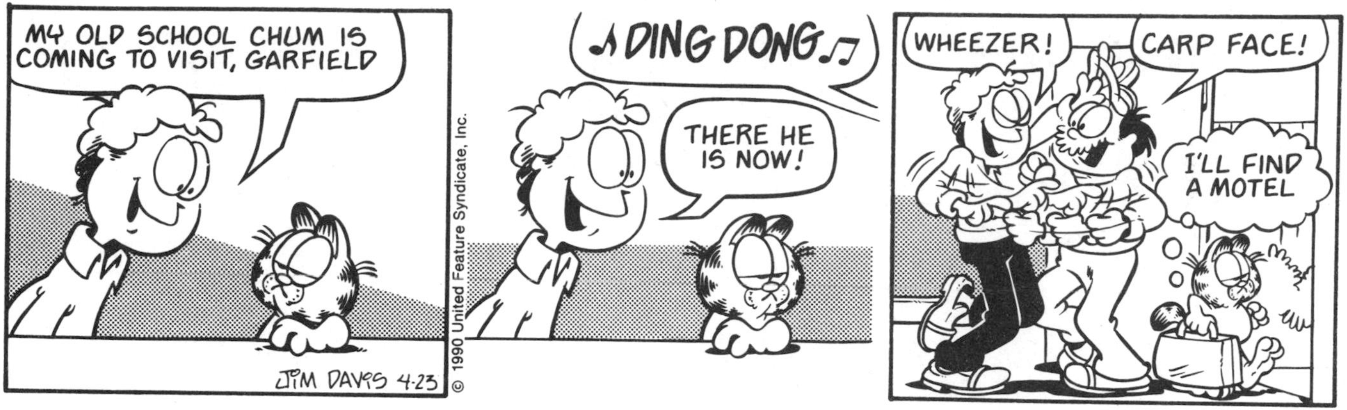
MY OLD SCHOOL CHUM IS COMING TO VISIT, GARFIELD
JIM DAVIS 4-23
© 1990 United Feature Syndicate, Inc.
DING DONG
THERE HE IS NOW!
WHEEZER!
CARP FACE!
I'LL FIND A MOTEL

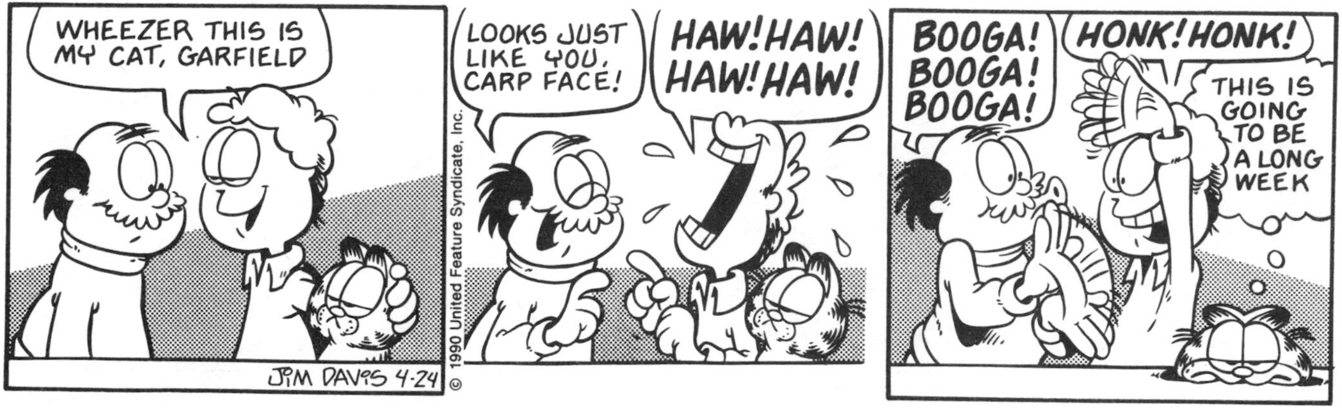
WHEEZER THIS IS MY CAT, GARFIELD
JIM DAVIS 4-24
© 1990 United Feature Syndicate, Inc.
LOOKS JUST LIKE YOU, CARP FACE!
HAW! HAW! HAW! HAW!
BOOGA! BOOGA! BOOGA!
HONK! HONK!
THIS IS GOING TO BE A LONG WEEK

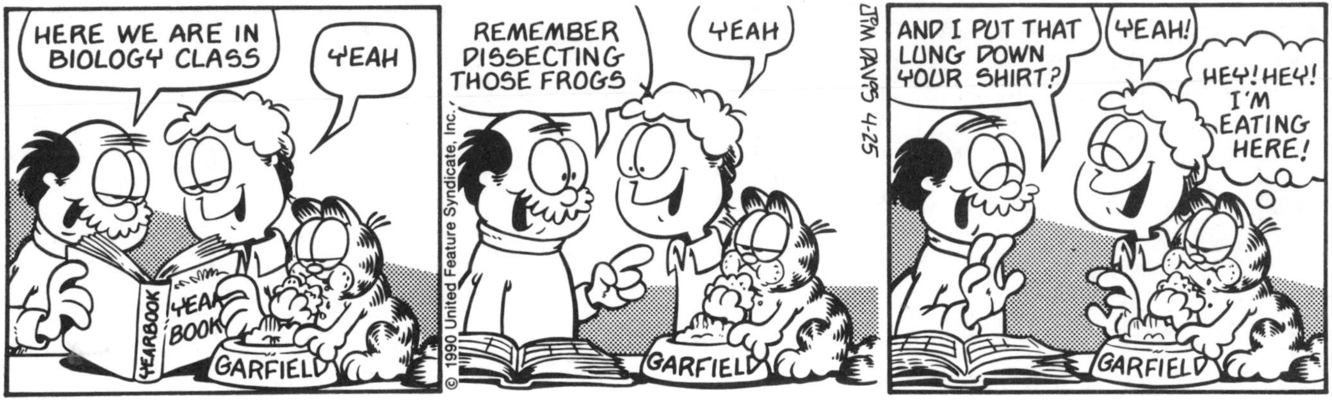
HERE WE ARE IN BIOLOGY CLASS
YEAH
YEARBOOK
YEAR BOOK
GARFIELD
© 1990 United Feature Syndicate, Inc.
REMEMBER DISSECTING THOSE FROGS
YEAH
GARFIELD
JIM DAVIS 4-25
AND I PUT THAT LUNG DOWN YOUR SHIRT?
YEAH!
HEY! HEY! I'M EATING HERE!
GARFIELD

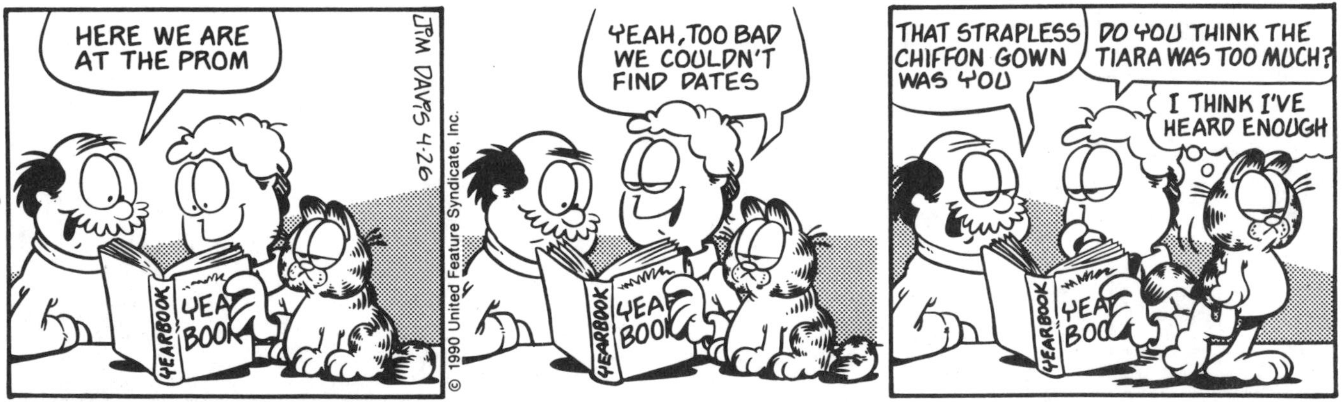
HERE WE ARE AT THE PROM
YEARBOOK
JIM DAVIS 4-26
© 1990 United Feature Syndicate, Inc.
YEAH, TOO BAD WE COULDN'T FIND DATES
YEARBOOK
THAT STRAPLESS CHIFFON GOWN WAS YOU
DO YOU THINK THE TIARA WAS TOO MUCH?
I THINK I'VE HEARD ENOUGH
YEARBOOK

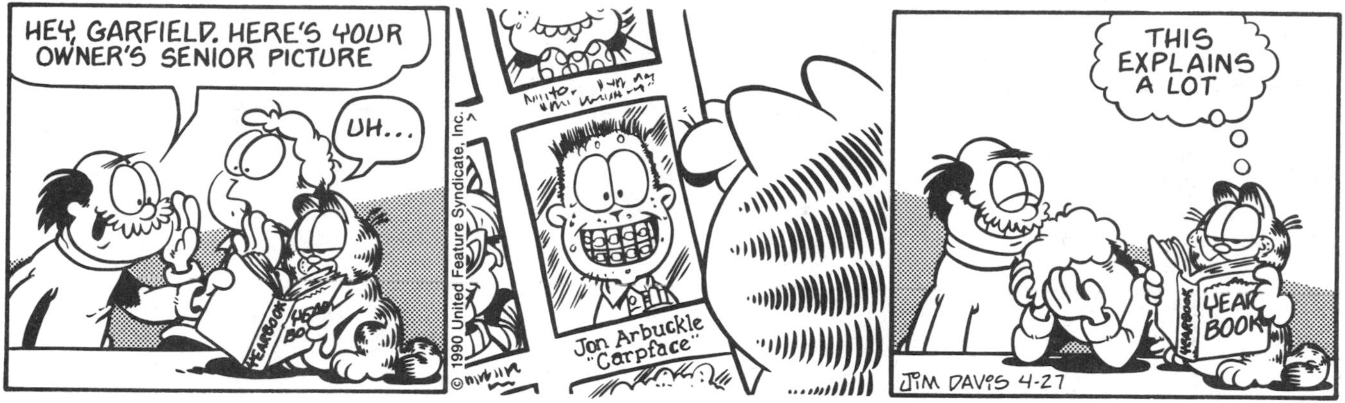
HEY, GARFIELD. HERE'S YOUR OWNER'S SENIOR PICTURE
UH...
YEARBOOK
Jon Arbuckle "Carpface"
THIS EXPLAINS A LOT
YEAR BOOK
JIM DAVIS 4-27
© 1990 United Feature Syndicate, Inc.

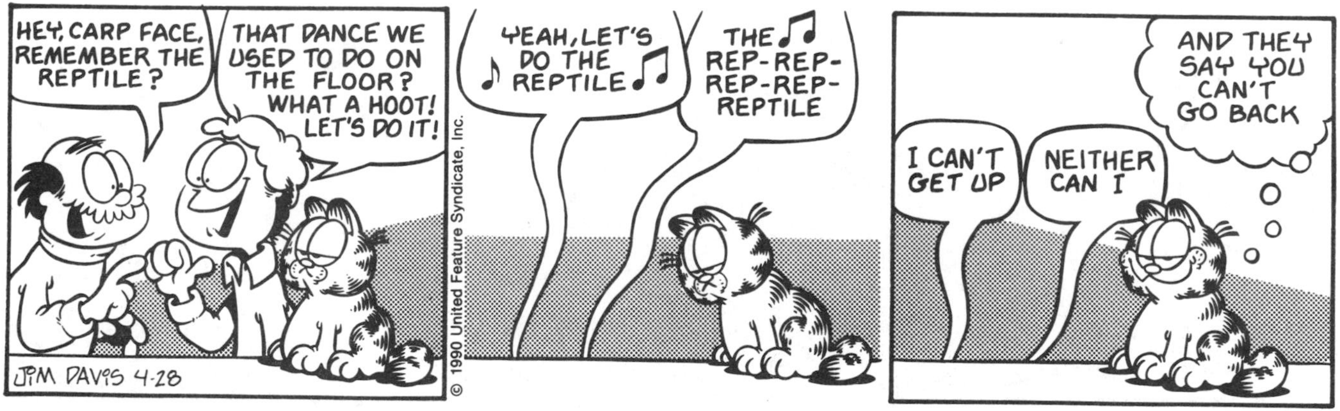
HEY, CARP FACE, REMEMBER THE REPTILE?
THAT DANCE WE USED TO DO ON THE FLOOR? WHAT A HOOT! LET'S DO IT!
YEAH, LET'S DO THE REPTILE
THE REP-REP-REP-REP-REPTILE
I CAN'T GET UP
NEITHER CAN I
AND THEY SAY YOU CAN'T GO BACK
JIM DAVIS 4-28
© 1990 United Feature Syndicate, Inc.

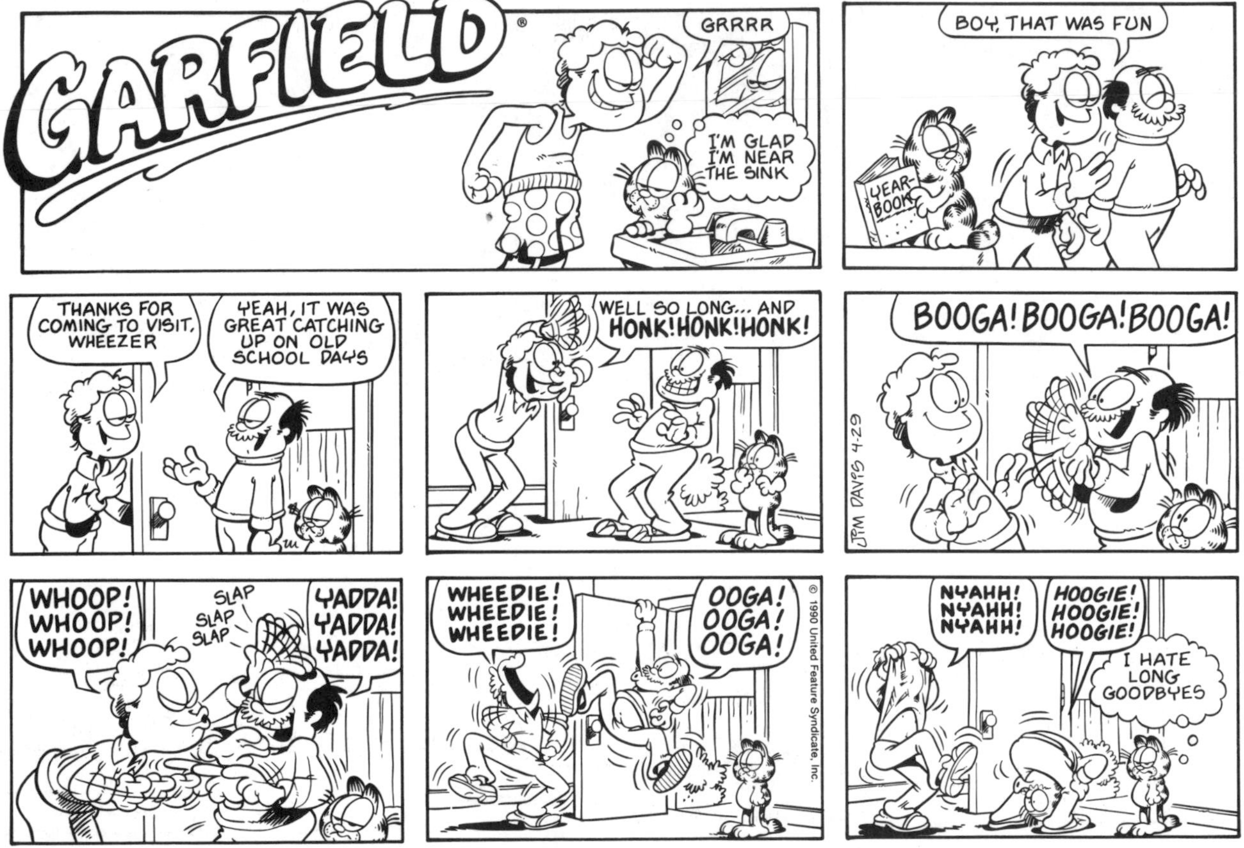
GARFIELD®
GRRRR
I'M GLAD I'M NEAR THE SINK
BOY, THAT WAS FUN
YEAR-BOOK
THANKS FOR COMING TO VISIT, WHEEZER
YEAH, IT WAS GREAT CATCHING UP ON OLD SCHOOL DAYS
WELL SO LONG... AND HONK!HONK!HONK!
JPM DAVIS 4-29
BOOGA! BOOGA! BOOGA!
WHOOP! WHOOP! WHOOP!
SLAP SLAP SLAP
YADDA! YADDA! YADDA!
WHEEDIE! WHEEDIE! WHEEDIE!
OOGA! OOGA! OOGA!
© 1990 United Feature Syndicate, Inc.
NYAHH! NYAHH! NYAHH!
HOOGIE! HOOGIE! HOOGIE!
I HATE LONG GOODBYES

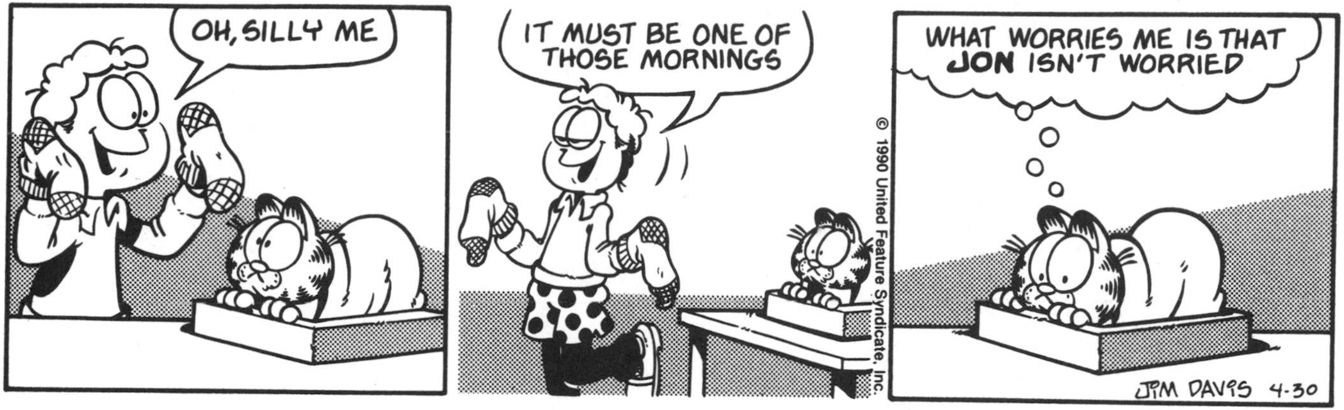
OH, SILLY ME
IT MUST BE ONE OF THOSE MORNINGS
© 1990 United Feature Syndicate, Inc.
WHAT WORRIES ME IS THAT **JON** ISN'T WORRIED
JIM DAVIS 4-30

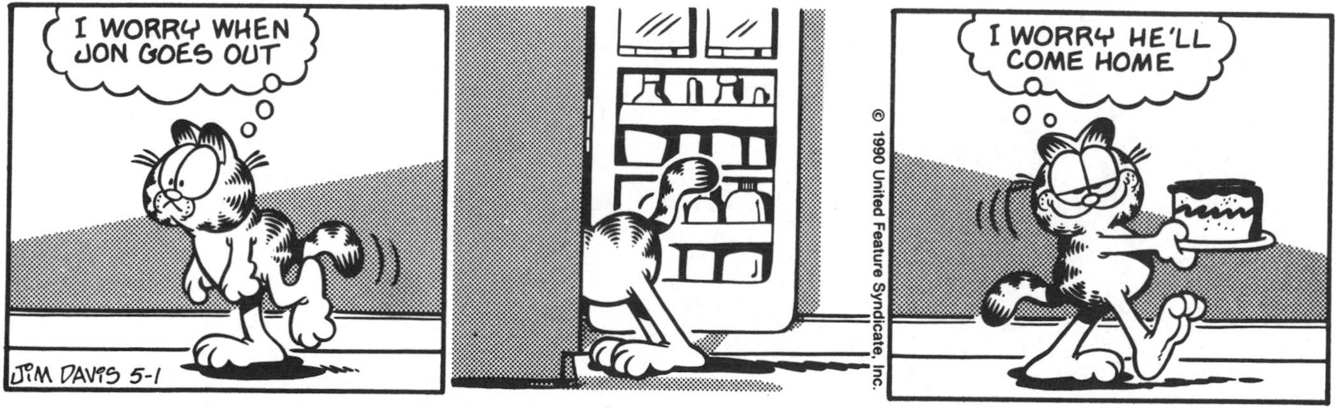
I WORRY WHEN JON GOES OUT
JIM DAVIS 5-1
© 1990 United Feature Syndicate, Inc.
I WORRY HE'LL COME HOME

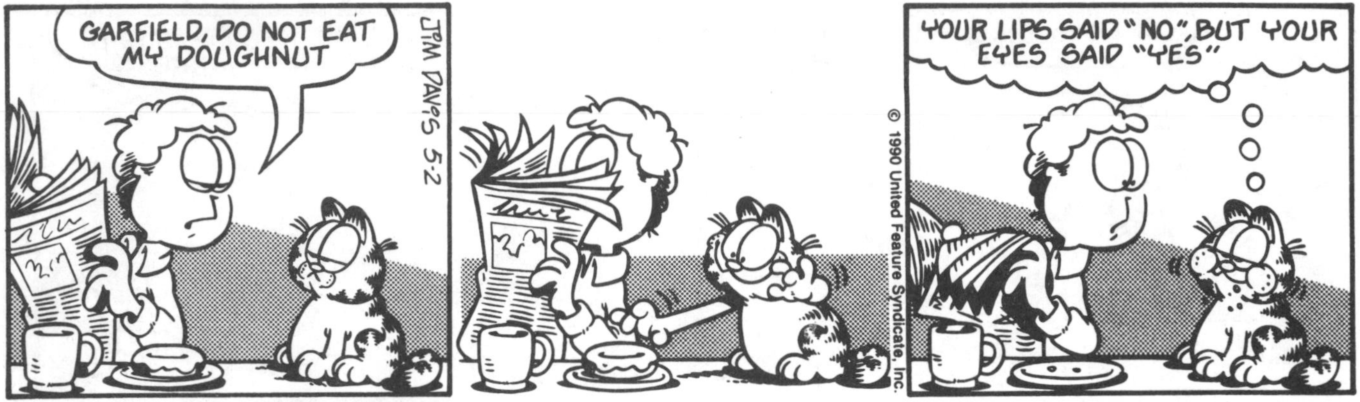
GARFIELD, DO NOT EAT MY DOUGHNUT
JPM DAVIS 5-2
© 1990 United Feature Syndicate, Inc.
YOUR LIPS SAID "NO", BUT YOUR EYES SAID "YES"

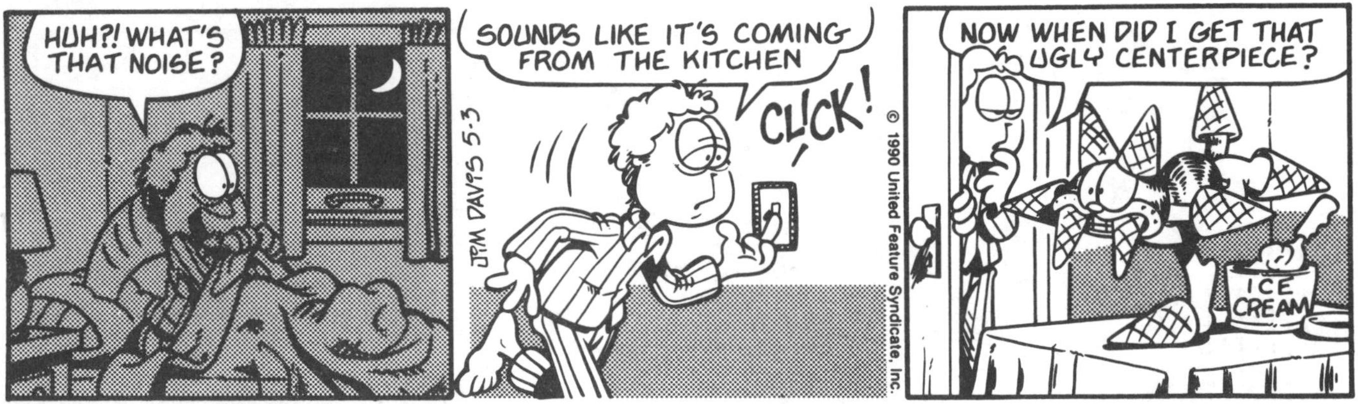
HUH?! WHAT'S THAT NOISE?
JPM DAVIS 5-3
SOUNDS LIKE IT'S COMING FROM THE KITCHEN
CLICK!
© 1990 United Feature Syndicate, Inc.
NOW WHEN DID I GET THAT UGLY CENTERPIECE?
ICE CREAM

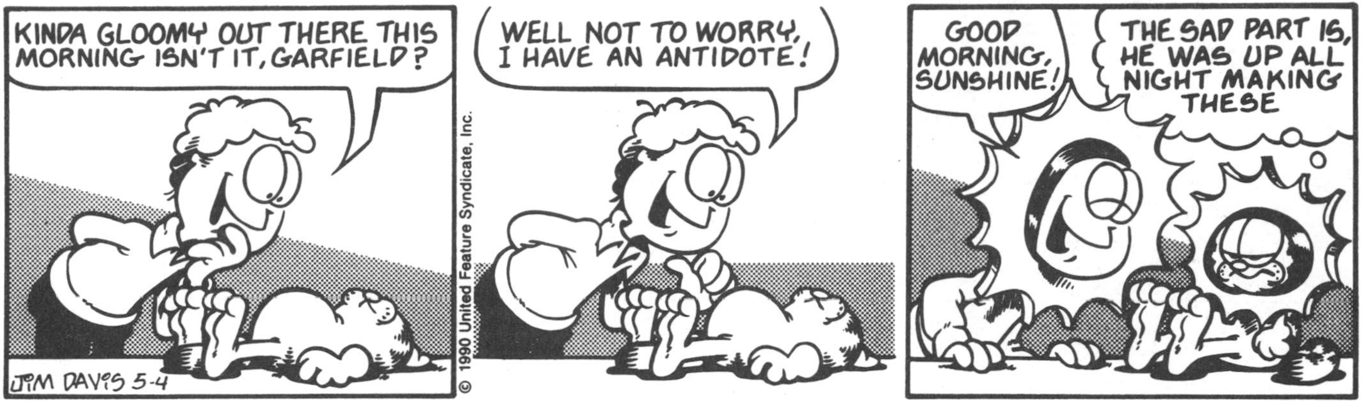
KINDA GLOOMY OUT THERE THIS MORNING ISN'T IT, GARFIELD?
WELL NOT TO WORRY, I HAVE AN ANTIDOTE!
GOOD MORNING, SUNSHINE!
THE SAD PART IS, HE WAS UP ALL NIGHT MAKING THESE
JIM DAVIS 5-4
© 1990 United Feature Syndicate, Inc.

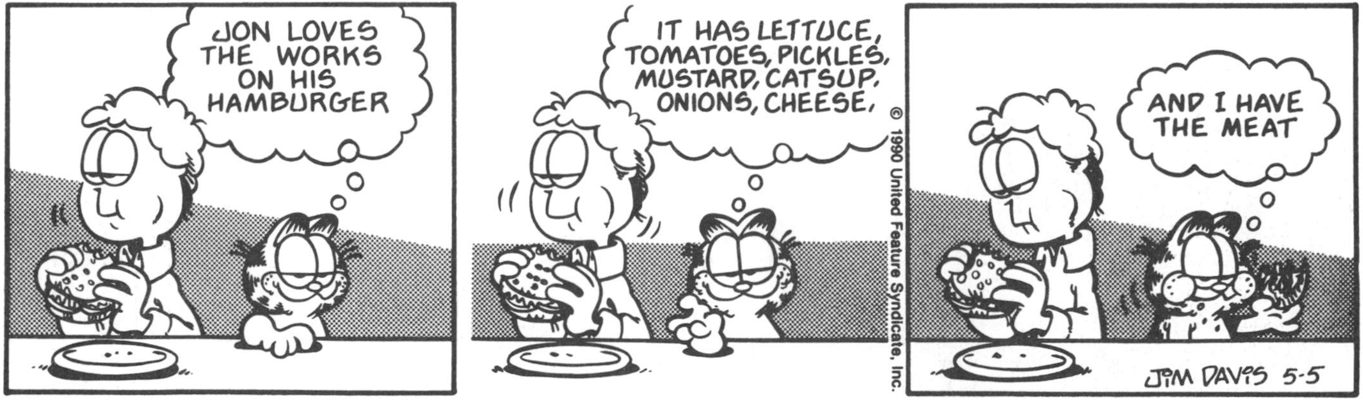
JON LOVES THE WORKS ON HIS HAMBURGER
IT HAS LETTUCE, TOMATOES, PICKLES, MUSTARD, CATSUP, ONIONS, CHEESE,
AND I HAVE THE MEAT
JIM DAVIS 5-5
© 1990 United Feature Syndicate, Inc.

Ask a cat.

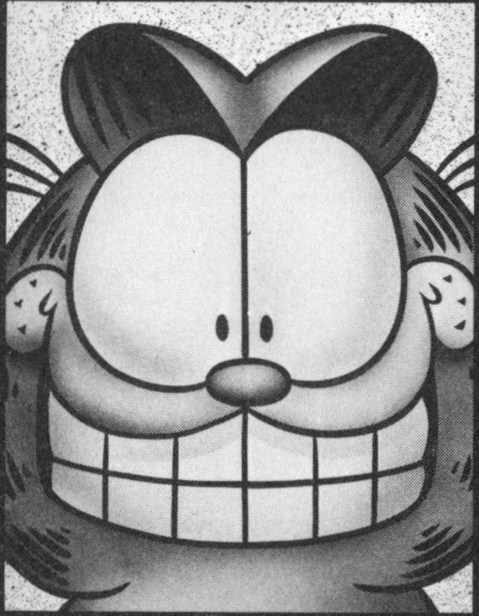

Q: Why does a cat always land on its feet?
A: Because it beats landing on its face.

Q: Can cats see in the dark?
A: Yes. They see a whole lot of dark.

Q: Is there more than one way to skin a cat?
A: I have given your name to the authorities.

Q: Why do cats eat plants?
A: To get rid of that mouse aftertaste.

Q: How often should I take my cat to the vet?
A: As often as you would like to have your lips ripped off.

Q: Should I have my cat fixed?
A: Why? Is it broken?

Q: Why do cats spend so much time napping?
A: To rest up for bedtime.

Q: How much food should my cat eat?
A: How much have you got?